MW01140622

VOICES FROM THE

ODEYAK

The completion of this book
is a celebration
to the memory of my Mother
Rebecca Brenzel Posluns

VOICES FROM THE *ODEYAK*

Michael Posluns

To Leah
"A fellow traveller"
with love from
Dad

NC Press Limited

Toronto 1993

Front Cover and Insert Photo:
  Odeyak at Crown Point, N.Y. on Lake Champlain
Back Cover Photos:
  Top: Stopping on the shore of Lake Champlain
  Second: Landing at Fort Ticonderoga
  Third: *Odeyak* Travellers meeting re-enactors at Fort Ticonderoga
  Bottom: Trucker Larry House with *Odeyak* guide Josh Gordan
Copyright, second top photo: ©Charles B. Moore, 1990
All others: ©Nancy Papish, 1990

©Michael Posluns, 1993

No part of this publication may be reproduced, stored in a
retrieval system, or transmitted, in any form or by any means,
electronic, mechanical, photocopying, recording or otherwise,
without the prior written permission of NC Press Limited.

Canadian Cataloguing in Publication Data

Main Entry under title:
Voices from the Odeyak
Bibliography
Includes index
ISBN 1-55021-070-X
1. James Bay Hydroelectric Project – Public opinion. 2. Hydroelectric power
plants – Environmental aspects – Quebec (Province) – Great Whale River
Valley – Public opinion. 3. Conservation of natural resources – Quebec (Province)
– Public opinion. 4. Native peoples – Quebec (Province) – Great Whale River Valley.
5. Odeyak (Canoe). 6. Public opinion – Quebec (Province) 7. Public opinion –
United States. 8. Community organizing 9. Environmental activism
10. New England, New York State 11. Aboriginal rights 12. Environmental eco-
nomics
I. Posluns, Michael, 1941-
S934C3P67 1993   333.7'2'09714111   C92-094990-8

We would like to thank the Ontario Arts Council, the Ontario Publishing
Centre, the Ontario Ministry of Culture, Tourism and Recreation, the
Canada Council and the Government of Canada, Department of
Communications for their assistance in the production of this book.

New Canada Publications, a division of NC Press Limited,
Box 452, Station A, Toronto, Ontario, Canada, M5W 1H8.

Printed and bound in Canada

Contents

Foreword
By Pete Seeger

From Pete Seeger's greetings to a reunion of Odeyak travellers and hosts at the Beacon Sloop Club, on April 11, 1991.

To read the headlines in the newspapers, to listen to television, you would think that Americans are selfish people who are only interested in their own pleasure. You would think that Americans don't feel any concern about the lives of other people. You would think that American people are not concerned about the land that they are taking from the Indians up in the north of Canada so that they can have cheaper electricity. I think the newspapers are wrong. I think the television doesn't tell us the whole story. I think there are millions of Americans who will say "No."

When they realize that we are taking the homes of people who have lived there for thousands of years, people who took care of the land as they hunted and trapped and fished and who want to keep on living on their land — there are Americans who will say "No. That's not fair to take their land. We may have to spend a little more for our electricity. But we'll find something. We can learn how to use solar power. We can start using wind power." There are a whole lot of things we can do rather than to take away the land that belongs to these people.

A hundred and fifty years ago, a few rich people owned most all this valley. One man, for example, had two million acres. Sixty thousand farmers had to pay rent to him. And they bowed low whenever he passed by. It was like Europe. The time came that the farmers started an illegal organization. They met at night. Their signal was to blow a tin horn. It was the horn which the women would use to call the men in to dinner from working in the fields. When the farmers met at night they would plan not to pay their rent to the rich man. When the sheriff came to evict the farmers who had not paid their rent, the farmers blew their tin horns again. All the farmers who heard the horns being blown came on their horses and surrounded the sheriff. They forced the sheriff to put up his hands, seized the eviction papers and burned them. Sometimes they tarred and feathered the sheriff.

The first year the *Clearwater* was sailing on the Hudson River I sang a song at one of the river-front festivals about such a sheriff, "Big Bill Snyder." An old man came up to me and pumped my hand saying, "My grandfather shot Big Bill Snyder!"

The reason I am telling you this story is that it is a pattern that used to happen in America many times, where farmers or working people put up a struggle. At first, it looked like their struggle would be lost because there were just a few prepared to struggle and the rich people were so powerful. But because they put up a struggle, eventually they won.

At first, it looked like the farmers had lost. All the leaders were in jail. Some were going to be hanged by the neck. But then their story got into the newspapers. People in New York City and in Buffalo and in Albany said, "Its not right. These farmers should be allowed to own their own land." And eventually they won.

In the past, there were two peoples for which this pattern of struggle did not work: African-Americans revolting against slavery and Native Americans trying to stay on their ancestral lands. When the Indians tried to fight for their land, they were kicked off.

You are a small group of people. But now, because you are struggling you are going to find more and more people who will listen to you. What you are doing now is going to win, I think. It has a chance because you are working together and you were prepared to travel all this distance to meet the people who might be able to help you.

All I know is that history is full of surprises. There are many people who are very rich and powerful and many people who study books and think they know a lot. But there is not a single person who has been able to predict the surprises that happen in history. Nobody predicted that Abraham Lincoln would sign the Emancipation Proclamation. Nobody could have predicted in the earliest days of organizing that it would one day be possible to join a union without having to keep it a secret for fear you would lose your job. Who predicted what would happen when a young Black minister named King led a bus boycott in Alabama in 1956? A lot of people never believed that women would vote.

I think there are a lot of surprises liable to take place now. The keys are struggle and communication. This world will be shared or there will be no world.

Preface

This book is about the voyage of the *Odeyak* from the mouth of the Great Whale River to Manhattan in the spring of 1990. The story is important for a number of reasons. For me, the greatest of these reasons was the opportunity to learn the larger story of the Crees and the Inuit of Great Whale, including their history and their concerns for their future.

It is primarily told in their *voices* for the simple reason that it is their story. Some controversies arise from using the *voices* of the original participants. This is my opportunity to respond, at least to the major controversies. *Voices from the Odeyak* is a testimony to the willingness of the Crees and Inuit of Great Whale to protest against the destruction of their communities in a peaceable but quietly profound way.

There is a popular view today which finds the telling of history suspect. History, it is said, is a selective tale that makes no attempt at balance or merely a distraction from the excitement of the present. The denial of history is intimately bound up with the denial of fact. During my visits with the Crees and the Inuit, in the winter of 1990 and the spring of 1991, I was struck by the deep respect of the elders for education and an honest examination of facts. They re-affirmed the belief that if an environmental assessment process were open, fair and thorough, their view would prevail. This faith stands in stark contrast to the contemporary disregard for history in urban and academic circles, and the near-contempt for fundamental facts among government agencies with significant control over the Great Whale communities.

The accusations about factuality made against the Crees and their friends by a number of Québec political leaders, has lent the very notion of factuality a political intensity it would not otherwise deserve. During the campaign to cancel the New York-Hydro contract, Premier Bourassa and his Deputy Premier, Lise Bacon, repeatedly charged that environmental groups making critical comments in the U.S. were distorting the facts. Yet, neither their Government, nor Hydro-Québec, were prepared to disclose the evidence required for a full public debate either on an energy policy for Québec or for an environmental impact assessment of the Great Whale Project. The Governments of Canada and Québec, while objecting to the versions of the facts presented by small American environmental groups, denied the existence of whole species of animals. They also denied the existence of whole bodies of law. If government officials show a contempt for factuality, it is not because they do not believe in fact but because the denunciation of their opponents' accuracy is a subterfuge by which to avoid public debate.

Avoiding or forbidding debate on major political issues is a strategy which goes hand-in-hand with the denial of fact and a contempt for the historical experience of other peoples. Perhaps the most contemptible example was the charge made by the Honourable Lise Bacon that the Crees were not Quebeckers if they challenged her Government's policies at a protest rally in New York City. If so, then the charge that the entire Cree campaign was engineered by a Madison Avenue advertising firm was, for all its silliness, no less malevolent.

The most objectionable aspect of the accusation is that it imputes incompetence to the Crees in particular and First Nations in general. That Crees could not organize campaigns and lobbies on their own seems to be a refrain. The Catch-22 to the implied incompetence is that the use of advisors by Native political leaders somehow makes them less legitimate as Aboriginal leaders. Gotcha! If Native leaders seek professional advice it is a sign of incompetence. If they take advice they are accused of abandoning tradition. Gotcha! What would happen if we applied the same standards to political leaders in Québec, Ottawa or Washington? The question needs to be asked by every North American with any kind of egalitarian pretensions.

I was recently asked, by a Québécois acquaintance who works in Ontario, what I was doing these days. I mentioned this book on Great Whale. The notion that a book on *La Grande Baleine* might be written, or even conceived, anywhere outside Québec aroused this person's instant wrath. Perhaps this ordinary Quebecker's anger was a mere echo of the Deputy Premier's. I am inclined to hear something deeper. The image of Québec as a powerless and persecuted minority which should not be measured by the same standards as other states in North America may, perhaps, have had some basis in the *ancien regime* that ended with the election of the reform Liberal government of Jean Lesage in 1960 and the nationalization of Québec's hydro-electric resources by Mme. Bacon's predecessor as Energy Minister, Rene Lévesque. The idea that people outside Québec cannot discuss the flooding of an area almost the size of France, and the destruction of a way of life which unites the Crees of Whapmagoostui with Crees all around the inland seas of Hudson and James Bays, is absurd and insulting.

My own experience collaborating with First Nations voices began in 1970 at Akwesasne, a community whose records go back many hundreds of years but which has, more recently been divided by the New York-Ontario-Québec borders. My impression from eight years of paralegal work and journalism at Akwesasne was not that Québec officials were notably more hostile than those in the other two jurisdictions. Worse than hostility was their failure, from the time they began to assert an independent presence in the mid 1970s, to distinguish their basic attitudes to First Nations cultures from those of the dominant North American culture.

As different as Akwesasne may be from the Great Whale communities, there are also some geopolitical and historical facts which they share. One is the proximity to a border. The high water mark at Great Whale is the boundary between Québec and federal Canadian lands. The adjacent islands and waterways are important to the economies of both communities. The use of an interprovincial, possibly an international boundary, to divide a people from their livelihood appears to be another way in which the current Québec policies resemble nothing so much as the historic federal Indian policies in both Canada and the United States. Lastly, the denial of the Aboriginal experience as part of contemporary history is a political strategy which goes back to the earliest attempts to drive the First Nations from the eastern seaboard.

When we remove the First Nations voices from contemporary history we diminish our own reality as much as we diminish the reality of the First Nations. When Euro-Americans travel to any other part of the globe we learn to understand how to live like human beings in those places largely by looking at the historical experience of the indigenous cultures. When we deny the reality of the First Nations' experience in North America, we are refusing to learn about our own back yards the way we accept learning about other places.

The question raised by Great Whale is not a different question for Québécois than for other Euro-Americans. We need to ask whether the most fundamental principles of law and decency are to be offset by the expansionist impulses of mega-corporations. We also need to ask whether our own sovereignty really stands over against the sovereignty of the original peoples. And is that sovereignty advanced by the denial of other peoples' experience?

Acknowledgements

The primary challenge of writing an acknowledgement is accepting that the full extent of my indebtedness is quite possibly beyond words. Any attempt to express the full range of my gratitude would surely produce another entire book. My task is made easier, in this respect, by acknowledging the very great and real debt I owe to all the people whose names are mentioned in the course of the book. I am indebted to everyone who was gracious enough to answer my questions, in the Great Whale communities, in Chissasibi and down south. Theirs are — *The Voices* — from which I built this book.

Among all the many people who graciously indulged my questions I am especially indebted to the elders of Whapmagoostui and Kuujjuaraapik who shared their own life stories in assisting me to sketch the history of parts of their communities and their relationship with the land and the animals that continue to sustain them. Mina Weetaltuk, a much loved Inuit elder told me, "It doesn't take so many words to understand these things." What she said came from the depths of her commitment to the land and to her community. Her statement also struck a familiar chord; it was something my own Mother might have said under similar circumstances. The generosity of the elders, leaders and young people of the Great Whale communities, and of their hosts along the entire route, in providing me with interviews and with source materials was so great that I need to emphasize my own responsibility for the final selection of material.

Six of the original *Odeyak* travellers came with me to re-trace the trip the following year: Mina Weetaltuk, Caroline Weetaltuk, Joseph Petagumskum, Larry House and Matthew Mukash. Their insights and recollections at each stopping place along the entire route made the original adventure come to life in my mind.

Robbie Niquanicappo spent many hours with me before I began formal interviews in the Great Whale communities. His questions helped me to become clearer about my own mission. His questions and his stories helped me to prepare to meet the other people I would interview. Luis Egurun, an organizer with the Grand Council of the Crees' James Bay Task Force, gave me my earliest introduction to the Great Whale communities. He also provided some insights which could only have come from a person with deep personal ties in both Montréal and Whapmagoostui and for whom English and French were both second languages. Father Tom Martin offered many insights into the Great Whale communities' religious life and the role of the institutional church in enabling the voyage of the *Odeyak*.

Emily Masty is a person to whom I am most especially indebted. At the end of a long school term, while she was teaching her Grade Six class, she found time to arrange meetings with each of the elders who appear in the book and to translate their answers and their stories. John Petagumskum's answer to my question about how freshwater seals are different from marine seals — "their esophaguses are bigger." — inspired me to dig deeper at each stage of my research. Caroline Weetaltuk shared the inner sanctum of her father's workshop and the unimaginable expanse of ice and sky bridging the waters from the Kuujjuaraapik coast to the channel islands.

One or two people in each place along the *Odeyak's* route provided me with an overview of their region that helped to organize the many bits and peices. Nancy Papish and Doris Delaney each pulled together a very large number of loose ends. John Mylod reinforced my certainty about the chronology of the latter part of the voyage by cross-checking dates and times both with his own calendar and with the log of the *Clearwater*. Jeff Wollock provided an historian's sense as well as a New Yorker's love of Manhattan. His presence at the earliest announcement of the *Odeyak* voyage, and again in Hull and at Manhattan, provided me with a most fortunate overview of the whole sequence. Kenneth Deer and Michael Canoe also provided special insights from their perspective, escorting the *Odeyak* through traditional Mohawk territory. Jim Higgins provided a perspective on Vermont and its deeper connections to the message of the *Odeyak* which could only have come from someone who had absorbed an intimate river's eye view of the North as well as of his own state.

Bill Hoyt, a Member of the New York State Assembly from Buffalo, was another arctic canoeist who offered me some early insights into the politics of his state. The week before Governor Mario Cuomo cancelled the larger New York contract with Hydro Québec, Mr. Hoyt died.

Several other people contributed to my research far beyond their apparent role in the telling of the story. Jim Dumont, the Vermont attorney for the Grand Council of the Crees, explained the Vermont legal issues to me while he baby sat one Saturday morning. Lesley Becker provided further background on the town and village meetings of Vermont. Karen Lohr provided a perspective on the James Bay issue rooted in her experience as a southerner and as a leading Sierran.

Robert Shipley edited a much longer manuscript to the point where it might offer a much more enjoyable reading. Caroline Walker, the publisher of NC Press Ltd., introduced Robert and me. Howard Norman, whose *Wishing Bone Cycle* of poetic renderings of Cree trickster stories, from the other coast of Hudson Bay, provided continuing encouragement when I was searching for a home for Voices.

Paul Wertman, my former seatmate at the Narayever Congregation in Toronto and a community development consultant with the Oujebougoumou Band, began the series of introductions which led to my being welcomed into the homes and schools where I interviewed the *Odeyak* travellers. Brian Craik, the Director of Federal Relations at the Grand Council of the Crees encouraged me "to write something that would endure." The Grand Council has been generous in their support of my research. Billie Diamond, the first Grand Chief of the Crees and Matthew Coon Come, the Grand Chief at the time of the *Odeyak*, each offered their very personal historical perspectives at very early morning breakfasts.

I completed *Voices* while I was beginning a graduate program at York University. Two professors in the Faculty of Environmental Studies were more than generous in their support for this work. Mary Bernard reviewed chapters two and three. Professor Liora Salter's Policy Research course provided the ideal forum in which to explore the tension between federal policy directives and rulings of the Federal Court, an exploration which forms the basis for much of chapter eight.

The illustrations in this book were contributed by people for whom photography is another way of carrying on the *Odeyak's* message of sharing: Nancy Papish of Schenectady, N.Y., Charles Moore of Glens Falls, N.Y., Rob Rondon of Stormville, N.Y., John Puleio of Burlington, Vt., Isaac Masty of Whapmagoostui, and Lois Glenn-Karp, of Paradox, N.Y.

A number of children helped me find my way around both the Great Whale communities of Whapmagoostui and Kuujjuaraapik and around Chissasibi. Their willingness to ask me questions often re-assured me in my role of interviewing their parents and grandparents. Their capacity to ask probing questions in two, and sometimes three languages, is an example to contemporary journalists and scholars.

My most special debt is to my partner-and-friend, Marilyn Eisenstat, who walked with me through my many doubts and uncertainties and sharpened my vision with an early editing of two sample chapters.

The Cast of Characters

The Odeyak Travellers

From the Cree Village of Whapmagoostui
Dick, Gibert; Cree hunter and elder
Dick, Robbie; Chief of Whapmagoostui
George, Matthew; Cree hunter and elder
House, Larry; Odeyak's transport driver (from Cree Village of Chissasibi)
Kawapit, Abraham; Whapmagoostui financial director
Kawapit, James; Cree hunter and elder
Mamiumscum, Noah; Cree hunter and elder
Mamiumscum, Weemish; Cree hunter and elder
Martin, Tom; Anglican priest at Great Whale
Masty, David; Whapmagoostui Band administrator
Masty, Isaac: Whapmagoostui school superintendent
Masty, Stella; student from Whapmagoostui
Mukash, Matthew; Grand Council of the Crees community liaison worker, elected Chief of Whapmagoostui in 1992
Niquanicappo, Robbie; Deputy Chief of Whapmagoostui
Pepabano, Randy; student from Whapmagoostui
Petagumskum, John; Cree hunter and elder
Petagumskum, Joseph; Cree hunter and elder
Symes-Grehan, Marie; Great Whale Hydro Task Force Assistant

From the Inuit Village of Kuujjuaraapik
Bennett, Sarah; Kuujjuaraapik school teacher, town councillor
Fleming, Robert; town councillor of Kuujjuaraapik.
Fleming, Sappa; Mayor of Kuujjuaraapik
Fleming, Jeffrey; son of the mayor
Mickeyook, Mary; *Odeyak* traveller
Thrasher, Willie; Inuit folk singer and *Odeyak* traveller
Tukatuk, Alec; information officer for Makivik at Kuujjuaraapik
Tukatuk, Heather; *Odeyak* traveller
Tukatuk, Samuni; *Odeyak* traveller
Weetaltuk, Billie; designer and chief builder of the *Odeyak*
Weetaltuk, Caroline; one of builders of the *Odeyak*
Weetaltuk, Mina; wife of boat builder Billie Weetaltuk

Weetaltuk, Redfern; assisted in building Odeyak

Grand Council of the Crees (of Québec), Leaders, Staff and Advisors Appearing in the Story

Coon Come, Matthew; Grand Chief of the Crees (of Québec)
Craik, Brian; Director of Federal Relations
Dumont, Jim; Vermont attorney
Goodman, Ian; an energy consultant from Boston
Mainville, Robert; Québec attorney
Martel, Doris; organizer from Québec Cree headquarters at Nemaska
Moses, Ted; International Ambassador of the Cree Nation
Namagoose, Bill; Executive Director
O'Reilly, James; Québec attorney

Other Friends of the Odeyak

Alsop, Denny; environmental activist from Massachussetts
Canoe, Mike; Mohawk canoeist from Kahnawake, escorted the *Odeyak*
Chamberlain, Roland; Algonquin canoeist who accompanied *Odeyak*
Chase, Kim; French speaking Vermonter who helped host *Odeyak*
Cox, Sam; Chissasibi economic development officer
Cree, John; Mohawk Chief at Kanesatake
Delaney, Doris; member of the North River Friends in the Albany area
Deer, Kenneth; Mohawk canoeist from Kahnawake
Gibson, Canon Joel; St. John Divine Cathedral, N.Y.
Gonda, Ray; Atlantic Chapter of Sierra Club
Higgins, Jim; Vermont environmentalist
Hoffman, Bob; past president, Vermont Trappers' Association
Kistabish, Richard; Grand Chief of the Algonquins
Levine, David; the Learning Alliance in New York
Lyons, Oren; Chief of the Onandaga from near Syracuse, N.Y.
MacAusland, Steve; Cree speaking freelance New England journalist
Martin, Susan; co-ordinator of *Odeyak's* Vermont trip
Matchewan, Jean-Maurice; Barriere Lake Algonquin Chief
Mylod, John; Executive Director of the *Clearwater*
Napartuk, Thomasee; Inuit dog team driver
Natashaquan, Andrew; one of Odeyak's builders
Pachanos, Viola; Chief of the Chissasibi Cree
Papish, Nancy; member of the North River Friends in the Albany area
Petawabano, Smally; Mistissini Chief
Sam, Josie; Chissasibi high school guidance counsellor
Seeger, Pete and Toshi; founders of the *Clearwater* network
Singer, Beverly; Indian activist and Sierra Club member
St. Francis, Homer; Chief of the Abenaki Nation at Swanton, Vermont

Tapiatic, Sam; Chissasibi hunter
Walters, Bob; president of Ferry Sloop, Yonkers N.Y.
Webb, George; co-ordinator of *Odeyak's* Vermont trip
Wollock, Jeff; research director of Solidarity Foundation in New York

Canadian and Québec Political Leaders and Officials
Bacon, Lise; Québec Energy Minister
Bouchard, Lucien; Canadian federal Environment Minister
Bourassa, Robert; Premier of Québec
Burnet, Robert; Hydro-Québec's VP for Native Affairs
Caccia, Charles; Liberal MP from Toronto
de Cotret, Robert; Canadian federal Minister of the Environment
Drouin, Richard; President of Hydro-Québec
Fulton, Jim; NDP Member of Parliament from British Columbia
Robinson, Raymond; Federal Administrator of *James Bay and Northern Québec Agreement*
Rouleau, Justice Paul; Judge in the Federal Court
Siddon, Tom; Canadian federal Minister of Indian Affairs and Northern Development
Skelly, Robert; NDP MP from British Columbia, Native Affairs critic
St. Julien, Guy; Conservative MP from Northern Québec

American Political Leaders and Officials
Clavelle, Peter; Mayor of Burlington, Vermont
Cuomo, Mario; Governor of New York
DeLeon, Dennis; New York City Human Rights Commissioner
Dinkins, David; New York Mayor
Friedlander, Miriam; New York Councilwoman
Kunin, Madeleine; Governor of Vermont at the time of the *Odeyak* trip
Messenger, Ruth; Manhattan Borough President
Reed, Meg; Assistant to New York Senator Ohrenstein
Snelling, Richard, Governor of Vermont
Stallone, Hank, Mayor of Yonkers, New York
Steresenger, George; Aide to Vermont Governor Madeleine Kunin

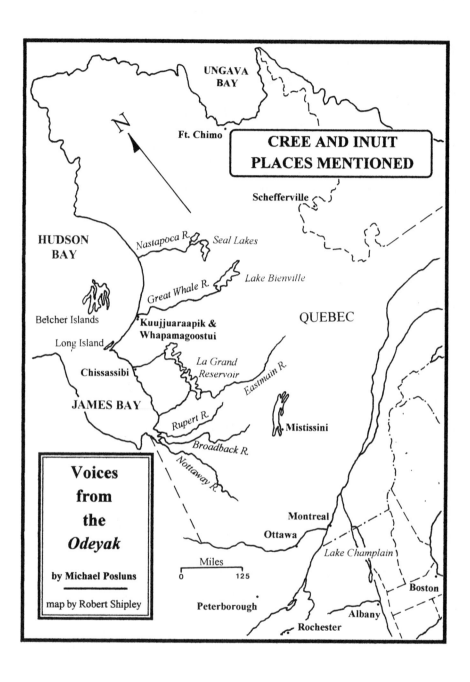

UNGAVA
BAY

N

Ft. Chimo

**CREE AND INUIT
PLACES MENTIONED**

Schefferville

**HUDSON
BAY**

Nastapoca R.   *Seal Lakes*

Great Whale R.   *Lake Bienville*

QUEBEC

Belcher Islands

Long Island

**Kuujjuaraapik &
Whapamagoostui**

*La Grand
Reservoir*

Eastmain R.

Chissassibi

JAMES BAY

Rupert R.

Mistissini

Broadback R.

Nottaway R.

**Voices
from
the
*Odeyak***

by Michael Posluns

map by Robert Shipley

Montreal

Ottawa

Lake Champlain

Miles

0   125

Boston

Peterborough

Albany

Rochester

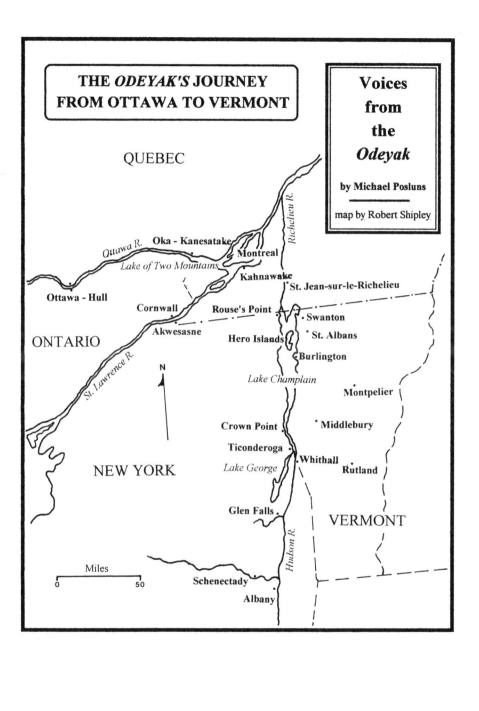

THE *ODEYAK'S* JOURNEY
FROM OTTAWA TO VERMONT

Voices
from
the
Odeyak

by Michael Posluns

map by Robert Shipley

QUEBEC

Ottawa R.

Oka - Kanesatake

Montreal

Lake of Two Mountains

Kahnawake

Richelieu R.

St. Jean-sur-le-Richelieu

Ottawa - Hull

Cornwall

Rouse's Point

Swanton

ONTARIO

Akwesasne

Hero Islands

St. Albans

Burlington

St. Lawrence R.

N

Lake Champlain

Montpelier

Crown Point

Middlebury

Ticonderoga

Whithall

Lake George

Rutland

NEW YORK

Glen Falls

VERMONT

Hudson R.

Miles

0   50

Schenectady

Albany

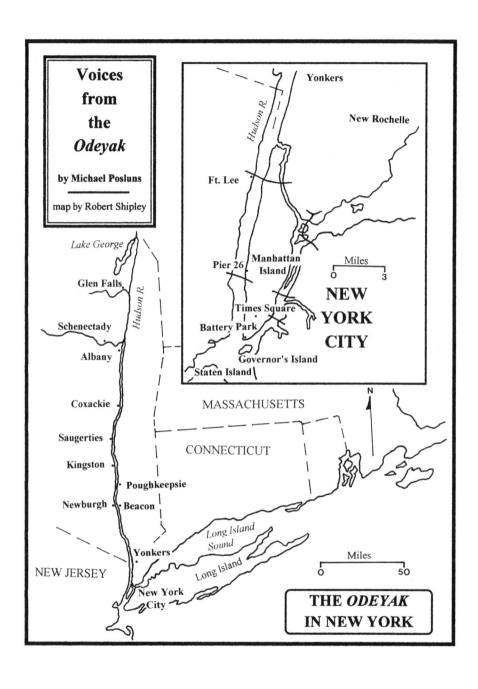

**Voices
from
the
*Odeyak***

by Michael Posluns

map by Robert Shipley

Yonkers

New Rochelle

Hudson R.

Ft. Lee

Pier 26

Manhattan
Island

Miles

0   3

**NEW
YORK
CITY**

Times Square

Battery Park

Governor's Island

Staten Island

Lake George

Glen Falls

Schenectady

Hudson R.

Albany

MASSACHUSETTS

Coxackie

Saugerties

CONNECTICUT

Kingston

Poughkeepsie

Newburgh   Beacon

Long Island
Sound

N

Yonkers

NEW JERSEY

Long Island

New York
City

Miles

0   50

**THE *ODEYAK*
IN NEW YORK**

Chapter 1:
Manhattan Transfer

The Big Apple

The reporter in the News Radio 88 traffic helicopter told listeners that he had spotted two canoes going down the river. He said it looked "like somebody had a new idea for commuting to New York City."

The boats spotted from the helicopter were no ordinary craft. One was the *Odeyak*, the other its Mohawk escort. The *Odeyak* is a large freighter canoe with its stern quarter covered like a kayak. The name came from *Ode* which is Cree for "canoe " plus the *yak* suffix in the Inuit word *kayak*. Almost ten feet longer than a standard 16-foot canoe, *Odeyak* had been built in the traditional way by bending cedar strips around a mold. It weighed several hundred pounds. The bow end replicated the "Cree canoe " in which the people of James and Hudson Bay had paddled into the interior of the Ungava Peninsula for the last five generations. The stern end was an invention of the builder, Billie Weetaltuk, a 72-year-old Inuk elder and a master boat builder.

Odeyak had been built just the month before at Great Whale River on Hudson Bay, more than twelve hundred miles north-west of Manhattan. Now it was in the shadow of the Palisades, entering the jaws of the Big Apple. When the two communities at the mouth of the Great Whale had decided that their best chance to stop the forces threatening to destroy their villages was to travel to New York City for Earth Day, Billie had built *Odeyak* in less than three weeks. The *Odeyak* was accompanied by an ultra modern, super light 26-foot Kevlar ® freighter, from the Mohawk community of Kahnawake on the St. Lawrence.

On the morning of Thursday, April 19, 1990, shortly after the sun had come up, a crew of paddlers climbed down into *Odeyak* from the old Ross quarrying dock on the Jersey side of the George Washington Bridge at Ft. Lee. Another crew boarded the Mohawk escort. As the two canoes were making ready, a Cree hunter called to a pair of geese flying low over the river. One of the geese turned to answer the hunter's call. To Bob Walters, "It felt like a good omen, a perfect touch for the final day's paddle." Walters was president of *Ferry Sloop*, an independent group of local river people affiliated with the *Clearwater* network, who had hosted *Odeyak* in Yonkers, New York.

The two canoes pulled away from Ross's Dock and headed downstream, riding the tide toward New York Harbor. Andy Hudak, a gentle man somewhere in his 40's and a long time Hudson River canoeist, would guide the two boats from the north in his own canoe. Guiding the *Odeyak* on its final stretch into Manhattan was a prospect which excited Andy. *Odeyak's* departure was scheduled to ensure its arrival at two successive downtown points at times suitable to the media. The two downtown destinations were Pier 26 on the Hudson River and Battery Park around the tip of Manhattan Island.

The early morning paddle had been prompted as much by wanting "to catch the ebb tide going down " as by the need to co-ordinate with the media. The constant effort to juggle, if not to balance these two forces, natural and human, had been the story of *Odeyak's* journey the past five weeks. There was a need to reach out to friendly faces both directly and through the media while also learning to go with the flow on unknown waters at springtime. Portaging around ice clogged channels and opening barge canals weeks before their official season, *Odeyak* had kept to a schedule that would bring the voices of the Crees and the Inuit to Times Square for Earth Day.

Ross's Dock was particularly suitable as a final point of departure. The television crews — naturally interested in covering the final day, "the winning goal " of the *Odeyak* trip — could not help but catch the Manhattan skyline behind the high-sided, photogenic boat. All along the trip, such planning as happened had been an effort to play off the physical realities of travel against the lures required for good media sound bytes. Along with these considerations there were also the human needs of the travellers and their hosts. Whenever these three realities coalesced a strong sense of the miraculous pervaded the travelling community.

Ron Ingold's shad fishing poles were the one remnant of traditional river life visible in the early morning light. Nowadays, Ross's Dock is used mainly for summer picnics. Ron and his forebears have fished shad at that site for five generations. The incongruity of the gill nets a few miles above Manhattan, which are much the same as those used by the Crees on the Great Whale, may help explain why a New York radio reporter, speaking from a helicopter, would describe a canoe paddling downstream on the ebb tide as a *new* idea for commuting.

"There was a bit of misadventure that morning," Robbie Niquanicappo recalled with a smile. Robbie N. was the Deputy Chief of the Crees of Whapmagoostui (Whap-mawg-stwee). "Somehow our bus driver turned left when the truck transporting the *Odeyak* turned right and we got separated." So the better part of the hour before sunrise had been spent driving around looking for *Odeyak*, the vessel whose very arrival in Manhattan was the purpose of their trip.

> By then everyone was getting worried, "We've lost *Odeyak*. Today's the final day! How could this happen?" Everybody was wringing their hands until the bus and the *Odeyak's* truck finally met up. Then everything started to come together.

What was unusual was not the misadventure but the wringing of hands. *Odeyak* had been on the water or on the road for five weeks and a day. The boat had been accompanied by two crews of ten people each, plus elders, leaders, and speakers from two villages. Because many of those had brought their families the *Odeyak* travellers as a group numbered close to sixty people. An intense month of organizing had accompanied the period when the *Odeyak* was actually under construction. But a month was hardly enough time to ensure food, lodging, speaking engagements and appointments with major political figures on a route from Ottawa through Montréal, along the Vermont shore of Lake Champlain and down the Hudson River to New York City.

In the absence of adequate time, the Great Whale people simply relied on the many promises from one or another group along the way to take care of all the necessities in their area. What was surprising was not the misadventures. Many of those had arisen from promises of support made by people whose good will exceeded their capacity to deliver. There was also a touch of naïveté from the Great Whale-based organizers who relied rather heavily on such promises. Far more surprising than the mishaps was the frequency with which *Odeyak* connected with hosts who provided both hospitality and a network of contacts in their own communities. It was this grassroots network which had become the main source of opportunities for the travellers from the north to share the concerns which had prompted the voyage of the *Odeyak*.

The wringing of hands was surprising because, as Father Tom Martin observed, the Crees and Inuit often "cope with life through last minute changes." Martin was the Anglican (Episcopalian) priest from Great Whale who had flown down to be with the travellers for the final days of their journey. But to lose *Odeyak* just when it was to be launched on "the final leg of the journey" after five weeks of travel, often sleeping on the floors in church basements or community halls, scraped against "the air of expectancy " that Robbie N. felt running through his people as they waited for the truck hauling *Odeyak* to descend the steep, winding road to the dock. If Bob Walters took the response of the Canada geese to the calls from the northern hunters as a "good omen," for Robbie N. the sound of the geese carried a much more mixed message.

> I remember feeling very homesick. A lot of us were thinking about how the people back home were getting ready for the goose hunt. In a week or so we would be getting home. As we watched *Odeyak* preparing to head off for New York City there were some Canada geese paddling around in the water. Seeing the geese there only made it worse. So a few of us practiced our calls. Of course, the TV cameras instantly swivelled to whoever was calling the geese. I think they were amazed that the geese actually reacted to what we were doing.

Kenneth Deer, a leader of the Mohawk Canoe Club at Kahnawake, a reservation community near Montréal, had helped make some of the early connections for the *Odeyak* travellers with his network of canoeists along the upper Hudson. Kenneth had paddled in the stern of the Mohawk escort as far as the U.S. border at Alberg, Vermont, before heading back to Kahnawake. Now he had re-joined the trip for the final day.

> It was a good day for a paddle. It was calm. You could see the skyscrapers in the distance. We knew where we had to go. When we left we could see millions of people around in this huge metropolis who were just oblivious to us as we paddled down this river. It was like a culture shock to be suddenly surrounded by New York City. There was a certain feeling, an anticipation of what would happen when we arrived at Battery Park.

"It's probably 12 miles from Ross's Dock to the Manhattan skyline," Bob Walters estimated. When *Odeyak* and her escort had pulled out from the Dock and the paddlers were working to find the rhythm of the river they began the chant they had developed, three weeks earlier, going up the Richelieu River, from the St. Lawrence River into Lake Champlain. "We could hear the echo off the rock of the Palisades as they started to chant, '*Odeyak, Odeyak.*' "

James Kawapit, a venerable elder who had spent his life canoeing along the Great Whale River and on the lakes and smaller rivers in the northern bush, had developed a fascination with the braces and pillars of the bridges crossing the Hudson. A man who had not seen a bridge until his maturity now found himself paddling under one after another. As *Odeyak* made its way downstream each bridge was a little larger than the last. Launching from Ross's Dock gave James the chance to have the kind of close look at the George Washington Bridge enjoyed by very few New Yorkers. James remembers how he felt, looking from the river up into the hills.

> I was in the other boat, not in the *Odeyak*. I felt very happy that it was such a beautiful day when we would finally reach our destination. When we first

started out on the trip, New York City looked very far away. So when we finally got there I felt a great happiness. I thought about all the people who helped us along the way. Then I remembered that before we left we had been told that people would be praying at home for our trip to be successful. So I thought of all the people whose prayers and good deeds had helped us to finally reach New York and I was very happy about that.

Pier 26 and Battery Park

When *Odeyak* and the escort had finally left and were well down the river from Ross's Dock, the rest of the travellers got back on the bus and headed for Pier 26 where they would watch the *Odeyak* finally land in Manhattan. For the length of the bus ride, Robbie N. could put aside his role as Deputy Chief and tend to other duties.

> When they finally left, the rest of us piled back on the bus. My little boy was really cranky that morning. It was kind of early for him to be on the bus. We put the kids back to sleep. I made sure I was on the left side of the bus because we were across the river from New York. We were sitting in the bus as it was driving toward Manhattan when somebody said, "Look!" I looked out the window and I saw New York City with its towers. Everybody gave a small cheer, "We made it!"

> I remember cameras snapping all around me as people tried to get a picture through the bus windows. A lot of us wanted to preserve that first sight of New York forever. It didn't matter that we were in a moving bus. I remember feeling very apprehensive about getting into New York because we had heard so much about the City. People there are crazy, weird. People get killed there every day. All the rest of what you see on TV. So although we were happy to be there a lot of us were very apprehensive.

The television image of New York City was the one clear picture of their destination shared by all the *Odeyak* travellers, Crees and Inuit, young and old, men and women. Soap addicts and news junkies in the Great Whale communities had access to the same channels enjoyed by couch potatoes on the Hudson. That image would shape the way the Inuit and the Crees dealt with the City as much as their scheduled appearances at Times Square, St. John the Divine Cathedral and the United Nations.

Stella Masty was a 14-year-old high school student when she set out to win the essay contest which would give her a place on the *Odeyak* trip.

> At first, I really didn't want to go because I was afraid of white people. Ever since I have been watching television I have been learning about people being racist and that scares me a lot, like Black people being beaten up — and Indians how they were treated in residential schools — and I was afraid of going to New York City. You hear all these different stories about New York City. People say it is nice and they like it there. People say that they don't even want to go there because there is a lot of crime going on.

When the bus had climbed back up the Palisades on its way to Manhattan and the *Odeyak* was a speck on the horizon, Bob Walters stood on the dock "watching the current going down between Ron Ingold's shad poles," thinking back on the three days he had spent entertaining the *Odeyak* visitors in Yonkers and the three weeks he had spent preparing for their visit while the *Odeyak* was making its way south.

Richard Kistabish, the Grand Chief of the Algonquins, had camped "just in the park by the water so that we could sleep beside the river and leave when we got up." He and his friend Roland Chamberlain were travelling without their families and had all the latest equipment. They were enthusiastic canoeists and had set out an hour before *Odeyak*. Grand Chief Kistabish had welcomed *Odeyak* to an Algonquin conference in Hull, the Québec side of Canada's national capital, the day after the *Odeyak* had been launched from Victoria Island in the middle of the Ottawa River. Ottawa and Hull are at the southern end of the Algonquin's traditional territory. He had been so taken with the commitment of the travellers from Great Whale that he had decided to join them for the final trip into New York City. When Richard and Roland had left at the crack of dawn there was nobody on the river. A couple of hours later they found themselves in quite a different situation.

> We were surrounded by large, high powered boats and ferries. It became quite dangerous for a while. The ferries cross the river very quickly and they don't seem to care about little canoes.

> So we decided to stay on the New Jersey side for awhile. While we were waiting for the *Odeyak* we went into a marina on the New Jersey shore and had breakfast. We had a wonderful view of Manhattan. It was a very nice restaurant. The manager was surprised to see people coming up from the river. He was more accustomed to limousines pulling up in front.

Odeyak did not stop for a limousine-style breakfast. But when they got thirsty they realized that, in the midst of all the excitement they had not brought a water supply. They knew by then that the Hudson is not a river from which a canoeist can slurp the water from a paddle. Kenneth Deer described the water at the mouth of the Hudson as "pretty murky." When your canoeing experience is centred on the St. Lawrence River near Montréal, the Hudson by New York is not so very much worse. The northerners had, by their last day, made a joke about whether the water of the Hudson might eat through the canvass cover on their canoe or whether the oil on top of the water would provide the extra coat of paint the boat needed. In the absence of drinkable water, Kenneth Deer engineered a solution from the Mohawk escort.

> We had to stop somewhere to try to get something to drink. There was a ferry restaurant. Two young boys went and found us some bottled water.

They thought it was pretty strange seeing these two canoes from the north pull up at their ferry dock. Then we shared the water with the *Odeyak*.

From the ferry docks the *Odeyak* and the Mohawk escort, now joined by the Algonquin Grand Chief, headed toward Pier 26 on the Manhattan side of the river. As this small fleet came into New York Harbor "we were met by a group of canoes and kayaks who had come out to greet us," Kenneth recalls.

Jeff Wollock, the research director of Solidarity Foundation, was waiting at Pier 26 when *Odeyak* arrived at 8:30 a.m. The Foundation is a New York-based, research-centred group that supports indigenous people. Two of Jeff's colleagues had gone out to Staten Island at 5:00 o'clock that morning to hire a tug that would serve as a press boat. Jeff had been in touch with the Crees since they met at a conference in Montréal at the beginning of February. He had not quite believed his ears when Matthew Mukash announced that the Great Whale villages were about to start building a boat which they would take to New York in time for Earth Day. Jeff is a seasoned traveller and a dedicated New Yorker. He knows the places in his City which continue to be occupied largely by Aboriginal people of the same First Nations who lived there before the Dutch proclaimed the area New Amsterdam.

Jeff had arranged for the local press when it was expected that *Odeyak* would leave from the pier at the foot of Dykeman Street. He was "personally a little embarrassed" when Denny Alsop insisted that it leave from Ft. Lee. Alsop was the environmental activist who had first suggested the Great Whale people come south and he had been doing the bulk of the publicity work for the *Odeyak* as it travelled through Vermont and upper New York State. He had developed a genius for slipping into town the day before the arrival of the Aboriginal travellers. Denny was committed to having *Odeyak* make a series of major "media hits" of which the arrival in New York City would be the biggest. If Jeff did not share Denny's vision of how to capture the media, he did understand the inner workings of New York. Jeff had a different idea of what it would take to make even a small dent on such a Big Apple.

Jeff Wollock recalls that when he arrived at Pier 26 at 8:30 that morning, he was very relieved — perhaps pleasantly surprised — to find all the loose ends finally coming together.

There were all the Cree and Inuit on the pier. Everyone was there. Everything was just as it should have been. I was tired but it all felt good. The press was there getting on the press boat. Everything was working out perfectly.

Pier 26 was the place at which the regular *Odeyak* crew stepped out of the boat to make room for a crew of Cree and Inuit leaders. Matthew Coon Come, Grand Chief of the Crees (of Québec), had arrived the day before specifically to join *Odeyak* travellers from Great Whale for this last mile and to be with them on Earth Day, three days later. Ted Moses, past Grand Chief and the Crees' International Ambassador had come in from Geneva to be with *Odeyak* in New York City. Sappa Fleming, the Mayor of the Inuit community of Kuujjuaraapik, had travelled with *Odeyak* for the entire course of the trip. Robbie Dick, Chief of the Crees of Whapmagoostui, had left his hospital bed in Montréal to join *Odeyak* at Vermont. Robert Fleming was a town councillor of Kuujjuaraapik. Matthew Mukash, the Cree community liaison worker who had only become the Hydro Task Force Co-ordinator the month before *Odeyak* project got underway, would succeed Robbie Dick as Chief of Whapmagoostui, two years after *Odeyak*. Robbie Niquanicappo, the Deputy Chief of Whapmagoostui, and David Masty, the Whapmagoostui Band Administrator, also joined the other leaders for the final paddle.

Sarah Bennett, an elementary school teacher, had worked with the Inuit children throughout the trip. Now, in her capacity as a town councillor, she would join the other leaders to paddle the very last stretch from Pier 26 to Battery Park. Sarah was one of only two paddlers who started at Ross's Dock to continue from Pier 26 to the Battery. Sarah, a very cool lady in her own space, had some very mixed feelings about sitting in a canoe in New York Harbor.

> I was one of the paddlers when we came into New York Harbor. For myself, I was quite nervous. There were so many people there. Native people, media and other people. I felt nervous but it was a good feeling at the same time to have made this trip and finally get to the place we had set out to reach.

> Going down the river to the Battery, I think that was when it really hit me about the scenery. Wow! This is New York! Look at those skyscrapers! There's the Empire State Building! My eyes really opened!

> Looking up at Manhattan from the river we could really see the smog. A very dirty smog, not just white clouds, it was almost yellow on top. The river was also dirty but not as much as I thought it would be.

Richard Kistabish was also awestruck by the experience of sitting in a canoe in New York Harbor.

> It is really an experience to paddle into New York City. The sight of the skyscrapers of Manhattan from where I was sitting in a canoe in the middle of the Hudson River put me in a state of shock for quite a while.

Kenneth Deer summed up his experience very simply, "You feel pretty small when you paddle a canoe past an aircraft carrier."

Robbie Niquanicappo recalled the paddle from Pier 26 to Battery Park in terms peculiarly suited to a boat full of leaders.

> They had told us, "Don't paddle. Just float." The tide was going out at the time. They wanted us to arrive at a specific time and if we paddled on top of the tide we would arrive too soon. So we basically sat there and let the current carry us out toward Battery Park. Then when we got to the Battery they had us paddle around in circles so they could take pictures, especially with *Odeyak* in the foreground and the Statue of Liberty in the background.

As *Odeyak* and its escorts came around the tip of Manhattan Island, in sight of Governor's Island and the Statue of Liberty, the strange squat canoe encountered the *Clearwater*. The 108-foot long sloop built by Pete Seeger and his friends to become the flagship of a movement to clean up the Hudson River turned in majestic salute to the *Odeyak*. The *Clearwater* network of sloop clubs had provided the largest part of the hospitality to the *Odeyak* all the way down the Hudson. But the sloop itself had been sailing in the lower regions of the river. According to the ship's log, it had set sail that morning with a class of school students and was off Governor's Island when it sighted and acknowledged the *Odeyak*.

Once the paddlers had taken in the skyline and recovered from the shock, and once enough time had been spent on the water to allow every possible photo opportunity, there remained the complex challenge of landing. A good deal of work had been done in advance simply to find a place where it was possible to land a canoe at Battery Park. It turned out to be an extremely complicated task.

John Mylod, the Executive Director of the *Clearwater* has an intimate knowledge of New York from the water. "The wharf area around most of Manhattan is quite high off the water so there is no easy place to haul a canoe in and out." Taking advantage of the ebb tide meant arriving in the harbor when the water was at its lowest level. The *Odeyak*, unlike a conventional canoe, could not be lifted easily from the water, "So it was necessary to have some sort of floating dock arrangement."

In New York Harbor such sites are very limited. Once such a place is found, permission to land must first be obtained. As John Mylod points out, around New York, "You can't do anything without getting insurance." Regarding the myriad of tasks essential to the *Odeyak's* visit, Jeff Wollock frequently said, "It's hard to do stuff like this in New York." Fortunately, through the diligence of the Solidarity Foundation, a floating dock was found at Battery Park. John Mylod described the landing site.

> They were to land at a place known locally as the *Petrel* dock. The *Petrel* is a sailboat that was well known ten or 15 years ago for taking charters around the harbor. The *Petrel* dock is right next to the Staten Island Ferry

Terminal and a Coast Guard dock. I'm not sure if the *Petrel* is still there but local mariners know it as the *Petrel* dock.

Jeff Wollock was "pacing up and down the sea wall like I was waiting for a baby to be born" when the *Odeyak* finally arrived at the *Petrel* Dock beside Battery Park. Jeff had ridden from Pier 26 with Marie Symes-Grehan, a community organizer from western Canada who had moved east at the invitation of the Crees, to help in their resistance to the Great Whale Hydro Development Project. Once the Cree and Inuit councils had decided to build *Odeyak* and take it to New York City, Marie had become the key southern tactician. It was she who had done the largest part of the telephone outreach during the month before the trip, making initial contact with the groups which had hosted the *Odeyak*. All along the way, it was Marie who had filled in most of the gaps that could be filled at each of the stopping places over the three weeks before this final arrival in New York.

Six hours after the paddlers had left their lodgings in Yonkers, the *Odeyak* finally landed at Battery Park. There was a crowd of perhaps three hundred people. Robbie Niquanicappo recalls that, "When we landed everyone started cheering. The cameras were going. And we were welcomed. That was our official landing at New York City."

The official landing was met by a group of New York religious, civic, and legislative leaders, each of whom made a short statement welcoming *Odeyak* and expressing concern about the role played by their city in relation to the wider environment. Canon Joel Gibson from St. John the Divine Cathedral had played a key role in ensuring a turnout of local dignitaries. He was joined at the landing by Human Rights Commissioner Dennis DeLeon, Councilwoman Miriam Friedlander, and Meg Reed, District Assistant to State Senate Minority Leader Manfred Ohrenstein. Battery Park is in Sen. Ohrenstein's district. It is also in Councilwoman Friedlander's district.

Gilbert Dick, a much respected hunter and elder, rejoiced quietly to himself as he watched his younger brother, Chief Robbie Dick, do the public performance at which he had become so adept in front of the collection of cameras and microphones.

We were just glad that we did what we had set out to do. When we started we could not know if we would make it that far. We had never been in another country before. This was our first trip, for most of us. Only the leaders had been there before. My brother, the chief, had been in New York City before, around 1970.

For Robbie Niquanicappo, the press conference and the traditional ceremonies following it were:

Pretty much a blur because by then I was tired from the high. My stomach was in knots. And I had my first taste of New York food at Battery Park ... the greasiest pizza I have ever had. My little boy didn't seem to care. He had a great time chasing the pigeons around. He wondered if they were ptarmigan and asked if I was going to shoot them.

Jeff Wollock was both thrilled and at the same time, disappointed with the media response.

Everyone was there: AP, CBC. They were all there. The point was what got into the media. The Canadian papers covered it. It was on the front page of a couple of Montréal papers, the Toronto Star (a beautiful picture with the World Trade Centre in the background). Do you think that anybody covered it from New York? The New York Post had one picture with a little caption. The New York Times had nothing. The News had nothing. The Newsday had something but they held it until Earth Day.

New York is the press capital of the world and it is harder to get press here than anywhere else, because there is so much competition for what is newsworthy. There aren't that many local papers. And one mistake that we made was not contacting the local papers. There are local papers, they are usually freebies. We had not contacted any of the local papers in Manhattan. They would have covered it.

Each of the three Native leaders who spoke at Battery Park had a similar message. Chief Robbie Dick summed up their position afterwards. "We are here to tell your governors and leaders not to buy power from Hydro-Québec." The survival of his community, he said, depended on the capacity of New Yorkers to abstain from Québec power.

The Grand Chief of the Crees (of Québec), Matthew Coon Come, was the first of three speakers to make the connection between New York City and the future of the Great Whale River.

There is jubilation in my heart but also a cry, knowing back home that our lands can be flooded. Today we have arrived in New York. We have come a long way to make a public awareness of why we came here.

You must know that Phase One of the James Bay project was built in our own back yards. We negotiated a land claims settlement to achieve what other Canadians and Quebeckers were receiving; health and social services, administration of justice. We signed that agreement when we reasonably thought that the Government of Canada and the Government of Québec could respect their commitments and implement their obligations. But what good is it to have an agreement that falls onto the Trail of Broken Treaties?

Now we are facing two massive hydro-electric projects: One called Great Whale River and the other called Nottaway-Broadback-Rupert Rivers. These major rivers are going to be diverted to flood an area half the size of

Texas. Eight major rivers will be diverted. This is like damming the Hudson a hundred miles above New York and leaving the mouth of the river where we are now without fresh water.

We have still an economic base in the resources of that area. Some people call us primitive because we still hunt, we still fish and we still trap as a way of life. That is our economic base. We have protected that land, we have protected its animals so that there are still animals there to sustain our families. The environment is still clean.

Now they want to destroy the Great Whale the way they destroyed the environment on the La Grande! The first James Bay project was neatly exempted from any environmental impact assessment. We live on that land. We are only ten thousand people but we occupy and use every square inch of that land of 144,000 square miles. Now they want to destroy the Great Whale! If you destroy and divert those major rivers you will have affected a sensitive animal habitat. Our main diet is fish. From the first project we know that the fish have become so contaminated with mercury that now we are told that we can no longer eat the fish from the La Grande River.

We know what the impacts of the La Grande project have meant for our people. The Great Whale Project — damming all the major rivers flowing into the Great Whale — will have a cumulative effect over and above its immediate effects. These cumulative impacts will represent a cultural genocide for us!

We are here to tell you, you Americans, that you are contributing to the threat that is facing us! It is Wall Street that is financing those projects. You are contributing to the environmental damages in Québec. You are dumping your problems into our back yards!

There is an environmental rácism going on here. Why is it that projects of this magnitude can be built in the homelands of indigenous people? If these projects were built near your cities in America there would be an outcry. When it happens on Indian lands they ask us to move over. "Move over, Indian! 'Cause we're gonna build!" We're saying we have to draw the line.

It is from our children as much as from our parents that we borrowed this land. We received this land from our parents so that we could protect it for our children. Our fight is to preserve the land so that we can return it to our children.

Chief Robbie Dick had been taken seriously ill after leaving Great Whale on the first leg of the *Odeyak* trek. He left a hospital bed in Montréal to rejoin the travellers from his community as they crossed into Vermont. Now, a few short weeks after heart surgery, he was standing in Battery Park to appeal to the people of New York, asking them not to participate in the destruction of his community.

As a symbol of our solidarity, the Cree and Inuit people of Great Whale

River in Québec, in their determination to stop the proposed hydro-electric development, dedicate *Odeyak* to our ancestors. It is through *Odeyak* that our ancestors are with us in spirit today. It is through *Odeyak* that they speak to us. It is through *Odeyak* that they give us wisdom and guide us in our struggle to save our homeland.

We are here with our elders, with our children and with our families to tell the people of New York State and the people of the world that our homeland, our environment and our Mother Earth is at stake. The proposed hydro-electric project, James Bay Two, will flood Cree and Inuit hunting and burial grounds and destroy the Cree and Inuit cultures as we know and practice them today.

The Great Whale project means the diversion of five major rivers in our area, the Great Whale River, the Little Whale River, the Boutin River, the Nastopoca River, and the Coates River. The head-waters of the Great Whale River, Lake Bienville, will be used as a storage reservoir. Eighty per cent of the water that now flows down the Great Whale will be held back from flowing down to the mouth. And that is where our communities are located. This also means the flooding of our most valued hunting grounds, the river valleys where the animal habitat is located.

We are here to tell you that if you buy power from Hydro-Québec you will be contributing to the disruption of our environment and our homeland. Our very identity as a people depends on what the land provides.

We are here to tell you to tell your governors and your legislators not to buy this power from Hydro-Québec. If they do they will be participating in a major environmental disaster. They should instead be looking at energy conservation and not contributing to the destruction of the environment.

Mayor Sappa Fleming said that he had come to represent the Inuit people of Kuujjuaraapik. He echoed the words of Chief Robbie Dick and added, "We need your support right now. We have come to ask for your help. We need your support."

Two years later, when Governor Mario Cuomo finally decided to cancel the contract between the New York Power Authority and Hydro-Québec, Lise Bacon, Québec's Deputy Premier and Minister of Energy would denounce the Crees for destroying the great dream of Premier Bourassa. But on that Thursday in April of 1990, Hydro-Québec's attitude was not much different from the CTV reporter who had filed his story before any of these speeches were made. Even before Mayor Dinkins' representative, Dennis DeLeon, had welcomed *Odeyak* with a promise to look at alternative sources of power, Canada's second major news source had already announced that New York was, "A city where such events are daily occurrences and are quickly forgotten. It is also a city which believes its need for cheap Canadian electricity is far more important than the lives of 75 paddlers from Québec."

Hydro-Québec had made its presence felt at Battery Park, as it had at every major stop since Burlington, Vermont. But Hydro had not taken the Crees and Inuit seriously enough to appreciate the possibility that an entire grass roots movement might spread through New York State and, indeed, throughout New England, in sympathy for two Native peoples fighting for their survival.

Robert Burnet, Hydro-Québec's Vice-President for Native Affairs, had appeared earlier in Albany and presented himself once again at the press conference in Battery Park. Another person representing herself as a journalist at the press conference turned out to be a local freelance advertising copy editor hired by Hydro-Québec to trail the *Odeyak*. She had been following the boat since it arrived in New York State. The New York Power Authority (NYPA) does not appear to have participated in this surveillance activity directly. Most of the time NYPA officials remained far enough in the background that they were much less conspicuous than Robert Burnet and his colleagues from Hydro-Québec, at whose disposal NYPA had placed their local facilities at several points along the *Odeyak* route.

The very presence of representatives of the Mayor and the Dean of the Cathedral meant that the *Odeyak* had accomplished what would be described, in military terms, as its first tactical objective. As Gilbert Dick said, the purpose of *Odeyak's* five week trip was:

> To tell the world that we are here. We are also people like any other people in the world. We're not something different. We're here to fight for our rights, to save something that people want to destroy.

Earth Day — Times Square

When the official welcome to New York City was over, what remained was to find accommodation for sixty *Odeyak* travellers of all ages, preferably a place which could support the different dietary needs of Inuit elders, hearty young men and fussing children. If the official welcome had been more thoroughly planned, accommodation had fallen between the cracks. Communication between trip organizers such as Marie Symes-Grehan and host groups such as Solidarity and Indian House had been haphazard. At the end of the official welcome there was no place waiting to receive the *Odeyak* people and to give them a break after the eight hours of travel and the presentation that had already been completed by lunch time.

Marie frequently felt that she simply had to rely on the ability of local hosts to do what they could for hospitality. The pressure on her to deal with all the other matters, such as speaking engagements, appearances and planning of major events, combined with the need to care for her own two-year-old son, made it necessary to rely on local hosts to plan accommodation.

New York City presented special accommodation problems. Accommodation in smaller cities and mid-size towns had been provided by local environmental groups. The *Clearwater* affiliates along the Hudson had long ago assigned hospitality to crews from their own clubs. Previous exchanges with the Kahnawake Canoe Club, home of the Mohawk escort accompanying *Odeyak*, made the extension of this hospitality fairly straightforward. In Vermont, a couple of groups who share facilities at the Quaker Meeting House in Burlington had been able to offer billets in their own homes. It simply was not very far to anyplace else in the State. In Manhattan, networks might be found for any number of political causes but not for accommodation for sixty people. Certainly not in private homes. And the kind of church basement arrangements which had worked out in the Adirondack area above Albany were also not likely to be found here.

Jeff Wollock and his colleagues clearly recall Marie saying that accommodation had to be free. "We might have been able to put people up for free but they would have been scattered all over the city. That would have been ridiculous, the logistics would have been totally impossible. They had to stay in more or less one place." Beverly Singer, an Indian activist and Sierra Club member in New York City called Jeff on March 15 to say, "I've actually got accommodation for them in New York City. But it's not free. We're going to have to raise the money. It's not terribly expensive." For weeks before the *Odeyak's* arrival, reservations had been held at the new student hostel that Beverly Singer had found. Unfortunately no money had been raised to cover the costs. "Marie's attitude was that she wanted the churches to pay for it. She said that the *Odeyak* had the backing of the Anglican church and that it was the least they could do."

Although Jeff had become convinced that this "was a personal issue of Marie's" he was not prepared to make unilateral decisions. Nor was Doris Martel, a Dene woman who had been sent from the Cree headquarters at Nemaska, in northern Québec, to assist Solidarity Foundation in planning *Odeyak's* Earth Day activities. Two days before *Odeyak's* arrival, when no down payment had yet been made, the hostel cancelled the reservations. A Buddhist group offered their basement space and said that they would try to clean it up.

This was the destination for the *Odeyak* bus when it left Battery Park. When Robbie Niquanicappo surveyed the broken windows, the lack of beds and the inhospitable appearance of the neighbourhood, he was prepared to sleep in the bus. Chief Robbie Dick also surveyed the site. He turned to Robbie Niquanicappo and said, "The people won't stay here. The place is really not fit for human beings. We'll have to put them up at hotels." After a brief discussion with the driver, everyone boarded the bus again. They headed for the Lincoln Tunnel. The *Odeyak* travellers stayed the weekend at a modest but safe-looking motel in New Jersey.

The motel in Jersey with defined forays into Manhattan turned out to be an ideal solution. It was not only the elders who found the Big Apple intimidating and perhaps even threatening. Stella Masty, the Cree high school student who had developed a reputation as an orator for her speeches at schools all along the route recalls the time in New York City with the least fondness.

> When I was in New York City I found it very difficult. I'm not used to so much loud noise, pollution, smoke. There were always a lot of people on the streets. It seemed that everyone was talking at once. And traffic noises all the time! So I didn't much want to spend time outside.

> The people looked strange with all their different styles. Their hair, their clothes were quite strange. Most of the people I saw were in suits. Except at the Earth Day celebrations most of the people were dressed more the way we dress, sort of casual.

Stella was already afraid of New York City before she went. Isaac Masty, Stella's father and the Whapmagoostui school superintendent, agrees that his people were not as comfortable in New York as they had been in smaller centres. "We didn't really know what to expect when we got to New York," Isaac says. Television stories about New York had already convinced one of the most sophisticated adolescents in the Great Whale communities that a walk to the convenience store was a dangerous adventure in Manhattan. Apprehension about New York had been a recurring topic of discussion during the long hours of travel in Vermont and New York State. Isaac was pleasantly surprised to find that New Yorkers were not as different from other people as the reputation preceding them might suggest.

> The way people accepted us and responded to us was not any different than the people in Vermont. I guess it depends on who you meet. But I can say for myself that I did not meet anyone who made me think that part of our trip was not successful or that we were offending against someone in our presentations. Nobody gave me that impression among all the people that I met.

Isaac was one of the very few *Odeyak* travellers to ride on the New York subway. Robbie Niquanicappo found that he had seen so little of

New York that he could not really compare it to the big cities he had often visited in Canada.

> We stayed together at the same hotel. Whenever we went out it was in the bus. We'd go straight to where we wanted to go, where we would meet people who already knew and cared about us. We rode around and looked at the city but we really did not get to know it at all.

The Jersey motel also meant frequent passages through the Lincoln Tunnel. The first time that the bus went through the tunnel, "Everyone was amazed. When we told the older people, 'We're now under the river,' I know that I was looking around for leaks, wondering if the whole thing was going to collapse." When the initial anxiety had passed, the tunnel became a new source of humor for some elders who often mix their wisdom with wit.

When the welcoming ceremonies at Battery Park ended and the other *Odeyak* travellers had set out in search of accommodations, Larry House and Randy Pepabano loaded the *Odeyak* onto a truck with a specially built rack, as they had done so many times before, and headed for St. John the Divine Cathedral. *Odeyak* would stay on display at the Cathedral until Earth Day.

Larry was a young man from Chissasibi, the Cree community downstream from the series of dams making up Phase One of the James Bay Project. He had been hauling the *Odeyak* on a red pickup truck whenever it had to travel by road. Chissasibi is the town where the road from southern Québec into the Ungava ends. *Odeyak* had left Great Whale on a sled hauled by a dog team on a three day trip to Chissasibi. When the Chissasibi band had been asked to lend their support to the expedition from Great Whale, Chief Viola Pachanos had recruited Larry House as a volunteer driver. Randy Pepabano, one of the two students chosen to represent the Cree high school at Great Whale, became Larry's assistant. At some of the portage points, Larry and Randy had to double back for the Mohawk escort. Sometimes, when a local guide had no other way to transport his canoe, they retraced the portage route a third time.

The only time that Larry House got lost was when he volunteered to haul Richard Kistabish's canoe back to Yonkers at 10:30 on the Saturday evening before Earth Day. Richard Kistabish, the Grand Chief of the Algonquins, had made no arrangements for storing his canoe until he got to Battery Park. Three hours after everyone else had left the Park, a truck arrived to take his canoe to Indian House where they managed to bring it into the office after removing a door and a window. When Richard's travelling companion, Roland Chamberlain, broke his leg, the day before Earth Day they became eager to head for home. Their car and camping

gear were in Yonkers. Their canoe was in a second floor office in downtown Manhattan. The trip to Yonkers was uneventful. It was only when
Larry tried to find his way in the middle of the night from Yonkers to the
hotel on the New Jersey side of the river that he found himself thoroughly
turned around. Larry and Randy made it back to the motel in time for a
few hours sleep before it was time to fetch the *Odeyak* from the Cathedral.

Earth Day was why *Odeyak* had come all the way to New York City.
Earth Day was why, after living more back-to-back than side-by-side for
fifteen years, the two villages at the mouth of the Great Whale River on
Hudson Bay near the tree line on the Ungava Peninsula, had reunited.
Earth Day, for the Inuit of Kuujjuaraapik and the Crees of Whapmagoostui, was their great opportunity to tell a world that hardly knew of their
existence that their future was imminently threatened.

The Earth Day ceremonies devoted to re-uniting Times Square with
Mother Earth brought together as wide a variety of New Yorkers as were
likely to gather for a common purpose. It included everyone who could
find a way to think of themselves as "environmentally concerned."

Earth Day at Times Square, for the *Odeyak* travellers from Great
Whale, was five minutes long. The first five minutes of the Times Square
ceremonies were given to the *Odeyak* people. After five weeks of icebound
rivers, windblown lakes, crowded buses, camping in church basements
and fire halls, beef stew and other potluck dinners, the Cree and Inuit
leaders had five minutes to make their appeal to America.

Odeyak owed its place at the top of the Times Square agenda to the
care and support of many different people. Jeff Wollock had come back
from a meeting in Montréal with the news that the Great Whale communities were making the trip. "When you get down to organizing something like Earth Day, it gets a little crass because everyone wants to get
into the act." Solidarity Foundation is a research support centre for Native
communities. Solidarity had a close working relationship with the Learning Alliance. David Levine, at the Learning Alliance, carried the appeal
for giving time to the *Odeyak* to the Earth Day organizing committee.

Denny Alsop, who had been doing much of the publicity for the
Odeyak ever since it left Montréal *en route* for Vermont, also had his line
of communication into the Earth Day organizing committee. Denny had
dreamed of presenting *Odeyak* to the ten thousand people gathered to
turn Times Square into a sacred place since before the boat was built or
named. "People have seen canoes on television for years and years.
Odeyak took that cliché and changed it to something unique. It was not
just the paintings on the sides. Its shape, its depth, its size. Everything

about *Odeyak* made it visible." Denny had a vision of six media hits. Times Square was the climactic moment.

Denny Alsop's and David Levine's campaigns may have crossed wires as often as they crossed paths. If the new boy on the block helped to ensure a decision that was already well on its way he won few friends in the process.

Lorraine Canoe and Oren Lyons, two famous speakers from the Longhouse, the traditional Iroquois Confederacy with its centre at Onandoga, near Syracuse, New York, had been early candidates to speak at Earth Day. When Lorraine Canoe heard that the Crees and Inuit were making the journey to appeal for support at Earth Day she had offered her place to ensure that they would have an opportunity to be heard. "If it will give them more time they can have my time."

"What can we say in five minutes to a crowd for whom even our names sound strange? How can we share our concerns and win friends without taking time to spell out who we are?" A year later, long after the smaller upstate and New England papers had understood that the word *Eskimo* was a Cree epithet, *The New York Times* would still use the Cree swear word to refer to the Inuit. A great deal of time was spent over the two preceding days pondering what to say to a crowd of ten thousand so that they would no longer be strangers. "The people at Earth Day didn't quite know what we were about when we put the *Odeyak* on stage," recalls Matthew Mukash.

The only events which preceded *Odeyak* were the official introductions from Manhattan Borough President Ruth Messenger and the Mayor of New York City, David Dinkins. Mayor Dinkins chatted with the Cree and Inuit children sitting on the overturned *Odeyak* during Ruth Messenger's speech. After the Borough President introduced the Mayor she called on "the Cree and Inuit of the Great Whale River of northern Québec! " It was *Odeyak's* turn.

Odeyak was carried onto the stage. Caroline Weetaltuk, one of the *Odeyak's* builders, and a paddler and peacemaker throughout the trip, led the chant the paddlers had used at successive landings, "Odeyak! Odeyak! Odeyak!" Then, without sparing time for introductions, Matthew Coon Come, still holding a tall Cree-style paddle, thundered his message to the crowd.

> The James Bay Two hydro-electric project will destroy our people, the forest, whales, the seals and geese. A vast wild and beautiful land as large as this state will be drowned. I do not believe that you want four billion dollars of American money used to cause this environmental crime!

There is no choice between nuclear or coal, between oil or hydro. The choice is between wanton waste and conservation. In the Amazon we are trying to undo the damage. With James Bay Two the harm of a major ecological disaster can be stopped before it happens!

Ask Governor Cuomo why he signed the death warrant for eight wild rivers to be destroyed.

Stop Hydro-Québec! Stop James Bay Two!

Then, in his most characteristic move, Matthew Coon Come said thank you in two Cree dialects, French and English as he asked New Yorkers to work with the northern peoples to leave a better world for their children and grandchildren.

Chief Robbie Dick mixed some metaphors in a way that was at first confusing to a New York audience.

Odeyak is a struggle for a right to life! A right to culture! A right to Mother Earth!

Help us! Save our rivers! Our land!

Sappa Fleming, besides being Mayor of Kuujjuaraapik, is also an accomplished Anglican lay preacher. His way of working an audience in his second language was to start with a text and let the message follow.

President Kennedy said, "Ask not what your country can do for you. Ask what you can do for your country." One thing you can do for the country is to tell your government not to buy electricity from Hydro-Québec!

Then the *Odeyak* crew standing on the stage broke into the song composed by folk singer Willie Thrasher in the course of the trip.

Did you ever see geese fly high in the sky, my friends? Did you ever hear the wolf howl in the night? And the Crees and the Inuit are singing their song. And I believe they're gonna stand tall!

When Willie succeeded in having the crowd fill Times Square with the chanted refrain the elders were content. They had done what they came to do. Their leaders had given the message that could be given in the time available. The chant which had grown out of their paddling song had been taken up by a crowd larger than the entire Cree population of Ungava. It grew to unite the full variety of humanity gathered at Times Square on Earth Day, 1990.

When the *Odeyak* returned to the Cathedral of St. John the Divine after leaving Times Square both the vessel and the people travelling with it joined the service. Some very general plans for their participation had been made between the Cathedral's sub-Dean, Joel Gibson, and Tom Martin, the priest from Great Whale. The plans were, however, quite loose and did not yet involve any of the other leaders of the service. Father Martin recalls walking into the Cathedral "at five minutes to eleven, carrying the *Odeyak*," with pretty much all the rest of the travellers following behind the boat. "I was trying to explain to the chief sidesman who we were. He was not finding my explanation very credible. Finally, I said, 'Where is Dean Morton?' " Father Martin had only just met the Dean of the Cathedral when he introduced himself at Times Square.

When Joel Morton, known in New York City as the "Green Dean," introduced Mayor Sappa Fleming and Chief Robbie Dick he stressed the way in which the three thousand people praying in the Cathedral that Sunday were implicated in the threat facing the Great Whale communities. He said that the Mayor and the Chief had brought their people to New York to protest, "because it is we in New York who purchase the electric power that is being generated by this project. So we are very implicated in the destruction of their way of life." The Dean's emphasis on the complicity of the congregation is particularly noteworthy in light of the conspiratorial interpretation of the events of this period which later became central to the hyper-nationalist views of some Québec journalists.

Sappa Fleming and Robbie Dick both appeared either more comfortable or more revved up at the Cathedral than they had at Times Square. Sappa Fleming spoke first.

> Today we have finally come to tell people what is going to happen to our land. We know what happened when James Bay One was built twenty years ago. We are feeling the effects of it today. If they build James Bay Two on our river we will feel the effects of it for many years to come.

> So we have come from afar to tell people that we need your support. To environmentalists, to residents, to legislators. To everyone who is here on this Earth. We are telling them that this project is going to end our way of life. Our future, our children's and your children's future is threatened by this project.

> We have come to tell you these things because our government and your government are not going to tell you what is going to happen to our lives. It is up to the people who live up there to tell you that our future is in your hands right now.

> We are the chosen people, the ones who have been chosen to tell you who are here what is facing our people. Because New York is a big place, people from all over the world hear what is said here. So we have come here to tell you what is going to happen to our land. I need your support. Thank you.

Robbie Dick found the Scripture reading directly related to the point he had come to New York to share on Earth Day.

> We have come over a thousand miles to be with you today in this Cathedral.

Our governments are proposing a second phase of James Bay. Our people live off the land. Our economic base is what the land provides. Our way of life is threatened by the destruction of our environment.

We believe the Creator gave us a way to live on this planet. ... I heard today, in the reading from the Book of Genesis mention of a Great Flood. God showed Noah the rainbow sign that there will be no more floods. But we hear that a great flood is coming to our land.

We don't question what the Creator has promised but we question what mankind does to the environment. Without our environment we can not survive as a people.

We need guidance from our elders. They are here with us in spirit. They wanted us to take this message to the people of the world. Every dollar that is spent on exporting electricity from Québec, from our homeland, pays for the destruction of our environment. Please say no to Hydro-Québec. Thank you.

After the Mayor and the Chief had each spoken, the Dean proclaimed, "The boat is their work." *Odeyak* was brought into the Cathedral and followed the sidesmen down the main aisle in the offertory procession. It was placed at the foot of the altar steps. Everybody involved with the trip came down in the procession as well.

Although most of the people in both Great Whale communities are Anglicans, the service in which they took part on Earth Day was a new experience for everyone who had not been to a Cathedral or High Anglican service before. The children gathered around *Odeyak* as it sat in the offertory were startled to find their boat being blessed with incense. After that part of the offertory, the Inuit children sang a song in Inuktituut. After this point Father Martin remembers that things went less smoothly.

The spontaneous communication eventually broke down. The organist cut in and the Cree drummer was deferred until the close of communion. The song was one a Cree hunter sings to his prey for giving up its life for the hunter's survival. In Christian terms it could not have been more appropriate than as a response to communion.

Visiting the Shinnecocks

Missing the chance to meet the popular children's performer, Raffi, at a United Nations reception was the surest sign that *Odeyak* trip was not being managed by a Madison Avenue public relations firm. Next to the Statue of Liberty, what the *Odeyak* travellers most wanted to see in New York was Raffi. Coming out of the Cathedral at 1:00 o'clock in the afternoon, the Great Whale people, who had arrived at Times Square at 7:00 o'clock in the morning, headed for the nearest restaurants. It simply was not possible to hustle elders and children to yet another ceremony without a meal. When they arrived late at the United Nations the celebrations had already begun.

Their seats on the main floor were held only until the Earth Day celebrations began. When the churchgoers arrived late they were hustled up to the visitors gallery. During a slide presentation about Earth Day the presence of Cree and Inuit visitors from northern Québec was recognized. At the end of the celebration, a group called *Evergreen* from Toronto came up on stage. When they saw the *Evergreens'* leader, the children in the *Odeyak* group whispered to one another, "Its Raffi!"

Later, the group would learn that Raffi had also been eager to meet them. Access to the reception, however, depended on having been seated on the Assembly floor. Once the program was over, the churchgoers who had been shunted into the gallery upstairs, were hustled out by the security guards. Raffi would remain more elusive than the Statue of Liberty.

The Shinnecock Reservation at the east end of Long Island is not as big today as when it was confirmed to them in the 1600's. It was a fitting place to end a trip that had begun with a welcome at an Algonquin conference in Hull, Québec, and visits to Kanesatake and Kahnawake, the two Mohawk communities near Montréal. Crees and Inuit from the far north have very mixed emotions when they visit an Indian reservation in the south. After four days in New York City, a feast in a Native community was a welcome relief. Matthew Mukash, re-tracing the *Odeyak* trip a year later, remarked, as he drove into Kanesatake, how he had survived his university years by going out to visit friends there on weekends.

But northern people who continue to use a traditional hunting ground several times larger than the whole of Long Island can be forgiven for looking at southern reservations with a sense of foreboding. Matthew, for one, had expressed this foreboding four days earlier, standing on Ross's Dock, when he had wondered out loud whether the Great Whale River might look like New York Harbor some day in the future.

Monday, however, was a chance to relax in a homey atmosphere after the series of hurried salutations to Mother Earth the previous day. It was a place where children could play on the beach and a place where Taxicab Killer was not on the minds of young women or concerned parents. It was a place where they could visit with people who had lived on their island at least as long as the Crees and Inuit had lived in the Ungava.

Some of the Inuit elders had been born in a place called Long Island, down the coast of Hudson Bay from the mouth of the Great Whale River. Their Long Island shelters a sound at the point that separates the more southerly James Bay from the larger Hudson Bay. Transplanted to the larger, southern Sound, the northern Long Island would look like a smaller shadow of Long Island, New York.

A good place to visit on the last New York day. The *Odeyak* travellers came out to the Shinnecock Reservation on the bus. A mishap with the truck meant that the *Odeyak*, which was to have been launched a short distance away, would miss its final engagement. A great many people were sitting on the beach waiting for its arrival, but Sappa Fleming was able to try the waters of Long Island Sound in a kayak.

An outdoor supper was served just outside the Shinnecock's Presbyterian church. The visitors gave their hosts a bag of crabs which had been presented to them by a fisherman when they had stopped to watch him unloading his boat at Bellport. The large Atlantic crabs were a new experience for people from the near-Arctic. When David Masty, the Whapmagoostui Band manager came into the kitchen, he said that the crabs looked very good. His people had never eaten crabs before and "weren't sure how it was done." So the Shinnecock women showed the Crees and the Inuit how to eat crabs.

The Shinnecock's fishing weirs were a more familiar sight to the northern Natives. Their attachment to the sea was the surest sign that, as much as they may have adapted to the contemporary life of Long Island, there are important ways in which the Shinnecocks have retained a connection with their traditional past.

Goose Break

The 12-hour bus ride from New York to Montréal was devoted to entertaining children, telling stories and dozing. Dozing allowed time for dreaming. Two dreams were shared by anyone on the bus who was able to doze. Each had his or her own memories of the strange events that led to the decision to make the five week trip from the Great Whale communities on Hudson Bay to the Hudson River and New York City; and every Cree and Inuit heading north on April 24, 1990, was looking forward to getting home to take part in the first sign of the Arctic springtime, Goose Break.

Chapter 2:
Building the Odeyak

The Place to Which the Whales Come

Once, a man and his wife went to Florida on a late winter holiday with another couple. By the second day of their holiday, his wife and his friend could see that the man would never rest in the sunshine state. It was Goose Break, the month when the Crees of James Bay look for the big birds returning from the south. The man would not feel at ease until he was out on the land, sitting in the eel grass, listening for the familiar honk signaling the end of the long winter. Before the ice was gone, his people would begin to enjoy the food their land offers in the spring: goose and duck, whitefish and pike. The man was Robbie Dick, chief of the northernmost band of the James Bay Crees.

The place to which Robbie and Elizabeth returned has a different name in each of the languages spoken there. It is Whapmagoostui (Whap-mawg-stwee) in Cree, Kuujjuaraapik in Inuktituut, Great Whale in English, and Poste de la Baleine in French. Whapmagoostui is the only one of nine Cree communities located above Cape Jones, the point separating James Bay from Hudson Bay. It is the northernmost Cree community on the eastern coast of Hudson Bay. Kuujjuaraapik is the southernmost of 15 Inuit communities strung out along the coast of the Ungava Peninsula from Killiniq, at the Labrador border, around the northernmost point at Ivujivik and south down the coast.

The Cree name, given by people who come to the coast each spring from the interior, describes "the place to which the whales come," the Whale River. The Inuit name, given by people who traditionally came from the islands and from points up and down the coast to find the whales at the mouth of the river each year, describes the great size of the river. Whoever coined the English name, later translated into French, brought together the perspectives of the two original cultures.

Whapmagoostui is located on a flat, sandy, wind-blown point of land between the tidal mouth of the river and the open water of Hudson Bay. It is the only Cree village built on open land, the visible trees standing well beyond the settled area. When the wind blows from the west, it comes across hundreds of miles of Arctic waters. When it blows from the east, it passes over a desert mountain terrain, filling the open spaces in the village with drifting snow which mixes with the sand. The hillside becomes terraced with waves of packed snow, bordered with a milk chocolate edging.

The village consists of half a dozen rows of houses, strung along a grid. Except for the very few remaining federal houses from the late 1950s, all the houses are quite new. Each string of houses is a mix of three different designs built by the band council in the fifteen years since the Crees signed *The James Bay and Northern Québec Agreement*.

The easiest way to tell where the Cree village of Whapmagoostui ends and the Inuit village of Kuujjuaraapik begins is by the houses. All the Cree houses of Whapmagoostui are bungalows raised enough for the basement windows to admit good light. The Inuit houses are two storey structures standing on stilts sunk into the sandy soil, a design ideally suited for the permafrost of the more northerly Inuit communities where it is not possible to dig basements. The distinctly northern design of the Inuit houses lying to the west of the main street, closer to the bay and farther from the river, sets the Inuit and Cree communities apart from one another. Beyond the airport, at the end of the narrow point, is the tank farm supplying fuel for the houses in both communities as well as for the skidoos which seem as numerous as the people.

The two main stores of Great Whale are on the Kuujjuaraapik side. The Northern, successor to the Hudson Bay Company, is diagonally across the street from the Kuujjuaraapik Municipal Office and the Inuit Co-op. The convenience store, on the Cree side, is a few short steps from the town line and almost cheek by jowl with the Anglican church building which serves both communities, each in their own language. Of the two public eateries, the short-order snack bar in a shack beside the airport building provides the more palatable food and the Air Inuit Hotel, the more expensive. Beyond these five establishments, cash is not a big item in Great Whale.

Up the hill and out of sight from the Chief's office is the white ghetto, the residence of Québec government officials, Hydro-Québec workers, the two non-Native constables in the provincial police detachment of four officers, and the non-Native teachers in both the Inuit and the Cree schools. Father Tom Martin, whose parish includes both communities, says that when the Crees have a public feast Chief Dick unfailingly invites the non-Natives as well as the Inuit, but very few whites accept his hospitality.

The grid patterns on which each of the two communities are laid out are at right angles. Whapmagoostui's runs parallel to the river while Kuujjuaraapik's is by the bay. The grids are the most visible benefit of *The James Bay and Northern Québec Agreement*, the modern-day treaty signed by Canada, Québec, Hydro-Québec, the Crees and the Inuit in 1975. Until the *Agreement*, Whapmagoostui and Kuujjuaraapik were one community with two, three or four names. Although each family undoubtedly had its preference, houses were built and tents were pitched where space was found. The *Agreement* required that a line be drawn between the Cree land, which would be declared a federal Indian reserve and the Inuit land which would be a Québec municipality.

The line between Whapmagoostui and Kuujjuaraapik became a very deep division in the years between 1975 and 1990. In 1975, the Inuit were the much larger community. By 1990, both villages numbered about five hundred people. Chief Robbie Dick says that the option given to the Inuit of relocating up the coast aggravated tensions between the Great Whale communities.

> When some of the Inuit from this community relocated farther up the coast, that contributed, in a way, to the difficulties for the Inuit who stayed behind because a number of their negotiators were among the ones who moved up the coast. The ones who stayed behind felt that they were not being taken into consideration. Their community land base is so small that people feel badly about it. But they did not realize that this would be an outcome of the relocation of part of the Inuit community.

Whapmagoostui received fewer benefits from the *Agreement* than the more southerly Cree communities, presumably because it was less affected by the earlier developments, particularly the La Grande Hydro-electric Complex and the road network into the southern Cree territory. One visible benefit is the bush plane that flies families from the village to their camps each fall and back in the spring, usually with a trip out for a few weeks at Christmas as well. A subsidy to trappers who spend extended periods on the land roughly matches the cost of two flights per family per year.

Throughout the territory of the James Bay Crees, the harvest lands or trapline areas are each held by a particular person. The Whapmagoostui harvest area extends to the edge of the barrens, bordering on the tundra. To offer the prospect of an equal harvest, each trapline must be significantly larger than at such southern points as Waswanipi or Mistissini. Even the traplines immediately south of the Great Whale River are considerably smaller than the ones at the northern end of the territory, near the Seal Lakes. Travelling as much as two hundred miles to their enormous traplines has given the Whapmagoostui people a certain fame for their prowess in covering great distances by canoe and on foot.

Within memory of the present generation of elders, people occasionally travelled 250 miles in mid-winter to trade into Ft. Chimo on the east side of the peninsula. More often, they went deep into the interior of the Ungava Peninsula where they would meet Naskapi from Schefferville and even from Labrador. Certain families at Whapmagoostui are known today as Naskapi families because of marriages begun on the interior plateau.

The Crees' pride in covering great distances, and enduring the challenges of bush travel, lends a special value to the radio network which maintains contact with the entire land harvested by the people of Whapmagoostui. The radio enables the community to extend a safety net to all its members. The life of the Cree hunting family has always relied on what would today be called "active listening." When a hunting family is not heard from, it is time to find if others on the radio system, families with neighbouring camps in the bush, or the pilots who fly families between their camps and the villages, may have seen them.

The Whapmagoostui Crees mostly live the way they always have. That means living on the land, hunting and trapping for months at a time through the sub-Arctic winter, and coming together to fish and to visit at the mouth of the Great Whale River during the short near-Arctic summer.

Robbie Dick's office and the band council chamber, on the upper floor of a very modern band council building, are angled to give the occupants a view of the entire village of Whapmagoostui as well as the hills and the bay beyond the river. The design of the room ensures that the Chief of Whapmagoostui always knows that the basic reality of the community is something other than the paper trail leading to his desk.

Robbie Dick, the Chief of Whapmagoostui, is a man as large as his hopes. Something in his frame and presence is reminiscent of Lorne Greene, not so much the Ponderosa cowboy as the man who read the news to Canada through World War II. If Robbie Dick read the news, people would start to believe it. On one of Robbie Dick's early public appearances in the south he testified before the National Energy Board. After the Board had already been told what damming the river would mean to the natural economy of the Great Whale communities, Robbie Dick explained how the loss of the traditional economy would also undermine the future of the Cree language. The language, he told the Board, is an expression of the people's relationship to the land. When he finally gets home from his office at 9:00 p.m. on a winter evening, Robbie is quite likely to spend a couple of hours skinning a caribou given to him by a hunter.

Robbie Dick, along with other Cree leaders, makes the same point time and again, that the main benefits credited to the *Agreement* by government are ones that all Canadians receive one way or another: municipal services such as public health, water and sewerage, education and vocational training for their children, and economic support for their primary industry.

Returning the Gift

On December 5, 1989, Grand Chief Matthew Coon Come, along with several other members and advisers of the Grand Council of the Crees (of Québec), went to Montpelier, Vermont. Their mission was to persuade the Public Service Board, a Vermont State regulatory agency, to reject a contract under which a group of Vermont utilities would buy their largest block of power from Hydro-Québec for the next 20 years. Steve MacAusland, a free-lance New England journalist familiar with Cree politics, had arranged for his friend Denny Alsop to meet with the Grand Chief and the other Grand Council leaders who would be attending the hearings. Alsop was an environmental activist with a special commitment to the cause of the James Bay people. When Denny met up with the Crees at the hearing room he was dismayed. He told Brian Craik, the Crees' Director of Federal Relations, that the public relations battle was about to be lost.

> If the story that went out was only about what went on in the hearing room, the Crees would lose. Simply because they did not have the slickest lawyers and could not make the most sensational statements. But this was a story about rivers, not about hearing rooms. I suggested that the Chief go down to a river bank and make his statement to the cameras against the backdrop of the river.

The nearest river setting was only a block away. When the hearing broke for lunch, the Crees invited all the camera people down to the river for a press conference. Once they had a visual that illustrated what the issue was all about, nobody wanted to use the footage from the hearing room.

Denny was invited to lunch with the Grand Council delegation. When everyone had finally ordered their meal the table became so quiet he thought they were about to say Grace. Matthew Coon Come turned to Denny and said, "Tell us your idea."

> What just happened on the river bank needs to be re-created over and over again in the consciousness of New England and New York State. I think you can do that by having the people who live at the mouth of the river build a large paddling canoe to become an ark, a symbol of their way of life, their culture. I don't know how you will do it. I know about the ice and how late the rivers are frozen. But I think that that canoe needs to come through your cities, over the border, through Vermont and down the Hudson River to arrive in New York City on Earth Day, next April 22.

I promise that if you work with me you will make a media story in every city along your route and people will know who the Crees are and will understand the issue.

After this outburst, Denny recalls asking himself, "Who the hell do you think you are making that speech to people you have never met in your life?"

Bill Namagoose, the Executive Director of the Grand Council, broke the silence. "Why do you want to do this for us?" he asked.

The answer went back 18 years to July, 1971, when Denny Alsop drove his grandfather's truck into Mistissini, the end of the road. Travel beyond this community on the edge of the Cree territory was either by canoe or by bush plane. Denny had arrived at Mistissini with Steve MacAusland and four other Harvard friends to begin a sixty day canoe trip down the Eastmain River. At that time, the Eastmain rose in the plateau north of Lake Mistissini and flowed eastward almost two hundred miles to James Bay. Eighteen years later, the Eastmain River had all but disappeared, most of its water having been re-routed into the La Grande.

The pickup that arrived at Mistissini brimmed with the finest and shiniest that America could offer. There were six Harvard students, film processing and moral support from *The National Geographic*, a donated Old Towne canoe and camping gear from Eastern Mountain Sports. But when Chief Smally Petawabano greeted the group he was clearly concerned at the prospect of six young whites taking on the big river. Denny Alsop had never met a Native person before. As Denny tells the story, he came to realize that, in a very special sense, they were coming under the care of the Cree chief. It was not only permission to travel through the Cree lands they wanted but advice about the route. The line on the map did not indicate the portages around the rapids or between the various lakes and rivers.

Seated in Smally's office, with maps and pencils set out, the students were ready to take notes about the best route. Smally began to talk them through the route by saying, "Go up to the third island and cut across to the mouth of the Wabassanon. When you've gone two miles there is a fallen tree on the left." When he had talked them through fifty portages over a distance of two hundred miles, the college men sat awestruck. This was a kind of knowledge they were not going to find at Harvard.

A couple of days above Eastmain, two weeks after losing their food packs and living on geese and pike and trout, the students came across a crew surveying a site for a bridge over the Eastmain River. When they arrived in Eastmain, two days later, they brought the news to the Crees that a Hydro-Québec surveying team was laying down lines on their land. The news that Denny, Steve MacAusland, and their friends brought with them was the beginning of James Bay Power Development in the area of Eastmain.

> When we told the chief and the people gathered around us what we had seen, we could see a cloud coming over their faces. We had arrived at East-main about the 28th of August, at the time when trapping families gather in their villages along the coast to visit and to fish. So none of the Eastmain people would have seen the helicopter traffic or heard the surveyors thrashing about in the bush two days' paddle upstream.

> We left knowing that there was an impending tragedy but without beginning to comprehend its size.

This journey was the greatest experience of Denny's life. He and his friends had paddled the rivers and walked the portage trails of the Crees, moving through their camp sites from the previous winter, past the grave sites of ancestors and children. It was, however, Steve MacAusland rather than Denny who remained in touch with Eastmain over the years. Steve spent enough time in Eastmain that he developed a fluency in conversational Cree.

Denny went on to become a canoe-maker who frequently designed and built canoes for particular and specialized needs. In 1988, when he was becoming increasingly alarmed about the forests and waters of his native state, Denny combined his knowledge of canoes with a basic knowledge of public relations and appeals to the mass media. He spent 33 days crossing Massachusetts from west to east, from the interior to the coast, in a state where the rivers all run north and south. Denny needed to go against the grain simply to make the people of Massachusetts aware of the sources of their water and how those sources are endangered.

Denny started to understand the media when he discovered the value of having a car phone in his canoe from which he could give interviews at each point of interest or at appropriate times of the day. Denny's media insights were reinforced when he reached Boston. An eight-person freighter canoe from which his friend, Steve, was filming his arrival was part of the fleet that came out to greet him.

Late in the summer of 1989, a short time after Hydro-Québec announced its plans for the Great Whale River, Steve called Denny from Boston. "The Crees are really going to fight this. And the first battleground is going to be Vermont." Steve understood that the Cree leaders had signed the *Agreement* under duress. Even so, he had found the signing so discouraging that it came to represent, in his own mind, the winding down of several years of intimate involvement with the Cree community at Eastmain. His conviction that the Crees were again prepared to fight had led Steve MacAusland to make contact with Brian Craik at the Grand Council of the Crees office in Ottawa. Brian told him there was an urgent need for a support movement in the States and a media campaign to get the message onto television. In sharing Steve's renewed commitment, Denny saw that he, too, had something to offer, and a way to return a gift.

At the Grand Council lunch in Montpelier, Denny Alsop considered carefully Bill Namagoose's question about why he wanted to do something for the Crees.

> Eighteen years ago, I made a journey from one Cree community to another, from Mistissini to Eastmain. For sixty days I travelled through your land. It was a gift from your people to me. I want to return that gift to you.

The conversation turned to the question of who in Great Whale could still build a canoe. Denny knew that he had been accepted by the group.

Matthew Coon Come explained that the decision did not lie with the Grand Council but with the local band council. Denny would need to go to Whapmagoostui to present his idea. The Grand Council members at the lunch in Vermont agreed that they would seek the support of the Grand Council for whatever decision Whapmagoostui made on Denny's proposal. On January 22, 1990, six weeks after the lunch in Montpelier, Denny Alsop was on his way to Whapmagoostui.

The Canadian Air flight attendants announced the destination of flight 748 as "Val d'Or, Radisson and Kuujjuaraapik." Denny had done well to come in on the evening flight from Albany to Montréal the night before. The plane left Dorval Airport at 7:10 a.m. Four hours later, when the breakfast flight arrived in Kuujjuaraapik, it had travelled a little better than 650 miles north. It had also gone almost two hundred miles west, to a point due north of Peterborough, Ontario, or Rochester, N.Y.

Coming in on the last leg of the flight, the vista Denny saw was very different from his memory of the Cree territory around Mistissini or Waswanipi. The flat coastal plain is punctuated by massive outcroppings of rock and long, winding streams. On the edge of the treeline, the few trees are spindly black spruce, widely spaced and slow growing. The soil is thin and more than half of what smaller maps show as land is in fact water. This Great Whale River terrain is blessed with the winter daylight missing from the higher Arctic.

The only non-air access to Great Whale in the winter is a one hundred mile snowmobile trail through the bush from Chissasibi or a longer route on the ice of the James Bay and Hudson Bay coasts. The Canadian Air flight is the one large plane which flies into Great Whale every week-day. It is supplemented by two regional flights: a daily Air Creebec milk run which connects all the Cree communities with Val d'Or, the regional capital of northern Québec and the Air Inuit flight to the Inuit communities around the Hudson Bay-Ungava coast and to Iqaluit in the eastern N.W.T. Kuujjuaraapik is the air gateway to the Arctic, the transfer point from all points south to all points north. The map places the mouth of the Great Whale River slightly north of 55 degrees. That is 11 degrees or eight hundred miles south of the Arctic Circle. But for Inuit heading south, or anyone else heading north, it is the gateway to one another's worlds.

Early January proved to be a good time for Denny to visit the Great Whale communities. Some of the trappers who came out of the bush shortly before Christmas had not yet gone back to their traplines. The ground was snow covered, the river had just frozen down to the mouth, and the Bay had just begun to freeze.

The Whapmagoostui Band Council building would be the envy of any community council for its combination of beauty and efficiency. The sounds of telephones, fax machines and computer printers tell visitors that this is a thoroughly modern and up-to-date administrative centre.

There is no smoking in the Whapmagoostui Band Council offices except in one room. When Denny walked into that room, a small crowd was gathered around a board table drinking coffee, talking in Cree, laughing and bumming cigarettes. One man in particular began to engage him in conversation, even, after a while, to befriend him. Robbie Niquanacappo clearly wanted to know what had brought Denny to Whapmagoostui. Robbie let Denny know his own background in some detail. He also let Denny know that to speak to the band council it was necessary to speak to him first.

Robbie N. is the Whapmagoostui Band Council's gatekeeper. He sets the agenda for the monthly band council meetings. He is the one who decides whether a matter merits the Council's attention. Prior to the meeting, Robbie listens to each person who wants to present a proposal to the council. He particularly meets with outsiders who have a pitch to make to the Council. A monthly meeting can go for a few hours in the afternoon or evening or for several days.

Robbie's scheduling can be as crucial to an outsider's reception by the Council as the actual presentation. The rhythm of life in Whapmagoostui is different from the rhythm of most of the places from which visitors come: Montréal, Ottawa or Québec City. Big city visitors have been known to convince themselves that the importance of their visit calls for a certain kind of urgent response to the message that they bring.

Robbie Niquanacappo is one of a growing number of young Cree leaders who are sophisticated both in the ways of the cities to which they travel and in the ways of the bush. For his birthday, the winter following the *Odeyak* trip, the people who knew Robbie N. best each presented him with something that touched a major part of his being. Robbie's parents, who had just returned from three months in the bush, honored him with a special feast including his favourite delicacy, beaver tail. The night before, his wife, Joan, had given him a video camera.

The view from Robbie Niquanicappo's office is not very different from the one from Chief Dick's office. Robbie is the Deputy Chief. His office is right next door. Robbie is an active listener but not one to suffer fools gladly. When he was first introduced to Denny Alsop, Robbie found himself greeting a tall, scruffy American wearing a red checkered lumber jacket.

> This guy comes in, plumps himself down and starts telling me about this crazy idea that he has for a trip, a canoe trip of all things! A canoe trip from here to New York City for April 22nd! The first thing I thought, when he talked about a trip to finish on April 22nd, was the ice on the rivers.
>
> Right then and there I nearly threw him out of my office. The idea was just too crazy to think about. But he started talking about why he wanted to do it, why he wanted the Council to hear him. It had to do with Earth Day on April 22nd and helping bring the message about the James Bay project. That part sounded good but the canoe trip, I was not too crazy about.

For Denny, the root of Robbie's scepticism surfaced when he asked, "What group are you with?" When Denny said that he was not associated with any group, Robbie asked again, "Audubon? Sierra Club? Who are you? Where do you come from?" Denny tried to convince Robbie that he had no affiliations, that he was simply trying to return a gift to the Crees and offer Whapmagoostui a way to capture the hearts and minds of his corner of America. Robbie, meanwhile, had a much more immediate and practical thought on his mind.

> As a matter of fact, I was not even too crazy about letting this guy in to see the Council. I decided to let him into the Council, if only to save myself the trouble of kicking him out myself. The more he talked the more I thought, "Maybe, just maybe. Crazy enough to be good."
>
> I had already finished the agenda. Normally, when people come to see me at the last minute I put them at the end of the agenda. But I put this one on first thing. I figured that might put him off balance. "If he's going to trip himself, it will be now."

While Robbie N. was speculating on the sanity of his visitor, Denny's own concept of his mission was undergoing a radical revision.

> When I finally was able to share my whole idea with Robbie Niquanacappo, I understood that this journey was not something about me. The journey had to belong to the Crees. If what I had to offer was not about Denny but about the Crees, I needed to cross that barrier before I went into the Band Council meeting.

> Robbie spent two or three hours chain smoking cigarettes and getting me to talk and telling me about himself. Somehow, he reconditioned me into thinking about how this could be a Cree thing rather than another Denny project.

Denny was surprised but pleased when Robbie said that he was putting him on the Band Council agenda for that evening. Steve had warned him that one way the Council protects the community is by letting visitors experience the community for awhile before expecting them to be ready to speak.

Robbie introduced Denny to Marie Symes-Grehan. "This is the person we hired to help us work with your culture." Marie reinforced Denny's own new perspective.

> White people have been trying to do things for Native people for centuries. It does not work that way. It has to be theirs or it does not work. In that way, they are no different than we are. Your biggest job will be to listen, to understand where your idea fits with their needs. Their need is not to be led, not to be helped. You want to find out if they are going to receive the gift.

Five hours after Denny arrived in Whapmagoostui, after travelling and being awake more than 24 hours, he walked up the spiral staircase and went into the Council meeting. As well as the six band councillors, the band manager David Masty and his financial director, Abraham Kawapit, were also present when Denny came into the council chamber. Matthew Mukash, the secretary of the James Bay Task Force, and Marie Symes-Grehan followed Denny into the room. Chief Robbie Dick introduced himself to Denny and shook hands. He drew a seating plan showing the names of all the people in the room with their roles and positions. Then he invited him to speak. Denny stood up and told the Council his idea.

> When I had begun to sketch the idea and had referred to the thing I was visualizing as a "canoe," the Chief interjected and referred to the boat as a "UFO, an unidentified floating object," everyone in the room laughed. Robbie Dick's humor simply dissolved whatever tension I might have felt in the room and in myself. I felt that he had given a signal that he was prepared to help it all come together.

When Denny mentioned his discussion with the Grand Council members in Montpelier, Chief Dick asked whether the Grand Council was really serious about their support. When he was told that the Grand Chief had remarked that a picture of a dog team hauling the boat across the ice on a sled would make "a great visual," Robbie Dick asked, "Well, will the Grand Chief paddle this canoe to New York himself?"

Chief Dick's humour turned the council's attention to the very real questions of who would do the work that would be needed to make the idea a reality. Robbie Dick asked Denny to show the Council the route he had in mind. Denny drew a map on the blackboard showing the eastern North American continent from Hudson Bay to New York City. He listed the major cities they would be sure to touch: Montréal, Burlington, Vermont, Albany, New York. Beside New York City he wrote, "Earth Day, April 22."

When the question arose about who might be able to build an appropriate boat, there was no doubt at all that the Band Council would ask Billie Weetaltuk, an Inuk from Kuujjuaraapik and one of the most respected and longest established canoe builders on the coast. The mention of Billie Weetaltuk helped bring the discussion around to the need to involve the Inuit community. Robbie Dick emphasized the importance of a joint project, "They are half of the community here."

The Whapmagoostui Council agreed to think about the idea overnight. In the meantime, Matthew Mukash and Denny would discuss the idea with Sappa Fleming, the Mayor of Kuujjuaraapik.

The hour was late and the air was cold when David Masty drove his snowmobile from the band council office to his home with Denny Alsop sitting behind him. When Denny fell into bed, very soon after the two men had come into the house, a sense of tranquil acceptance wound down the adrenalin on which he had been running much of the time since leaving Montréal twenty hours earlier.

The Healing Vessel

Although Matthew Mukash was part of a team assembled by the Grand Council, he was working under the direction of the band council. As Director of the Band's Hydro Task Force, his job was to organize the community's appeal for southern support. Matthew was born on his father's trapline. When he was 13 his father told him that he had to leave the bush and go away to school to learn the new ways. Since then he has spent 16 of the last 27 years studying. One reason for his academic success is that he was one of the few northern students to miss the residential school system. His father wanted him to go to a school in Québec where he could learn French. Like other Cree leaders, he has transferred the tradition of travelling in the bush to travelling between their village and the city.

The morning after the Whapmagoostui Council's meeting, Matthew and Denny met at the Kuujjuaraapik Municipal Office, with Sappa Fleming, the boldly diminutive Inuit Mayor who, five weeks later, would invoke the memory of John F. Kennedy in his minute of glory at Times Square in New York City. Councillor Sarah Bennett, Robert Fleming, and Alex Tukatuk, an information officer for Makivik, the Inuit regional organization, joined the meeting.

Matthew laid the groundwork for Denny's proposal with a strong statement of good will:

> For many, many years our two communities have been living side by side in a divided house. We've known each other for thousands of years. This James Bay *Agreement* has really divided us. We used to go to the same dances. We used to share food with each other. We used to help each other out in the bush. Since the James Bay *Agreement* we have forgotten to share. Now Hydro-Québec sits in the background and gloats at us. This is a chance for us to do something together.

Matthew introduced Denny as a person who had brought an idea to the Crees, "and we," Matthew told the assembled Inuit councillors, "would like to share it with you. We would like you to participate in it and to own it as much as we do." The Inuit Mayor and councillors were clearly moved by Matthew's gesture. After Denny had gone through his proposal, Sappa asked, "Has the band council approved this?" Matthew said that they had not yet announced a decision but that they would likely do so the next day. Sappa clearly saw an opportunity to register the Inuit decision to participate before the Crees had formally decided to participate themselves. He said, "We approve the project! But we have one condition. If this boat is to represent both our peoples it must be half-canoe but also half-kayak, as a symbol of the two nations working together."

Everyone in the room agreed that that was the way to go. Matthew Mukash got out a pencil and paper and drew a picture, which he labelled "Unidentified Floating Object, January 23, 1990." Matthew had drawn his vision of the hybrid Sappa had requested. The canoe (*ode*, in Cree) was no longer a canoe, it had become half-canoe and half-kayak. Matthew, the Cree building engineer, at Sappa Fleming's direction, had sketched the world's first odeyak.

Denny's boat building heart sank at the very idea of a hybrid. He was not even confident, at that point, that there was anyone in Great Whale who could build a respectable canoe, let alone anything that could sustain a long and difficult trip. He reminded himself of Marie's instruction, "Let them do it themselves. They know what they are doing."

Everyone went out to the office kitchen and made tea. When they brought their tea back into Sappa's office they chatted for awhile. Sappa agreed to step outside and make a statement on Denny's video recorder. Denny began to understand that he no longer owned the gift he had given.

The instant and intuitive appeal of the *Odeyak* to the pragmatically inclined leaders and traditionally minded elders of the two Great Whale communities sprang from an element no outsider could possibly have appreciated at the time. The Inuit of Kuujjuaraapik and the Crees of Whapmagoostui had lost something in recent years that they had enjoyed together for the last six or seven generations, the possibility of living in relative peace and harmony and sharing a common village space. The *Odeyak* could become the instrument through which they could begin to heal the rift between their two communities.

When the *James Bay and Northern Québec Agreement* came into effect in 1975, there were, Robbie Dick says, already hard feelings about how it had been negotiated. Under the *Agreement,* each one gained jurisdiction over a portion of the land they had previously believed to be theirs while they saw the other gain control of the rest. Under the *Agreement,* village areas are called Category I land. Category II represents lands in which either the Crees or the Inuit have exclusive hunting rights. But at Great Whale, for seven generations at least, there had been, in fact, a tremendous overlap in hunting territory. The Crees had often hunted whales when they were plentiful in the summer. The Crees continued to follow the caribou onto the islands in the Bay just as the Inuit looked for the caribou in the interior earlier in the season. The semi-annual goose hunt each fall and spring, perhaps the most reliable source of food for both peoples, had never considered property lines at all. The *Agreement* made no acknowledgement of the overlap.

Under the *Agreement*, not only would the Crees and Inuit be excluded from one another's hunting territory, but neighbouring Aboriginal peoples — the Montagnais and Naskapi on the east and the Inuit from the islands of Hudson Bay, legally part of the N.W.T. — would also be excluded. According to Matthew Mukash, the whole discussion of land selection was beyond the vocabulary of both the Crees and the Inuit. Neither group had the previous experience, cultural attitudes or even linguistic facility required to discuss land ownership. The whole idea of drawing property lines simply runs against the basic reality of peoples whose food supply depends upon what they are able to hunt and gather in the forest or on the water.

Not only were property lines drawn between the communities, they were to have two very different kinds of administration. The nine Cree communities were much more directly affected by the initial hydro development projects of James Bay One. They were also concerned about preserving their constitutionally protected status. The Inuit, whose more northerly communities would not witness the effects of the megaprojects for decades, had historically enjoyed far less support from the federal government. They took a more open and trusting attitude to the province. The 15 Inuit communities agreed to become a regional municipality, with each settlement becoming a new Québec town.

As Robbie Dick explained,

Ever since then there have been problems of jurisdiction between the two communities. ... because in the area of the villages we have always both had all the same rights as far as anyone here is concerned. We and the Inuit had the same rights everywhere that we went. We could go and build a shed or a camp here or there. Now we can not do it without the authorization of their council and they can not do it on our land without our authorization.

The launching of the *Odeyak* as part of the public awareness campaign about how this community is threatened was designed to have the communities at least combine their strength in opposing the hydro project. It didn't mean that we were ready to do everything together. But there was this one thing that we wanted to do together. The *Odeyak* somewhat brought the community together again because we accomplished the one thing that we were all determined to do.

Robbie N., the man who first put the *Odeyak* idea on the council's agenda, summed up the complex motivations of the two communities' leaders, "Creating that unity was as important as the message we were taking to the outside world."

The Boat Builder

Billie Weetaltuk's boat shop is a boatmaker's dream. Sitting wedged between the road out from town and the drop down to the river, it is a very long shed filled with good light and abundant work space. Inside the shop, tools and pieces of wood and metal seem to be scattered randomly and interspersed with snowmobile parts.

Billie Weetaltuk, an Inuk who had just turned 70, had learned boat building from his father who made "white man's sail boats" in the Moose Factory area, the southernmost part of James Bay. Billie came to Kuujjuaraapik in 1963 from Cape Hope Island where he had lived hunting and fishing with his father. Like weathered craftsmen in most cultures, Billie has spent most of his adult life too deeply absorbed in his work to comment on what the weather is doing that day.

When Matthew, Denny and Peter, their Inuit translator, walked into his shop, Billie was busy working on a snowmobile engine mounted in a vice. Billie could speak quite good Cree and Matthew knew a little Inuktituut. Peter could translate very well and Denny talked with his hands, so the discussion began well. Billie was expecting them. He understood that there was a white man who wanted him to build a canoe. Billie asked Denny what kind of boat he was going to be building. Matthew pulled out the drawing that he had made in 45 seconds the day before. Denny said, "Twenty-five feet long, ten people paddling, down a big lake and a long river." Billie scratched his head for a minute, nodded up and down and said, "Yes, I can do that. No problem."

Denny was clearly uncomfortable. In his experience, designing a boat requires a lot of knowledge and a lot of sophisticated communication. A boat that has a long way to go through a variety of difficult waters requires very careful thought. Peter, the translator, had told Billie Weetaltuk that this boat had to look half like a kayak. How was this man going to design a boat with no more discussion than that?

As everybody was making ready to leave, Billie said, "I need the materials. I have not got any materials." Billie had stopped building canoes and was now doing mostly outboard motor and snowmobile repair. Matthew told Billie, "The Crees and the Inuit will pay you for it. How much will the boat cost?" Billie, who had had some unfortunate experiences collecting from fishermen for his work, also knew the difficulties of bringing boat building materials to Great Whale in the winter. Matthew assured Billie that the materials would be provided.

Denny was apoplectic at the casual way the matter was being handled. He turned to Peter and said, "Quick, Peter, ask him how wide the boat will be to go down the long lake." Billie could see that Denny was a white man needing reassurance. He pulled out his Stanley steel lock measuring tape and had Peter and Denny stand side by side while he measured across their respective backsides and held the tape up over their heads and showed them 40 inches. Denny was then convinced that Billie Weetaltuk knew what he was doing.

The next day, when Matthew and Denny returned to his shop, Billie presented a sample of each of the items that he required — sheathing, rib stock, canvass — with a list of sizes. Billie is basically a taciturn craftsman. He would never show anyone, outside his family, more than a glimpse of the deep happiness he felt at building the vessel with which the community would challenge Hydro. Denny would certainly never know how much time Billie spent sketching and drawing before he began to make the mold.

The idea of the *Odeyak* as a hybrid, half-canoe and half-kayak, may have been a wonderful political metaphor. As a boat that was expected to travel a very long distance, the *Odeyak* presented some serious design challenges. As Robbie Dick pointed out, a kayak is built for one person while a freighter canoe holds several. If the *Odeyak* were literally half-and-half, one end would have one person and the other four, six or more.

> If we had that many at one end and only one on the other — not only would it look peculiar, it wouldn't be stable. In order to fit more people into the boat and maintain the balance, only a quarter of the boat was built as a kayak. So that was the way it was built, but the symbol of it was for the two communities to travel together.

Billie's 28 year-old-daughter, Caroline, had been his builder's mate since she was eight, when she started helping out at his shop after school. According to Caroline, Billie had built some seven hundred boats when he decided to fix engines because the money was easier. Every wooden canoe is built around a mold and Caroline points out, for an interested visitor, the five different molds on which Billie has built this flotilla.

For Billie, there were two things that made building the one-of-a-kind *Odeyak* difficult. One was that he had to make the mold. With a finished mold and an experienced helper, Billie would typically make a boat in a week. The second difference was his lack of experience with the kayak design. Growing up as far south as Moose Factory, there were no kayaks around when he was learning boat building from his father. As a result, the *Odeyak* would take three weeks to build instead of one.

Billie was under doctor's orders to avoid heavy work but that did not slow his pace. He recruited his younger son, Morris, until he took on other work and was replaced by his older brother, Redfern. Andrew Natashaquan, a talented Cree builder whose experience with Billie went back as far as Billie's early years in Great Whale, came to join him. But the steadiest if least obtrusive helper in Billie's shop was Caroline. As the boat shed began to buzz with activity, Billie found that it was hard to sit still and supervise others. Caroline has succinctly summed up Billie's approach to having less strength and more help. "He was not going to work himself, but just make sure that we built it right. He told us what needed to be done and we did it. But as the work went along he started to work too."

Billie was able to start work quickly. The Cree Housing Authority provided the wood for him to build the mold. Knowing that the *Odeyak* was to be one-of-a-kind, Billie's mold did not need to be made with the permanence and solidity of the ones on which he has produced his life's work.

Denny had been asked to shop for the oak and cedar and canvass needed to finish the canoe. When he brought these supplies back to Great Whale, two weeks later, Denny went again with Matthew and Peter to Billie's shop. Billie opened the door to a space dominated by a newly completed canoe form, the mold around which the *Odeyak* would be built. While Billie stood silently beside him, Denny thought, "This is the most wonderful looking canoe shape. The cameras are not going to be able to pull away. If this thing is in the landscape they are going to have to focus on it."

Whatever its limitations as a vessel, the *Odeyak* would not have the problem of low visibility when seen from the land. Its high sides made it as close to a moving billboard as a canoe could be. It was perfect for the job it was meant to do. As a statement of the unity and the struggle of the Cree and Inuit peoples it could not have been better.

The time from Robbie Niquanicappo's decision to put Denny Alsop on the Whapmagoostui Band Council agenda until the *Odeyak* left the mouth of the Great Whale River on a sled pulled by a team of eight dogs, was a very short month. In any professional projection, a month would not have been time for the most experienced organizer to put together a canoe trip from Kuujjuaraapik and Whapmagoostui on Hudson Bay to Manhattan Island at the mouth of the Hudson River. Indeed, more seasoned planners might have shuddered and walked away from the prospect of finding lodgings for sixty people every night for five weeks in the cities, towns and villages of New England and New York. A veteran campaign organizer would have known better than to try to bring a large contingent of quiet, private northern Natives, most of whom could count their days in the south on their fingers and few of whom had ever before been to the United States, into a location where they would fan out to cover several events, all conducted in a foreign language.

The seemingly casual style of Cree planning, which works very well travelling in the bush where reservations and the staging of public events are not essential components, was complemented by an intense month of telephone networking that bore some resemblance to the early stages of any major political campaign. Matthew Mukash had only begun work as Task Force Secretary at the beginning of January. The principal planner, Marie Symes-Grehan, an experienced public relations worker, spearheaded the beginning of the campaign. A non-Native from western

Canada, dedicated to the Cree cause, Marie had a general familiarity with the territory into which the *Odeyak* would head. As soon as the idea of the trip took hold, the Task Force office came alive. Marie had brought a long list of contacts from her previous work in media. She and Matthew started to make calls to southern contacts everywhere along the route. There were, however, no routines or precedents which could be drawn from past campaigns because nobody knew of a campaign quite like this one. Gradually, as the *Odeyak* travelled from place to place a successful pattern would emerge. The discovery of that pattern would require a tenacity born from the dedication of the *Odeyak* travellers as well as from their friends and supporters along the way.

Sixty people were required to carry the message of Kuujjuaraapik's and Whapmagoostui's concern for their survival. To keep the *Odeyak* moving at a predictable pace in unknown waters would require two crews of ten people each. As well, each of the two communities would send its best speakers. The leaders needed the presence of the elders, men and women whose dedication to their people and accomplishment in traditional pursuits led the community to see them as models. The elders said that it was important to have both younger and older students to talk to the young people their own age down south. Travelling, in the Cree and Inuit traditions, is a family activity.

It was necessary to have a clear sense of what each person might contribute. Stella Masty and Randy Pepabano, two high school representatives, had won their place on the trip by writing essays about what the Hydro project would mean for the community's way of life. When Stella's father told her that a paper longer than five pages would not be read, she put her excess energy into polishing an essay, distilled from her grandparents' stories about what it means to be Cree. This preparation would help her to gain fame and recognition as she spoke in school after school along the *Odeyak* route.

The earliest publicity about the *Odeyak* was a blend of diligence and happenstance that would accompany the boat along the entire course of its trip. During the initial preparations every effort was made to avoid releasing news of the *Odeyak*. Halfway through the month the boat was being built, Father Tom Martin and his wife Mary Ann left Great Whale on a trip to Toronto. Just as they were leaving, Marie called Tom on the phone saying, "I better fill you in on some of this." The next day, when Father Martin walked into the national office of the Anglican Church to seek support for the expedition, the *Odeyak* story was on the front page of *The Globe and Mail*. Andre Picard, a reporter from the *Globe's* Montréal bureau, who was beginning a major series on Great Whale, had been given the scoop on the *Odeyak* while he was visiting the communities. Marie no longer needed to be concerned about how Hydro-Québec might react to the communities' plans.

Departing Great Whale

Denny Alsop had arrived and met with the Whapmagoostui Council on January 23, 1990. The next day he had met with Mayor Sappa Fleming and several Kuujjuaraapik councillors. The major materials for the *Odeyak* arrived on the 13th of February. Once the supplies were in hand, the building took a little less than three weeks. Now, on March 6, the Whapmagoostui Band Council invited every person living at the mouth of the Great Whale River to a feast.

The feast to dedicate the *Odeyak* belonged to both communities. The Inuit and the Crees each found the essential elements of their own way of life in the departure of the vessel that carried the message of their two communities. The newness and size of the gym at the Cree recreational centre made it the natural place to hold the feast. The dog team pulling the sled-mounted boat to the community centre took the long way from Billie's boat shop through the Inuit community and past the airport. The boat, strange sight that it was, became its own invitation to the feast.

The feast worked. Tom Martin recalls it as a time when he felt no division between the communities. A common sense of purpose and a realization that sixty of their members would be living together in distant and foreign places for the next five weeks had united the two communities.

The Crees and the Inuit each have a long tradition of oratory. The speakers at the feast each talked about the voyage on which the two communities were embarking together. In keeping with the ways of peoples who value both the insights of the young and the wisdom of elders, the speakers addressed the throng in ascending order of precedence.

Robbie Niquanacappo, the Deputy Chief of Whapmagoostui, thanked Billie Weetaltuk for his skill and leadership in building the *Odeyak* and also thanked Andrew Natashaquan for working steadily alongside Billie. Robbie pointed to the way the *Odeyak* was to leave the community and begin its way down south. Crossing the Bay by dog team, he said, was the traditional Inuit means of winter travel while following the rivers by canoe was the traditional Cree means of summer travel. Between its time on the dog sled and its time in the water, the *Odeyak* would travel on the back of a pick-up truck. This modern transport would bring the boat from Chissasibi to Ottawa.

Isaac Masty, inside a tent at Spring Goose Camp in May.

Laughing in the wind.

Odeyak travellers en route to Ottawa, March, 1990.

Trucking the *Odeyak*, Ottawa, March, 1990.

The *Odeyak's* first test run, the Rideau River at Ottawa, March, 1990.

George Webb, the *Odeyak's* first U.S. landing, Albert Vt,. March, 1990.

John Puleio, Mayor Peter Clavelle presenting Mayor Sappa Fleming of Kujjauaraapik and Chief Robbie Dick of Whapmagoostui with a "one world" flag at the Burlington Boat House.

John Puleio, Cree and Inuit men at the Burlington reception.

Isaac Masty, the *Odeyak* and a teepee in front of the Vermont State House in Montpelier.

Lois Glenn-Karp, a stern view, the *Odeyak* beached at Triconderoga, N.Y.

Lois Glenn-Karp, the *Odeyak* about to land at Triconderoga, N.Y.

Charles B. Moore, the Odeyak landed at Triconderoga.

Charles B. Moore, the *Odeyak* in the locks of the New York State Barge Canal.

Pete Seeger making music with the *Odeyak* travellers and members of the Beacon Sloop Club, Easter Sunday, 1990.

Isaac Masty, Crees and others carrying "One World" Banners at Times Square, Earth Day, 1990.

Issac Masty, the *Odeyak* in St. John the Divine Cathedral, New York City, Earth Day, 1990.

Sappa Fleming, Mayor of Kuujjuaraapik, could keep the rapt attention of an audience simply with the warmth of his smile and the sparkle of his eyes. He would be the senior leader on the trip until Chief Robbie Dick, who had been taken ill, was released from the hospital. Matthew Coon Come, the Grand Chief of the Crees, repeated his enthusiastic commitment to preserve his people's way of life. In front of committees, at meetings, and before street crowds, Chief Coon Come would deliver the same message over and over. His most essential message to the people of Great Whale, as he stood before the *Odeyak* for the first time, would become familiar. "We may have inherited this land from our ancestors, but we have also borrowed it from our children."

The blessing of the *Odeyak* by the Primate, the presiding bishop of the Anglican Church of Canada, the Right Rev. Michael Peers, was another moment in which the Crees and Inuit became one community. The hunters and trappers of Great Whale continue to express their respect for the animals through traditional observances such as hanging a beaver's skull from a tree where it will not be disturbed by predators. But they are also devout Anglicans. Almost every community leader is also a church leader. The presence of the Church as a mediator between these two communities and the great powers impinging on them goes back almost as far as the role of the Hudson Bay Company. As the Great Whale communities have increasingly come to speak for themselves, they have also welcomed the continuing support of the Church.

The feast had been prepared by Cree women with food provided by the Band Council. Bannock, caribou stew, beaver, fish and other northern delicacies were washed down with tea and coffee. Cake and cookies had also been added to the list of traditional festive foods. But this time everyone at Whapmagoostui-Kuujjuaraapik was included in the celebration. The supper was one of the last in which the travellers would be able to eat the foods to which they were accustomed. The music that followed was led by Matthew Mukash on the fiddle, a custom picked up by the Crees from the Scots, the Irish or the English somewhere over past generations.

Robbie N. announced that the official departure would take place the next morning at the Harricana line, the line where the world's longest annual snowmobile race ends when the racers who set out from Moosonee, at the mouth of the Harricana River, come off the ice of Hudson Bay and into the mouth of the Great Whale River.

By nine o'clock on the morning of Saturday, March 7, 1990, a crowd had gathered, young and old, Crees and Inuit. The *Odeyak* was again brought out of Billie Weetaltuk's shop. This time it was carried from the shop to the sled by the leaders from both communities. Great ceremony was made of securing the boat for the rough ride it would have across the ice. The *Odeyak* was an olive drab, as uninviting a colour for a canoe as might be imagined. Billie had saved the second coat of paint until he would be able to do whatever repairs might be needed after the boat reached Chissasibi.

As soon as the last dog was properly harnessed to the sled, the driver, Thomasee Napartuk, gave the signal. The *Odeyak*, sitting on top of a sled, lurched forward as the eight animals leaned into their traces.

Chapter 3:
The Whale and the Seal –
Traditional Way of Life

Commonality and Diversity

For the Crees and Inuit of Great Whale there is a sense of impending doom, a chaos that threatens the continuity through which order is given to the precarious cycles of the Creation. For them these cycles have been measured by the migrations of the caribou across the tundra from the north, the geese and ducks from the south, the fish that come to spawn in the river and the whales and seals in the sound. This sensitivity to nature, which permeates the world view of many traditional peoples, guides them in a path respectful of the Creation. They believe that following the path, observing the rituals of respect and telling the tales learned from the grandparents, helps ensure that the land and the water will continue to yield up their bounty.

The presence of this chaotic force, one which, unlike the cycles of the Creation, cannot be appeased by treading lightly on the earth and living harmoniously with nature, threatens the traditional sense of order. For his people, Whapmagoostui Chief Robbie Dick says that the very idea of such a large part of their land being put under water is incomprehensible.

> They just cannot understand why it has to happen. Those who know the land, those who have lived off the land, cannot imagine all that land being under water. For what? To convenience people in the States and in southern Québec? Why does it have to be our own back yard?

Robbie Dick conveyed the feeling of chaos his people see in their future when he compared the flooding of their land to Noah's Flood.

> The Bible teaches us, in Genesis, that when the water from that flood subsided, the Creator made a promise that the lands will never again be flooded. The same white men who brought us that good news now want to flood the land.

The discovery that there is an arbitrary force which cannot be appeased, but nonetheless demands respect, came long before Hydro-Québec announced its intention to flood their land. At the time of the *Odeyak*, the village of Kuujjuaraapik did not have a dog team of its own. To start the boat on its southward journey a dog team had been flown in from Povungnituk, far up the Hudson Bay coast. All the dogs of Kuujjuaraapik had been shot by the RCMP one day in the1950s.

Everyone then living in the community remembers the shooting. Although it is frequently mentioned, and was a major trauma in the life of Kuujjuaraapik, nobody who recalls it is able to tell why the shooting happened. Perhaps the question "why," the very idea that such an event might possess an explanation, does not resonate in the minds of the Inuit elders. Like the shooting of the dogs, what is beyond the understanding of the Great Whale people is the disrespect required to conceive of flooding the land.

Gilbert Dick, Chief Robbie Dick's older brother, says that the Cree and Inuit communities who are now facing the crisis of hydro-electric development on their land have a long history of sharing.

> We made friends with the Inuit the same as we would make friends with Crees who we did not already know. We got to know one another that way. Most of the Inuit and the Crees know one another very well. No one ever made trouble between the Inuit and the Crees. Not even the old people.

Emily Masty, a teacher, Whapmagoostui band councillor, and historian, points to the most tangible sign of longstanding co-operation. "There are some Inuit who speak Cree fluently and some Cree who speak Inuktituut fluently, even without formal education. We pick up each other's language."

Before the construction of the Distant Early Warning (DEW) Line radar stations in the 1950s, and long before the *James Bay and Northern Québec Agreement* of 1975, Emily says that relations between the Cree and Inuit were close.

> We all lived together. Maybe in different little neighborhoods but we were never unpleasant to one another. We simply respected each other's cultures. We would be friendly to one another, help each other. We also traded things we made with one another, especially since the Inuit made waterproof footwear from the sealskins. The Cree people had more store bought things because they had a greater variety and a greater volume of fur bearing animals to trade with the Hudson Bay. The Inuit only took foxes and the occasional polar bear. The Crees had otter, mink, marten, beaver and even ermine.

In the time of his youth, Cree elder James Kawapit also remembers a situation different from the current situation.

> Cree and Inuit hunted in the same place, on the Bay near the mouth of the river. That is where they took the whales. What I have not seen, but I heard a long time ago, was the whales being killed inside the river. That is

where they used to be hunted a very long time ago. But when I was young they were taken out on the Bay.

Inuit and Cree elders necessarily tell quite different stories, each basing their stories on the tradition that they received. Nonetheless, certain common themes emerge from the origins and world views of these two overlapping communities. One is the belief in the importance of story telling, as a way of educating the younger generations. Story telling leaves room for interpretation, thereby respecting the autonomy of the individual and avoiding didactic instruction.

Today's elders recall hearing stories from their grandparents which they, in turn, had heard from their grandparents. The communities' stories are never things of the past, but rather an ever present reality. As a result, in the late twentieth century, there is a collective memory that reaches back at least as far as the eighteenth century. This collective memory makes the people's history a presence in everyday life and conversation. This is something that few people in North American cities, with only written history and little or no connection to the land, can share.

Traditionally, as Emily Masty explains, story telling was centred around the fire or wood stove in the family tent, after the children were ready for bed. Many of the best stories are exemplary tales the elder heard not from his own parent or grandparent but from the grandparent of a listener. After all, the merit of the story comes as much from the listener's relationship to the source as from its intrinsic significance.

Perhaps the most frequently recurring and deeply rooted theme is the need to respect (even revere) the animals which sustain the life of the people. Perhaps the other most popular motif are stories about origins. These explain how the people came to the place where they live today. There is a sense in which all the stories the elders tell have both these themes. The people have survived for all these thousands of years because their ancestors developed a relationship of respect and reverence with the animals who have sustained them and kept them alive to this day.

The Cree of Whapmagoostui

"The Eeyou came to Whapmagoostui because it was the place where they could sell their furs in exchange for supplies." Emily Masty prefers the Crees' name in their own language. "Eeyou," like "Inuit," literally means "the People." The presence of a Hudson Bay Company post led to the development of a Cree village at this site. There had been earlier posts at different locations along this coast but when they were consolidated and trading for the whole area became centred at the mouth of the Great

Whale, the trappers began to bring their furs here. The Hudson Bay Company may also have moved to the Great Whale River because they found Crees there who would hunt whales for them in the summer.

Gilbert Dick recalls "whaling for the guys on the ship. Whaling was the only time that we had jobs. When it was over we would go back in the bush."

Emily Masty says that, in the days when the Hudson Bay Post dominated Whapmagoostui and the Crees transacted business with the factor, "no money was exchanged." She says that, "The money was in the background but the people never saw it. The store manager would say to himself, 'This beaver pelt is worth two dollars, so I will give this man two dollars worth of merchandise.' Because the people did not know that, they say that no money was exchanged." The men who went whaling were not given money, Emily says. Instead, they were given a beluga whale each.

> When the white people came and saw all the whales, the whites wanted the whales and asked the Crees to help them take the whales.
>
> But it became a kind of slavery. Why did the manager think that the whaling people needed a whale from him? If they had wanted a whale for themselves they would have taken one. I don't think that the old people see it as a form of slavery. But when you ask what they got for their labor they will say that they were paid slave wages. When the Hudson Bay found, for instance, that the people liked sugar very much they set the rate for a woman cleaning ten whale skins at one dollar's worth of sugar.
>
> When I stand back and look at our history it seems to me that what the Cree people were saying to themselves was, "Because we're here to hunt the whales anyway, and these strangers came to find whales for their oil and their skins, we might as well oblige them."

Emily Masty has been gathering the elders' stories, in Cree, on tape for years. These stories, which she has translated into English, have been given to her in the same form in which they were traditionally told around the fire in the teepee or the stove in the tent. Some of the most esteemed elders have given to Emily, word-for-word, the stories they heard as children from their elders who were also repeating verbatim what they recalled hearing. Emily says that the modern houses, with central heat and separate bedrooms, have disrupted the traditional teaching as much as television.

The history Emily plans to write will, she says, be told in two ways. There is "a factual history which can be told in a chronological order relating a sequence of events." Then there are the stories that "happened before there was Time, when humans and animals could change forms." This, she says, is similar to what the Aboriginal people of Australia call "sleep time." These stories belong to the history of the Eeyou because they depict the relationship between the People and the animals that continues to this day.

For example, to an educated young hunter a successful hunt still depends on the ability to communicate with the animals. Matthew Mukash explains.

> We have a spiritual relationship with the animals. When people have the power to communicate with the spirits of animals then they understand the animals the way people understand one another. You and I talk to each other in words. If you told me of your sickness I would know that you are sick because you told me so. The behaviour of animals is known by some Crees in the same way.

Matthew's understanding of this relationship comes from elders such as James Kawapit, a trapper who has spent his life on the land around Lake Bienville where his father also trapped. His way of knowing touches on the idea of the sacred.

> In the past, the Cree people here were sometimes helped by the animals. They knew how to look upon those animals with respect and with an understanding for their place in the Creation. This understanding had been handed down from generation to generation.

The Crees came to Whapmagoostui from two directions, some from the south and some from the interior. Emily's mother's great-great-grandfather, for instance, came from the south to hunt caribou. When he found the game plentiful, he stayed. Emily's family came to Whapmagoostui when the Hudson Bay Post at Richmond Gulf was closing about 1952. She was about three years old.

The distance Emily's ancestors came from the south is more than matched by the people who came to Whapmagoostui from the interior. There are, Emily says, many stories about Whapmagoostui people out on the land who would meet people "from the other side," meaning from the other side of the peninsula, from Labrador. People have always gone into the interior from Whapmagoostui. From time to time they would meet up with Naskapi from Labrador. James Kawapit is an elder whose ancestors were Naskapi from the Schefferville area. Whapmagoostui Cree and Naskapi understand one another's languages. Indeed, Whapmagoostui Cree is closer to Naskapi than to Algonquin, a language largely understandable to the Cree at the southern end of James Bay.

There was a time, not so very long ago, when the Crees walked all over the interior. "A man who is still living says that he and his father once went to sell their furs in Wabush. Another time they went to Ft. Chimo."

When he was still able to hunt, Matthew George followed the footsteps of his father and his mother's father until he reached, "the mountain range [where] the rivers flow the other way, toward Ungava Bay. That is where I hunted."

He says that he was never aware of any officials asking where they hunted until the Crees went to court, in 1973, to stop the James Bay hydro-electric development.

> As far as I know they have never come to ask us all that. It was only during the court proceedings that they asked the Crees how far they had hunted or where the best hunting was to be found. We said that our hunting covered the whole of northern Québec as far as Ft. Chimo, or Kuujurak now. Our people have been there at one time or another.

The practice of walking tremendous distances to tend their traplines and to sell their furs in exchange for supplies did not, Emily says, make the Crees nomadic. They moved from place to place to harvest the land. They knew that at a certain time of year certain animals were ready for taking.

Trapping begins in the fall and, apart from a break at Christmas made possible more recently through bush planes, continues to keep a family on their trapline through the winter. When people travelled by canoe to their traplines, the greater part of the year was spent in the bush. Families travelled upstream for as much as a month, to reach their trapline shortly before freeze-up. They needed to arrive in time to build or repair their cabin and to walk the trapline, marking the place where each trap would be set. Beaver lodges must each be checked before the freeze-up so that the trapper can count the number of beaver in each lodge. A lodge at which the numbers are too small will be left for the year. If there were not enough beaver on the trapline, the previous spring, the tallyman, the acknowledged head of the trapline, would have closed the line for the year. Then his family and any others with him might look to another tallyman to share his space with them for the year. One or two men on a trapline might take their catch to the post in mid-winter. The families came out when the ice began to break up in the spring.

The Crees came down to the mouth of the Great Whale as the newly spawned fish headed downstream and the whales came to the Bay to molt. James Kawapit says that, "the Eeyou came here during the summer months because of the abundance of game. That is how we came to be here." Noah Mamiumscum says that there were other attractions to bring the Crees there in the summer. "The whitefish were very plentiful at that time. Since the ships came and the settlement grew up, first with the Army and then the Québec Government, there are no more whales and no more whitefish."

One reason that the Whapmagoostui Crees have become accustomed to trekking such long distances is that the populations of the animals on which they depend rise and fall in cyclical patterns and sometimes also change the course of their migrations. The reasons for these upswings range from the natural cycles of the different species to the best and worst forms of human intervention. Matthew Mukash remembers when he first went caribou hunting, in 1976. "We had to go about 120 miles north to sight the first herd. It is a combination of many things that have brought the caribou back this way."

The low level flights by NATO aircraft training over Labrador, on the opposite side of the Ungava Peninsula, is one contributing factor Matthew cites. Hydro-Québec would like to take credit for stimulating the growth of the vegetation near the La Grande Reservoir resulting in an increased food supply for the caribou and for many smaller animals. They are less eager to take credit for the drowning of ten thousand caribou at the flooding of the Caniapiscau River. Neither does the utility want to share in studies about the effect on birds and small mammals of the layer of thick frost covering the trees and groundcover along the La Grande dams. This vegetation is the main food source for many of the animals through the winter. More important than the effect of mega-projects is the natural cycle of the animals and the vegetation that supports them.

> The animals would have come back to some extent around this time even if there was no interference simply because the upswing in their cycle was due about this time. When you've lived in the land for five thousand years you look to the stories on which you can rely from generation to generation.

Matthew George looks back three generations to trace the caribou that are more abundant today nearer the mouth of the Great Whale River.

> The caribou that come here originate in two different places. There is a caribou herd from the north that used to stay around The River That Has No Trees. This is the tundra herd that came south of Kuujurak. The other herd comes from the south. So there's two sets of migrations. My grandfather told stories of this caribou herd coming from the River That Has No Trees. He said that they went behind Lake Bienville back to where they came from. That is how long it has been that they did not come here until recently. We've known them to come here for six years.

In his community liaison role, Matthew Mukash has had ample opportunity to hear elders such as Matthew George and advocates for Hydro-Québec.

> It is true that some animals will go away for twenty or thirty years and then come back. Marten is one that has been in short supply in this area for thirty years now but is finally starting to return. I can tell you that their re-generation is not because of the hydro project.

The land is very productive right now. Animals that have not been around for awhile, such as the porcupine as well as the marten, are starting to reproduce at a very high rate. Even some birds that have been scarce for a while are becoming very abundant. Unfortunately, this is all going to be destroyed and the threat is coming at a time when the productivity is heading toward a high point.

Chief Robbie Dick compares his people's dependence on the land to southern farmers'.

They're just like farmers out there. In southern Québec, when you go down there, you see the city of Montréal, but you also see the farmlands extending as far as the eye can see. There are people living there. They have a livelihood. They go to the city too sometimes. Sometimes they go to other places. That is the same way our people are living on the land.

Now they want to build the dam and to destroy that land. That's somebody's back yard. That's somebody's garden. That's somebody's farmland. What would the other people think, in southern Québec, if that happened in their farmlands?

The Inuit of Kuujjuaraapik

For all the apparent differences, Alec Tukatuk uses the same image to describe the Inuit. Alec works at the Kuujjuaraapik Municipal Office as an information officer.

The effects of this project will be more disastrous to our food sources than to anything else. The main thing is food because the whole area is our farm. We don't have farms like in the south where there are different farms fenced off. Here it is one big farm. The animals we farm come in and go out. Some of them, like the migratory birds go a very long range. They go all the way down to Mexico.

The permanent settlement of Inuit at Kuujjuaraapik began when the U.S. Army needed a pool of local labour to work on the construction of the DEW Line station. The RCMP solved this labour shortage by re-locating Inuit families from along the coast, above and below Kuujjuaraapik and from the adjacent islands. Some of the families came from the Nastapoca Islands much further north along the coast, or Long Island, further south at the point separating Hudson Bay from James Bay.

But Kuujjuaraapik is much older than this recent history. Indeed, it has likely been a good place to camp in the summer since shortly after the last ice age. It is a good place to take whales after the ice breaks up in the late Arctic spring. It is also a place where there is sure to be fish in the meantime. As long as the river has been in its bed, the features which make it a prolific source of sustenance have transcended its constantly changing social history.

Since the coming of the Hudson Bay Company some four hundred years ago, the same animals that provided food for the Inuit were also the source of their most valuable trade items. Whale oil was one of their first major items of sale to the outside world. The same oil was used by the Crees to cook their caribou, moose, and fish. Until the present generation, the Crees looked to their Inuit neighbors for seal skin boots. These boots were the main item the Crees bartered or bought from the Inuit.

As an information officer, Alec's job involves transmitting material provided by Hydro-Québec to the community. He says repeatedly, that he has no stand. "Information has to be bland. It doesn't take sides." Alec is officially neutral on any question specifically about the Great Whale Hydro Project. About the history of his own community, however, he is a fount of knowledge and a master of the acronyms of the military and civil agencies that have been a powerful presence for many years. "The U.S. Air Force came in first. Two years later the Canadian Army took over. Four years later Canadian Marconi Company took over. Six or seven years after that DGNQ took over. From DGNQ it went to MTPA and then to SIQ."

Alec tells visitors that the Belcher Islands, seventy miles northwest into Hudson Bay, were discovered by Inuit from this part of the coast when they fled from a Cree raiding party in the 1700s. The irony of a forced re-location under RCMP supervision almost three centuries later appeals to his sense of humour. These bad old days also seem to have been forgiven by the Cree. Asked about the battles which led the Inuit to flee until they discovered the Belcher Islands, Cree elder Gilbert Dick waved such stories away as medieval history. "Oh, that was in the old days before we ever knew one another. We just knew that the other one had a different way of talking. So we thought they were a strange people."

Alec says that traditionally the Inuit were spread out all along the coast. There's a map in the other office that contains names all along the coast. We were never settled in one place for too long because when the animals moved we moved. Because the Inuit hunting takes place on the ice along the coast and off the islands, hunters are able to reach many of their families' traditional hunting areas. During the months when the Bay is in the process of freezing up or melting, day trips are the only way to go out onto the Bay. During those months, the Inuit continue to hunt for seals and ducks. Under better conditions, the Inuit go all the way to the Belcher Islands to find belugas and seals and fish. They also go some distance inland in search of ptarmigan and caribou and to fish on the rivers further up the coast. Alec's first contact with white men was when he started school in 1957.

I had started to go with my father to watch him when he was hunting. When I was just old enough to have a clear picture of him, my father fell in the water in January, the coldest month of the year, and got pneumonia. He died that year. So I started hunting very, very early in order to feed my mother and my brothers and my sisters.

"I was born south of here, thirty miles from here. In a camp. With no doctors, no nurses. Just naturally." Alec's family moved to Kuu-jjuaraapik before he went to school. "Because my father died in the camp and there was always a little group here that could look after us. So they did that and as I was growing I became more independent and brought in a food supply. When I had to go to school the other people fed us."

Alec says that the constant movement of the ice means that it is sometimes possible to go out only for a couple of hours. If a canoe gets stuck in the ice, the travellers can be stuck there for quite some time. And if a floe breaks loose from the larger ice mass, the people on a snowmobile can be even more uncomfortable.

When you hunt you have to be prepared to take any weather. The weather changes dramatically here at this time of year. It can change at any moment. We train ourselves how to watch the weather and to predict the weather. We try to know the weather before we go out. Every morning we try to foresee the weather before we listen to the DOT [Department of Transport] forecast. That's part of what it means to be a hunter.

When all signs say that it is safe to go out, the Inuit continue to travel ten to fifteen miles in their open outboard canoes to the places where they can find the animals on which their people rely. Reading the horizon to find both the seal and the storm cloud manifests their relationship to their environment. Alec Tukatuk sums up his own identity quite precisely, "I go hunting every chance I get. As a matter of fact, I would rather be called a hunter than an information officer."

A Brief Political History of Ungava

Chief Robbie Dick places Québec's presence in the Ungava Peninsula in a larger historical context.

The Québec government just arrived here 35 ago, in the '60s. Before that they were not even visible up here. The federal government was visible to some extent. But it seems like only yesterday that Québec was starting to appear up here in our territory and tell us that they own the land.

Indeed, the question of which government had jurisdiction over the Cree and Inuit of Ungava was not resolved until the *James Bay and Northern Québec Agreement* in 1975. Québec had acquired jurisdiction over the Ungava Peninsula from the federal Government in 1912, on condition that it negotiate a treaty with the "Indians." This 1912 requirement to settle the Indian interest in the land has long been taken as an early constitutional indication that both Ottawa and the British Parliament at Westminster recognized the reality of an Aboriginal title. No negotiations took place, however, until 1973, when the Québec Superior Court recognized an Aboriginal interest in the land and issued an injunction against further construction of the first James Bay hydro-electric project. When the Québec Court of Appeal lifted the injunction, they ruled that while this constitutional requirement might apply to the Cree it did not extend to the Inuit. The court said that the Inuit were not Indians in this sense. Nobody had ever signed a treaty with the Inuit. Since there was no precedent for such an agreement it could not be a legal requirement. Such was the attitude of the Québec Court of Appeal in 1973.

Perhaps nobody had signed a treaty with the Inuit before the 1970s because there had not been a compelling reason to have Inuit give up their land, or their interest in the Arctic ice floes, until then. The *Alaska Native Claims Settlement*, also a modern-day treaty, was signed with a series of Inuit villages as well as with the Tlingit and other Indians in the 1970s after oil was discovered on the north slope of Alaska. Lawyers for the Inuit of northern Québec wondered aloud whether the court's exclusion of the Inuit did not reflect a Québec dislike of the common law system in which the recognition of Aboriginal title had long been implicit. The Québec Appeal Court's notion that the lack of precedent was a proof of some incapacity was one the Supreme Court of Canada would go to some lengths to set aside in the following decade.

Whether the term "Indians" includes Inuit had arisen on an earlier occasion in northern Québec. During the 1930s, when crops were failing in many parts of North America, famine also visited the Ungava Peninsula. The caribou herd disappeared from the western side of Ungava. Little other game could be found. The Inuit, facing starvation, appealed both to Ottawa and to Québec for help. Both governments denied that they had responsibility for aiding the Inuit during a famine. Québec argued that the term "Indians" in the list of exclusive federal powers, in the Canadian Constitution, includes the Inuit. Ottawa, anticipating the circular reasoning of the Québec Court forty odd years later, argued that the Inuit were not included in the federal power over "Indians and lands reserved for the Indians" because Ottawa had never used its power to include them. The Judicial Committee, in a rare burst of plain sense, ruled that the Inuit were, indeed, Indians within the meaning of section 91(24) of the *British North America Act, 1867*.

The complete absence of Inuit representation throughout these proceedings is the surest sign that the Inuit were actually being treated very
much like Indians. Under an 1880s amendment to the federal *Indian Act*,
"Indians" were decreed not to be "persons." Under a 1927 amendment,
raising funds for the purpose of pressing Indian land claims was declared
a criminal offence. Neither the Inuit nor the Crees were ever consulted
about the various transfers of jurisdiction. Although the major disabilities
imposed through the *Indian Act* were repealed in a gush of post-war liber-
alism in 1951, it was a decade before Indians were given the right to vote.
These disabilities, nonetheless, play a part in the Inuit decision not to
maintain a federally protected status under the 1975 *Agreement*.

It is useful to remember that the RCMP was the main government
presence in the region until the mid 1960s when Québec became highly
enthusiastic about exercising its jurisdiction in the Ungava Peninsula.
When the Inuit were gathered from the islands to work on the DEW Line
in the 1950s it was the RCMP who patrolled both the islands and the
mainland. The boundary had been drawn some fifty odd years earlier, in
1912, but not put into effect until then. The *James Bay and Northern
Québec Agreement* brought another new set of boundaries that separated
the Cree and Inuit.

Canadian Boundaries — Native Realities

The drawing of the boundary began a process of dissonance, the creation
of a political reality quite out of line with both the social custom and the
physical reality on which it is based. This dissonance is one that has been
repeated along international, provincial and state boundaries throughout
North America. Wherever boundaries have been drawn in political confer-
ences by men who have never seen the land and for whom the separation
of a village from its sustenance is incidental, lines have often been drawn
in the most inopportune places from the standpoint of the communities
involved. The drawing of the line between Kuujjuaraapik and Whapmagoostui in the 1975 *Agreement* was a further evolution of the dissonance
which governments had been cultivating since the earliest Euro-American
boundaries.

The land granted to Québec in 1912 is known to northern Natives by
many names, to geographers as the Ungava Peninsula, and to Quebeckers
as Nouveau Québec. It extends from just north of Eastmain River on the
James Bay coast around Hudson Bay, Hudson Strait and Ungava Bay. On
the east, the Québec sector has been bounded by the Labrador border, at
least since a 1927 Judicial Committee decision. On the south, the 1912

extension is bounded by the Eastmain and a series of other rivers and a line of latitude. This boundary is the northern limit of an 1898 extension of Québec jurisdiction that embraced the land from Val d'Or to the Ontario border, up to James Bay and around the coast to Eastmain. Wherever the boundary is a shoreline, which is everywhere but the east and south, the boundary is the high water mark above the sea.

The area beyond the high water mark including the offshore islands, the sounds, bays and channels, were all retained under federal jurisdiction within the North West Territories (N.W.T.). These waters and islands along the coast are where the whales and seals come to feed off the fish and vegetation that proliferate in the brackish, half-fresh-half-salt water. The lake trout and other fish that travel up the rivers to mate in the fall spend the greater part of the short summer months in these channels. The massive numbers of geese and ducks that migrate each spring all make their nests in the eel grass that grows in the same brackish waters in the sounds, the channels and the river mouths. The fertility of these sounds and channels and river mouths sustains the Inuit who live along these shores. This fertility also gives the ice that covers the water for half the year as much value as the adjoining land, to the people who live there.

This boundary, between Québec and the N.W.T. separates Kuu-jjuaraapik village from the area where most of the Inuit still do the hunting which continues to provide the bulk of their food. The separation of the village from its sustenance began with the drawing of the boundary in 1912. But the boundary was inconsequential to the people who lived there until Québec began to exercise its jurisdiction. The pursuit of the *James Bay and Northern Québec Agreement* brought the situation into sharp focus.

Chapter 4:
The Bulldozer – James Bay One

The James Bay and Northern Québec Agreement

The young people in Great Whale today see development as an inexorable force that is burying their way of life. This image comes from something they have heard an elder say.

> What is happening to us now is like what happens to the land as a bulldozer moves over it. Wherever the bulldozer has moved everything is covered by a layer of gravel or sand or something that was not there before. Whatever was on top is not there any more; it's covered under. And that is what, it seems to me, that the white man has been doing to Indian people since the visitor people arrived here.

Perhaps this process began back in the 1950s with construction of the Distant Early Warning (DEW) Line. This string of radar stations across Northern Canada was designed to give the American military advanced warning of approaching Soviet bombers. Until that time almost the only non-Native people in the area had been a few Hudson Bay Company factors and missionaries. The presence of the U.S. Air Force and Army was quickly seen as a very mixed blessing. Besides bulldozers to build the landing strip and a golf course, the military introduced a cash economy. People who had been accustomed to "slave wages" for summer work plus barter for their harvest from the land suddenly found themselves able to be paid for year round work. Cash, of course, comes with a price. Alec Tukatuk, the Kuujjuaraapik information officer, speculates on what was lost. Alec's understanding of southern development today is shaped by the way his community experienced the occupation by the U.S. Army.

> The impact of that army system was not very good. We pretty well lost our culture. We almost lost our identity. When we were growing up, everyone worked together in order to survive. Today it is quite different. We tried to work with the new system which we did not know about, the system that is called civilization. Out there in the civilized world, it is each man for himself. When there are jobs, and a person starts to earn a salary or wages, then he becomes independent. He tends to move away from the family group.

Emily Masty was five years old in 1954 when the DEW Line construction began.

> The two things that really scared me as a young child when the Air Force were building here were the blasting — that really terrified me — and people with beards. But I really liked the oranges and apples. There wasn't any fruit in our store but the servicemen had them in their store. We learned very quickly to say "apples" and "oranges" to the men around the work site.

> There was a fence around the defence installation. Our people could not go in there except for those who were working there. The only time that they would have people come in was once a year around Christmas. The Army would throw a party, a big feast for the whole community, Inuit and Cree. Beef stew was the main course, and bread and cake, apples and oranges, and gifts for the children.

But the Army's brief introduction of the cash economy withered to a very few maintenance jobs once the construction was finished. Gilbert Dick says that as recently as 1960, people were once again coming to the post mainly to trade. Most of the families did not live at Whapmagoostui. "I remember thirty years ago. It is not too long ago that people stayed out on the land. All the Inuit were along the coast. The Crees were along the inland rivers and lakes. We [Crees] came here a couple of times a year to trade and to get together. We would come here in August for two or two-and-a-half months."

The present era began with *The James Bay and Northern Québec Agreement* of 1975. Not that all the changes that grew out of *The Agreement* happened right away, but when they happened their origins could plainly be traced to *The Agreement*. Most of the visible changes arising from *The Agreement* came to Great Whale only several years after the 1975 signing.

All the hundred or so houses set down along each of the two grid patterns that sit at a right angle to one another to form the villages of Whapmagoostui and Kuujjuaraapik, for example, have been built since 1985. The only exceptions are the few remaining prefabs across the road from the open field, the remains of the DEW Line landing strip, between the two villages.

When the first eight prefabs were built, under a Department of Indian Affairs and Northern Development (DIAND) building programme that lurched through the 1960s, Emily's family was one that received a house. The houses were being given to the elderly and to people who were known to have had pneumonia or tuberculosis. Emily's father had gone to the sanitarium twice. So his family was high on the list when the prefabs came in.

In the early '60s, when the Crees still only came to Whapmagoostui for the summer, they lived in tents. Sometimes, the tents had wooden sides. A few might have had a wooden platform. More often the floor consisted of carefully layered spruce boughs which provide a soft surface for sitting or sleeping and some degree of natural insulation. Some winter lodges, the homes where the Cree families spent the larger part of the year, were a pole construction, often more elaborate than the family's housing in the village. Today, when families go out for three months at a time, the canvas tents set on a wooden platform or lined with spruce boughs are the most popular housing in the bush.

Families living in wood frame tents who did not go to the traplines in the winter always moved across the river and into the woods during the coldest month. There was more shelter in the woods, Emily recalls. Firewood was also more accessible. The tent, adapted from the traditional Cree teepee, was meant to be erected in the bush among the trees where there would be a lot of natural shelter.

At the time of *The Agreement*, most of the families were living in DIAND prefabs. The prefabs doubled a family's living space without giving them a great deal more insulation from the elements. The houses sat on blocks a few feet above the ground. Foundations were still unknown and there was no running water. But they now had oil stoves instead of wood stoves. The first tanks, past Billie Weetaltuk's boat shop at the point, had been built for the military base. Others were added as a result of *The Agreement*. The solid, modern housing that has grown out of *The Agreement* is a blessing that has come at a steep price. Each version of Cree housing has brought improvements. The first houses were semi-detached for cost. This economy created friction when neighbors became tiresome or noisy. Since the second version, all the Cree houses have been free standing. Each wave of construction has had some new feature. A kitchen porch at the side and a small, enclosed porch at the front door, besides being useful, gives some distinction to the latest model of Cree housing. A few more houses will be built each year until the thirty or forty families waiting at the time of the *Odeyak*, and the new ones that come along in the meantime, each have a house.

The Inuit houses have much less variety. Almost all are the two-storey, blue semi-detached houses raised with a thorough insulation between the floor and the ground. This design was especially created for Inuit communities in the high Arctic where permafrost prohibits subterranean foundations. Further north, a heated basement would melt the permafrost and turn it into a soup. Although the sandy soil of Great Whale supports foundations on the Cree side, this seems simply to have become the standard design for Inuit communities. There is, however, another reason for the greater uniformity of the Inuit houses. The re-location of half the Kuujjuaraapik community to Ummuriaq also absorbed a great deal of both the creative energy and the financial resources available to the Inuit housing program.

A Sense of Uncertainty

Robbie Dick has a vision of adapting what is most helpful from the outside world while maintaining the Cree tradition. Symbolically, his vision centres around the new technology that has become affordable partly as a result of the *Agreement*. "We can adapt to what is good because a lot of things that are coming up are good for us. Also, when we see our people out there practicing their traditional way of life we know that those are the same people who have modern houses here in the village, they have skidoos and outboard motors. They're using aircraft to go in and out of the territory."

The Great Whale peoples, like most everyone else, would like the best of both worlds. They would like to have the new technologies, already visible throughout Whapmagoostui and Kuujjuaraapik today such as housing, council offices, school buildings, skidoos, four wheelers and television. These things will let them live a better life while they continue to live off the land that has sustained their ancestors. At its best, this is what modern life has allowed. Both people continue to depend on the land in real and substantial ways. The greater part of the food supply continues to consist of the fish and birds and animals that hunters bring home for their families. Most of the families spend a large part of the year on the land. The ones who work in the offices and, therefore stay in the village through the winter, spend the months of October and May, the two annual goose breaks, on the land. Men as different as Robbie Niquanacappo and Alec Tukatuk also spend the greater part of each weekend in the bush.

The real price for the benefits of the *Agreement* is not the separation of the Crees and the Inuit from their old ways. It would be hard to begrudge the hunter going miles out to sea in an open boat the safety and comfort afforded by the radio that crackles outside Alec Tukatuk's office. Nor does the sense of uncertainty come from the actual *Agreement*. The plain text of *The Agreement* was meant to guarantee their future. This is how the Crees and the Inuit read it. It is also how it was presented to the Parliament of Canada and the National Assembly of Québec. The uncertainty comes from the increasing apprehension that the two communities who have lived side by side for so long, sometimes as friends and sometimes like an old married couple, may not have a future.

The announcement of the Great Whale Project, by Premier Robert Bourassa in 1989, presented the Great Whale people with the prospect that what they believed had been guaranteed to them might soon be taken away. Robbie Dick found himself, like an Indian Chief in a bad cartoon. He had a treaty whose guarantees would last "as long as the river runs" and a government announcing that they would build dams to turn the rivers from their course.

The Agreement, in effect, created a special and unique kind of partnership among the five parties (the Crees, the Inuit, Canada, Québec and Hydro-Québec) each of whom had some interest in the land recognized, guaranteed and confirmed by the others. The two Aboriginal groups also received some financial compensation, largely in the form of debentures and bonds which were to become real money over the next fifteen years. But what led them to surrender their claim to the largest part of their ancestral land, most of the interior of the Ungava Peninsula, was the recognition of their title to the remaining land.

Imagining disaster was not the difficulty. What was "just not understandable" from the viewpoint of the Great Whale people was what was required to conceive building something so disastrous. Robbie Dick believes that his people would understand if Québec wanted to use the land to create rather than to destroy.

> It would be a different story if they wanted to build on the land for their own use. The Crees would understand that they don't have enough room down there. But they just want to take the water, not even for people in Canada, but to sell it to the States. Québec doesn't even want to occupy the land. They just want something off the land and, by God, they'll destroy the homelands of the Crees to get what they want. And that is just not understandable. For our people, anyway.

Robbie Dick does not mean that his people cannot imagine their lands being devastated by the flooding for a hydro-electric project. Almost every adult at Whapmagoostui and Kuujjuaraapik has toured the dam and the underground generating station at Radisson. Most of the Crees and many of the Inuit at Great Whale have family at Chissasibi where they can see the latest dam being built. Not only the leaders, but the elders and the trappers have all described what the project will mean for their land.

James Kawapit succinctly described the effect he expects the project will have on his trapping area.

> There will be a great impact on the animals. The fur bearing animals, otter, the beaver and the mink all have their own special habitats, places where they bear and rear their young. Through generations they have been frequenting those places. The hunters have also known where they were. Now those habitats will be destroyed.

John Petagumskum is the elder most often mentioned in Whapma-goostui. He is a tall man whose bearing gives an impression of a much younger man. John's many years on Whapmagoostui's most northern trapline have been kind to him that way. More important than his age, his voice and face have a gentleness that is commanding and his words have a humility that is inspiring. John offers a vivid description of some of the likely effects of the project. Some of what John observes is based on his own experience and beliefs but he also shows a considerable knowledge of the recent findings of scientists concerning such things as mercury contamination in the La Grande River system which has resulted from the previous flooding.

There will be many things that will hurt us about the project. One of the things that will hurt is that once the reservoir is completed we will look at it and know that many of our relatives' and ancestors' burial sites are underwater.

Once the reservoir is completed, lakes in that area that are known to be very good fishing areas, where the fish are big and healthy, will no longer provide the habitat to support the fish in good health. The fish will then move out to the bigger water of the reservoir that will be impure. So these fish will become sick and some will die. The ones that die will be washed ashore and eaten by the animals who will then also be contaminated. The birds who prey on the fish will also be contaminated.

Ptarmigan and rabbits feed from the trees and the willows in the winter. The animals who are still on the land when the reservoir is complete will be in a place where there will always be fog condensing over the reservoir through the winter. Wherever the wind blows it will carry this moisture with it. Wherever it deposits the moisture, in the willows or in the trees, their greenery and branches will be encased in ice. So the browse that those animals need to eat will be covered in a heavy ice. So even if the animals can reach the food that remains for them in this area, the ice covering the food will make them sick and unhealthy.

For us, the Crees, we will have no way of knowing which animal has the disease and which does not. So when we eat the diseased animal we may, in turn, become sick. The burial sites will also make the water contaminated. It is a belief about burial sites.

Alec Tukatuk, in his role as a hunter, reflects on what he has learned as an information officer.

When *The James Bay Agreement* was signed it was not mentioned that the Great Whale River area could be dammed and a hydro project made here. After it was signed we learned that section 8.13 where it says "other projects" included Great Whale. Around the second paragraph it says "sociological factors shall not be grounds to oppose or prevent the said developments." To me that was way too much to give away. And we feel trapped because of that. What does it mean to have an environmental impact assessment that leaves out sociological factors? The big question is whether contamination is included as an environmental factor or a sociological factor.

The question, "What does it mean to have an environmental impact assessment that leaves out sociological factors," would prove to be prescient. Eighteen months after the *Odeyak*, two courts, the Federal Court of Canada and the Superior Court of Québec, would focus on other parts of *The Agreement* to address substantially the same question. Mr. Justice Paul Rouleau, like Chief Robbie Dick, would describe the situation as "incomprehensible."

Among not only the elders and the leaders, but also the students and even the children, talk about appropriate behavior invariably comes around to the idea of "respect." Respect is a term heard at Great Whale more about the land, the water and the animals they sustain than about anything else. Perhaps even more than about "respect for elders." In the English spoken by the Crees and the Inuit, respect takes on a meaning closer to reverence than to the common use of respect elsewhere. Chief Robbie Dick gives a functional description of the term "respect."

> Our understanding is that we should only take what we need on earth and don't overuse or abuse anything. Leave something for the ones who will come along later. This is what we do with the environment: we just take the animals that we need and we don't overuse it. We try not to, anyway. Of course, there are always some people who do the opposite in any society.

> Now, because somebody wants to make money or to take more than their share, they don't even need to consider the welfare or the lives of the people of the land. Our people cannot understand that that is how some other cultures operate. They can not understand, "Why? Why does it have to be us?"

When James Kawapit speaks, his words reflect the presence of history in everyday life.

> My father was 87 years old when he died. All his life he was on the land and it was the land that kept him alive all those years. During all those years he taught me many things about how I should behave when I am on the land. He taught me many things until he passed away just last summer.

> We try to teach our young people to respect the animals in the same way that our elders taught us. We teach them that, even though there are many caribou around nowadays and have been for a number of years, that they are to kill only one caribou and that all its parts are to be used. It is the same way when we hunt geese and ducks in the fall. Even if there are many there that we could take, we take only what we need to feed our families through that season. Nothing is thrown away. Every part can be used for

something. If they kill many and then leave them lying about then we know that such disrespect will come back on us.

Beyond the numbers taken, James learned that the entire way of handling the animal taken had to follow the way of respect.

For example, if I killed a caribou and I did not follow the traditional ways of handling it, then I may anger the caribou spirit or I may also anger another animal by the way I treat that caribou. Therefore, that could result in my not being able to take more animals when I needed them.

The way you show respect to the caribou begins with the way it is butchered. Once the caribou has been killed, to show respect and appreciation, one of the female caribou from a large hunt, should be set aside and the whole thing cooked. Even the bones are crushed and boiled for drinking and all of its fat and everything else is cooked and eaten all in one festive meal. We make sure that nothing is wasted and nothing is allowed to go bad. Also, if something must be thrown away, you keep those parts in one place.

The skin of that animal should also be tanned right away so that by the next morning all the edible parts have been eaten and the skin has been tanned so that it can be used. Using the whole of the animal on the same day is how we show the animal spirit that we appreciate the life that has been given to sustain our lives; it is how we show respect for the animals that keep us alive.

When many caribou have been taken, the skin of a choice animal should be tanned as white and then decorated with colours and the edges fringed. The ones that I have seen in my younger days were stretched and hung outside to show respect to the caribou.

James' references to his youth do not mean that the custom has been abandoned. By not mentioning his own talents in preparing a caribou hide, which are highly esteemed both by his own community and throughout the Cree nation, he is simply acknowledging his elders as the source of what he is able to share.

I have heard it said, in the past, that people who very much wanted to have a caribou would sing a song. If the caribou liked the hunter's song then the caribou would freely give themselves. That is why the person was able to kill the caribou. I have heard my father singing caribou songs in this way. When we have been blessed with a large number of caribou I have been able to take part in such a feast myself. But I think that in my father's time these customs were followed much more precisely.

In a world where respect is owed, and is seen as providing the benefit of further harvest, the person who lacks respect is much more likely to suffer consequences.

One of the stories I heard about this understanding was about a group of people who saw a herd of caribou coming down to cross the river. Near the river crossing there was a falls. So the people scared the caribou for no good reason so that some of the caribou went over the falls and drowned. It is said that once the food that these people had gotten by killing the caribou in this way had all been eaten that the people could not find anything else to eat. It is said that most of these people starved to death because they did not respect the animals the way we have been taught.

One time, when the fat had been freshly made, a man was told to take that fat to another camp where the people were in need. Along the way he decided that it was too much trouble to go all the way to their camp so he simply hid the fat somewhere along the trail. Some time later the man who wasted the fat was beset with a slow, wasting illness. One of his legs simply withered and he suffered great pain. It is thought that this illness came upon him because he had allowed the marrow and fat of the animal to be wasted.

Another story I have heard about the caribou fat tells that when there is a feast and the caribou fat is being served we are told to wipe our mouths very clean and not have any fat on us when we go outside and leave the tent or house where the feast has been taking place.

The connection between respect for the animals and the threat facing his people's land is quite clear, "Because we were told by the Creator that we should look after everything very well. If we ignore this instruction I fear that something will happen to us as a result of our not looking after the land and the animals. Something will come upon us that will be not good for us."

What is beyond the understanding of the people of Great Whale about Hydro-Québec's plans is the total absence of the respect that shapes and informs their own lives. How else but in the total absence of respect could a person even conceive of devastating an entire land?

Stella Masty was already on her way to becoming an activist at 14 years of age when she travelled with the *Odeyak*. Her struggle to understand led her to ask her elders some hard questions. "Sometimes I talk with my grandfather and ask him, why do people want to flood our land?"

Well, certain white people are stubborn in trying to destroy everything. When they want to get something they have to destroy whatever is around it before they can reach the thing that they want.

For Crees, when we want something, we have to say a prayer to the Spirit. When we pray to the spirit of the animal, that is when we might be allowed to take the particular animal. Everything to us is a brother or a sister. There's no such thing as racism in our culture because we are all related to everything around us.

Crees give other people a higher rank than they give themselves. If a group of people were all hungry and only one person were able to hunt, that person would feed everyone else before he ate.

Part of what remains incomprehensible is the apparent duplicity the Whapmagoostui Chief finds in the statements of the Québec Government. Robbie Dick cites, from memory, a pivotal paragraph from the speech of Hon. John Ciaccia, special representative of Premier Robert Bourassa, on November 5, 1975, when he introduced *The Agreement* to a standing committee of the National Assembly. Mr. Ciaccia's speech has been included in every reprinting of *The Agreement*.

> In undertaking the negotiations with the Native peoples, we have followed two guiding principles, two principles of equal importance. The first is that Québec needs to use the resources of its territory, all its territory, for the benefit of all its people. The use of these resources must be reasonably planned. The future needs of the people of Québec must be anticipated.

For Robbie Dick it is the disparity between the first principle stated by Mr. Ciaccia and the reality of current Québec policy that is beyond understanding,

> He didn't mention anything about exporting power to the United States. Now they're saying that we agreed in the *James Bay Agreement* for these projects to be built. We say that we didn't. And we especially didn't agree to dam our rivers to export power to the United States.

Freshwater Seals

The problem of respect for the animals versus duplicity became a particular issue during the National Energy Board of Canada hearings on Hydro-Québec's application for export permits to New York and Vermont. Hydro told the NEB that there was no such thing as a freshwater seal, the animals for which *les Lacs des Loups Marins*, are named. A year later, Hydro issued a report stating that the freshwater seals were to be found in numerous lakes in the area including the largest, Lake Bienville.

James Kawapit spent his life hunting in the Lake Bienville area until he retired. His father hunted there before him.

> I have never seen the seals in Lake Bienville itself. I have only seen them in the other lake, the Lesser Seal Lake. I have seen my father kill some seals there. I have never killed any myself. We didn't hunt there much when I started hunting on my own. I have never heard, during all this time, that there were freshwater seals at Lake Bienville.

James Kawapit's description of the physical differences between freshwater and marine (or sea dwelling) seals is vivid and thorough.

The freshwater seals look different in that their fur is much darker. Their markings are more numerous and are dark. The marine seals are much lighter in colour. They also have different habits. The other difference is in the taste. The freshwater seals taste more like fish and their fat tastes different from the marine ones. The freshwater seals taste the same all year round but the marine seals' taste changes during the springtime and summer. The marine seals are stronger tasting in those seasons because of what they eat. They eat things at the bottom of the ocean. So the marine seals are better to eat only in the winter time.

One of the freshwater seals' habits is to lay around on the rocks around the shore of the lake in the fall. They do not lie on the ice.

John Petagumskum testified before the National Energy Board for the Grand Council of the Crees in reply to Hydro's claim of the seals' non-existence. He is something of an expert witness on the matter of freshwater seals. In his younger years he travelled by canoe far past the Seal Lakes. Today, very few of the other hunters who used to travel to the Seal Lakes still hunt. John says that he is "the only one who goes that far nowadays." John Petagumskum described the differences between the two types of seal not only from the outside but also from the inside.

Its esophagus is much larger and wider than the esophagus of the salt-water seals. This is because it has only one diet. They will take a big fish, bite it in half and eat it. This is one of the big differences.

The freshwater seal debate goes to the very heart of the Cree way of life at Whapmagoostui. The seal is accorded a particular respect because it is rare.

We hold it in such high respect because they are only found in the one area. The other communities don't have those seals. They are not found anywhere else but in these two lakes.

The seal is like the bear. In certain periods in the past, the black bear has not been very abundant. So only a few people managed to find and kill the black bear. The number of hunters who went inland to the areas where bears might be found was always much greater than the number of bears they were able to take.

Hunters of the past and even today have certain skills in hunting a certain animal. Some people have a skill for one animal and some for others. But for all the hunters who are skilled in hunting other kinds of big game, I have found that the seal is harder to hunt than any other game. This is not only my observation, it is also agreed by other hunters.

The seal also commands a special respect because it has been known to save the lives of Cree families in times of famine. When later asked about his testimony before the National Energy Board, John told three stories to demonstrate the special powers of the seal.

This story was told by Emily's grandfather, Sam. Once their family was hunting very far away from the post. That season they were very unsuccessful. They were becoming very hungry. Finally, Sam made a decision that his eldest son would go to the post to try to get some supplies. His younger son, Emily's father, would go with Sam to a place where the water is open and does not freeze over even in the depth of winter.

The first day that they were at the opening they sighted the seal but were not able to shoot it. The second day they returned and Emily's father got the seal. They were very grateful to have that seal because they had not had anything to eat since the others had left for the post to bring supplies. In an instant, they had been blessed with a great deal of food.

John's second story happened to an old man he knew in his youth at an even earlier time than the first.

One time, this man was with a hunting group who were also having no success, to the point that they were becoming very hungry. Not only had they been unable to take any animals, they had also not been able to catch any fish and had not eaten for some time. They had become so weak with hunger that the women were no longer able to chop wood and the men could no longer go outside to hunt.

The only two people who were able to continue to work were an elder woman and a man who could still hunt with a gun. Finally, the one elder man told his wife, "I am going to go out to hunt some ptarmigan."

While he was out he heard sounds that he had never heard before from someone or something in the mountains. He thought to himself, "It does not seem like that sound is coming from the air. Whoever makes that sound must be on land." So he decided to find out what it was. He didn't walk far before he heard the sound again. This time he felt certain he could tell where the sound was coming from. Soon he came to an area of willows and a frozen, snow-covered stream where there were imprints in the snow that had been made by a seal. He followed the seal's print for a short distance until he sighted it and was able to take it to feed his family.

This story was told by our great-great grandmother who said that if the man had not been given that seal the people in that camp would all have starved. She was pretty sure of that.

John's experience as a hunter leads him to reflect on this story in a way which further distinguishes between the freshwater and marine seals.

The seal must have travelled far inland by following the streams and gone into another lake. During the fall, while the water is freezing, the seals lie on or close to the rocks where it is warmer. When the seal would have tried to return, the stream in which he had travelled had frozen so that the seal could not swim down that stream. This forced the seal to travel, contrary to the usual custom of the seals, on the land or the ice on top of the frozen stream leaving its mark to be followed by a hungry hunter.

The third story told by John Petagumskum explained how the special respect accorded to seals is expressed through special rituals.

> When our grandfathers who are no longer with us would be given any big game, they would hold a feast. It is the same ritual for a seal. A feast is held in its honour and its meat is shared with everyone who is present. The other thing that has been done a long time ago and to this day is that its oil or fat can not be wasted or spilled in any way. So the seal must be handled with great care.

> One is not supposed to waste the seal or throw any part of it away or even to leave any part of the seal. It was thought that if a hunter killed a seal but let it go under the ice or he somehow lost the seal that the hunter would be met by some further misfortune. He would be unsuccessful in his effort to find other game once he had been careless with the seal. If there is a danger that the seal might sink or that it might get away after you have wounded the seal, you just do not shoot it.

John has his own idea about Hydro's reasons for putting out contradictory and unsubstantiated stories about the seals and the lakes where he has spent much of his life.

> At the beginning, I suppose they expected that people would believe them that there were no seals because the people in the south are not here and can not see the seals. We all know we would not have believed them. As for Hydro-Québec seeing seals in other places, maybe it is a possibility because we have not hunted them for a long time. It is possible that they have multiplied in these intermittent years. They do follow the streams flowing into the Lower Seal Lake and will also go downstream where the Lower Seal flows toward the Little Whale River.

Like James Kawapit, John Petagumskum has never heard of seals at Lake Bienville. "Maybe they are saying that now so that nobody will make a fuss if they are not so rare."

Matthew George tells a story about John Petagumskum which would be immodest for John to tell himself. In the summer of 1990, David Suzuki's CBC program *The Nature of Things* produced a two-hour documentary on the Great Whale River hydro-electric project. Twice during the summer John Petagumskum went to the Upper Seal Lake to look for seals with the camera crew.

> They saw the Hydro people there this summer where the seals are. They just had a tent and a helicopter. They were also studying the seals. John told me that they saw the Hydro people at the spot where the seals are usually to be found in the Upper Seal Lake by the rapids. That's exactly where they had put their tent. John made a strange discovery. They did not see the seals during the day. They only saw them at night. John figured that the helicopter that the Hydro people were using to look for the seals

was scaring them away. So the seals only came out at night. The seals had learned very quickly.

Matthew Mukash sees the teaching of the Cree elders as the very opposite of the dominant theme of urban culture.

> A lot of the understanding is deeper and more to the point than the understanding of engineers or biologists. In modern society, people tend to create parameters. Everything is done within those parameters. If you have actual experience of living in the bush through every change in the cycle of the year then you have a knowledge that goes far deeper than what can be learned with a slide rule or a microscope. We have a spiritual relationship with the animals. When people have the power to communicate with the spirits of animals then they understand the animals the way people understand one another.

Like their respective seal searches, the approach of John Petagumskum and the other elders to the struggle and to life itself is the very antithesis of Hydro-Québec's. John counters indifference with acceptance. Judging a visitor's interest to be sincere they tell the stories they heard from their elders, providing that the visitor asks to hear them. Matthew George suggests that it was Hydro's disbelief in the presence of the Crees that led the Crees to go to court, seeking an injunction to stop James Bay One, in 1973.

> At the beginning of the Hydro Project, the Québec Government couldn't believe that. They kept saying that the Cree and Inuit couldn't have been around this area for that number of years. They couldn't believe that even by word of mouth. It was then that they were taken to court because they couldn't believe that we were here all this time.

Matthew and John counter the duplicity and disbelief of Hydro and the Québec Government with their own transparency. Another elder, Noah Mamiamscum, who was still spending most of the winter in the bush at the time of the *Odeyak*, recalls how the military changed the landscape.

> Before there were any white people, except the Hudson Bay Company, there was no sand to be seen in this town. It was just vegetation growing over the soil and a few willows here and there. Since the white people came, they tore up the town and there is only sand and nothing that grows.

This is the spectre Robbie Dick says is haunting his community in the face of the hydro-electric project.

> Now that bulldozer way-of-being is slowly coming up into our territory too. This has happened to our brothers in the south and it is happening to us now. And this is the way it is going to continue to happen unless the people can take what is left of our culture and maintain it in any way possible, and save whatever is left of what the land provided, for our culture to have survived to this day.

Chapter 5:
A Canadian Wilderness

Over the Ice to Chissasibi

The sun was beginning to set into the frozen expanses of James Bay when the three men accompanying the sled-mounted *Odeyak* rode onto Ft. George Island at the mouth of the La Grande River. A small crowd had come from Chissasibi on their skidoos to greet the *Odeyak* as it entered their ancestral home. The welcome was brief: cheers, greetings, a sandwich and a cup of tea in one of the remaining homes. The travellers were all eager to reach Chissasibi before the daylight was completely gone.

Thomasee Napartuk from Povungnituk, the owner of the dog team, had flown "down south" for the occasion. He had had some time to get acquainted with his two helpers from Great Whale, Robert Fleming, an Inuk, and Weemish Mamiumscum, a Cree. Heavy winds on Hudson Bay had forced them to seek shelter, adding another day to the trip from Great Whale to Chissasibi. Even cutting across the peninsula well before Cape Jones to follow the Seal River from Polar Bear Mountain, the trip was still 160 miles, three days' travel with a dog team pulling a heavy boat in a wind.

The old village of Ft. George, the centuries-old home of the Chissasibi Crees, had stood on this island in the mouth of the La Grande River. In 1978, Hydro-Québec had determined that its furthest downstream dam in a series of five on the La Grande system, LG-1, would be built at the First Rapids. Until then, Ft. George had been a typical hunter's village, full of the small cabins favored by people who lived much of their year in the bush. The Hydro authorities told the Chissasibi band that with the irregular and extreme flows from LG-1 they could not guarantee that the island would not wash away. They offered $60 million to build a new village on the mainland. Today, Ft. George is a ghost town. A few families stayed, but eventually most of the village was razed.

Chissasibi is the Cree community that has experienced the greatest impact of the La Grande Project, James Bay One. Indeed, through the re-location of the village, the flooding of prime hunting, trapping and fishing areas and the subsequent mercury contamination, Chissasibi has been entirely re-shaped by James Bay One. The Chissasibi experience is exactly what Whapmagoostui and Kuujjuaraapik most fear will be the fate of their communities if the Great Whale Project is allowed to proceed. If southerners already knew the fate of Chissasibi, the message of the *Odeyak* could be reduced to a single sentence, "Don't let this happen to us."

When Thomasee finally brought his dogs to a halt near the Commercial Centre in downtown Chissasibi, he was cheered by four hundred people, a sizeable turnout in a community of twelve hundred. The *Odeyak* had arrived, late but safe at its first destination. With the travellers' blessing, a group of men lifted the *Odeyak* off the sled and carried it into the Commercial Centre.

Both Great Whale villages have intimate connections with Chissasibi. There is probably not a single family in Whapmagoostui who do not have relatives in Chissasibi. A number of Inuit families from Chissasibi had taken up the openings created by the move of a large portion of the Inuit from Kuujjuaraapik to Ummuriaq. When whales were still abundant, Chissasibi people travelled to Great Whale to hunt. Today, the traffic more often moves the other way. Almost every adult and adolescent from Great Whale has visited LG-2, the massive dam fifty miles upstream from Chissasibi. Chissasibi is also the site of the regional hospital, run by the Cree Health Board.

Viola Pachanos, the chief of Chissasibi Band, sees the re-location of her people as a disorienting upheaval to which they are still trying to adjust. The upheaval that began with the actual re-location of the village has been compounded by a series of subsequent events. All these events flow from the construction of dams and dikes that had been going on for 16 years when the *Odeyak* arrived in March, 1990.

The two most devastating events have been the flooding of the La Grande valley and the subsequent contamination of the enormous reservoir by methyl mercury. The flooding of the reservoir behind LG-2, the first of five dams completed in the La Grande system, had raised the water level by about 450 feet, or the height of a forty-storey building. The flooding has resulted in a massive, totally unanticipated release of methyl mercury into the water of the reservoir. When the fish became unfit for human consumption, the Chissasibi Crees had lost a major source of food. Cree hunters were, by the time of the *Odeyak*, suspecting that fish-eating animals were also showing signs of mercury poisoning. In 1985, the La Grande Agreement established special aid to Chissasibi in response to the unanticipated loss of their fishery. Six years later, moose and caribou were being found with organ damage. Hunters feared that these herbivores were also poisoned by the microbially released mercury.

Viola says that the biggest impact has come from the ease with which drugs and alcohol began to flow into the community after the opening of the road to Chissasibi from the south. The road building also brought the entirely new frontier town of Radisson, populated primarily by construction crews who came for the high paying, round-the-clock work. The workers made frequent trips to their homes in southern Québec and had no commitment to a northern community.

Josie Sam, a high school guidance and career counsellor, points to the trucks that come in twice every week and says that the road is a new source of food. While he thinks that the children have become healthier living in the new community, he also despairs at the thought of replacing the geese and ducks, on which the Crees have traditionally relied in the spring and fall, with chicken from the south. Nobody thinks that the highly processed food brought in by road (at an average of four times the price that it would cost in a southern urban center) is an adequate substitute for the wild food lost to the hydro projects. Although Josie Sam estimates that half the diet of the adolescents remains country food, medical consultants attribute the dramatic increase in diabetes to the introduction of foods containing high amounts of sugar and starch. The constant refrain, not only among Chissasibi leaders but also young parents is, "What will our children have to eat?"

The Commercial Centre, into which the *Odeyak* was carried, embodies the greatest strengths and weaknesses of the Chissasibi community in the middle of its first generation of re-location. The Centre is a miniature shopping mall on the ground floor of the Y-shaped building which defines the core of the re-located Chissasibi. The mall includes a bank, a hardware store, clothing stores, music and furniture shops, and a locally owned fast food service. Two of the store sites are occupied by the overflow from Band and Grand Council agency offices most of which are located upstairs.

But the major tenants of the Centre are not the stores and offices. The one feature which distinguishes Chissasibi's Centre from the mini-mall in other small towns is the sense that it belongs more to the people than to the landlord. The major occupants of this mall are the people, the older ones who go out on the land less and less and the younger ones for whom wage work is, at best, uncertain.

The sense of belonging reflected in the recognition that the covered mall is the most comfortable place to pass the time of day is a very mixed blessing. The instant new town of Chissasibi acquired an instant new package of social problems: kids with nothing to do, unemployment and alienation. Even teen-age suicide, previously rare among the Crees, has become a tragic reality. Some sense of these problems is visible walking through the mall. Larry House, a 25-year-old father of three, is the Chissasibi youth delegate to the Grand Council of the Crees. He believes the cluster housing and The Commercial Centre mall work against a traditional sense of community.

> The way they set up the new village was the way they do down south where they create bedrooms and they have everything centralized even though it is a small village. In Ft. George we had the Hudson Bay store at one end of town, the co-op and the post office at the other end, and the gas station toward the middle. Everybody walked all over the place.

> When we were on the island the old people used to gather down by the banks [of the river]. A lot of the young people used to go down to watch them tell stories or play checkers as they talked away. In the new village, all the old people have is the Commercial Centre. The old men sit around there and play checkers but, everyone is so busy doing everything else.

Chief Pachanos points to the difficulty of transferring social skills from the family bush camp to the larger village.

> When people come into the community they seem to have a different concept of how it is to live than when they are out in the bush. Out there they are self-sufficient and they share with whoever is there. Once they come into the community, the same people seem quite helpless. They want somebody to do things for them.

> For me, that downstairs [of the mall] is a real eyesore. We talk about trying to be environmentalists and conservationists and then litter our own community center. When the same people live in their camps they seem to take care of their space. They do not leave litter. In the community they are totally different.

Many of the challenges stemming from Chissasibi's re-location are reflected in a unique kind of generation gap. Chief Pachanos estimates that half the population is under the age of 25.

> People like myself and the older people who were born and raised on the island find it harder to adapt to this way of living. For the younger generation who have never lived in tents and teepees they think that this is the only way to live. One youth said, "You older people, your roots were over on the island. For us, this is where our roots will be."

Josie Sam is not at all sentimental about what was left behind on the island. As a guidance counsellor he sees himself clearly in the role of helping students to adapt to the reality of the new society.

> It is very hard to adapt to white society but they are learning. They want to try everything that they see. They're young. Some have tried to go out to hunt but not for very long. Three weeks and they have had enough. They are ready to start to learn something more about the white society. You can't blame them because the world is changing. We are not going to

be back again in the olden days. The world is changing and they are living with it now.

The Traditional Pursuits course offered by the school is criticized by some elders for rewarding people for learning their own culture. As a guidance counsellor, Josie Sam sees such courses primarily as a frill.

> The [fur] market is so low that the only thing that I can see now is to have a good time in the bush. They have the opportunity to learn but they will not be able to live on it. They can't live on it but they can go out there as a recreation, to enjoy the fresh air and take whatever you want to hunt. But why kill caribou or why kill moose if you're not sure if they are safe to eat. You might take a moose, but, God only knows if it will be safe to eat!

The initial loss of land through flooding and the subsequent devastation of the La Grande basin fishery and wildlife have become one prolonged and continuing event in the collective mind of Chissasibi. About half the traplines along the length of the La Grande lost substantial amounts of land which may add up to as much as one third of the land on which the community based its traditional economy. The greatest impact has been on the habitat of beaver and moose. There is a proverbial story about a beaver that responded to the rising waters by building its lodge higher and higher. When the beaver had built to a height of twenty feet and the water kept coming, the animal fled. Raising the water level several hundred feet wiped out both the places where beaver might build lodges in the river, or dams on tributary streams, and also the marshy shoreline where moose browse.

Sam Cox is a former game warden who now works on economic development. His speciality is tourism. If the Crees can gain an increasing role in the hunting and fishing based tourism of their region they will be able to apply their traditional skills in the cash economy. Sam also emphasizes that they will then be able exercise some much needed control over the visiting sport hunters and fishers.

On his office wall Sam has a map of the forty traplines covering the entire Cree territory. Each is shown with a number. Each trapline has its own tallyman, the person responsible for the trapping on that land. Sam's own family lost three-quarters of their land to the rising waters of the La Grande Reservoir. Their trapping area is shared by ten families with all the problems that implies.

> The camps are very close together now. We used to be all over. Now we're all situated along the highway. It is very hard to reach the places we used to go. In the summer, it gets very rough. In the fall and spring the water level is rising and falling and it is hard to travel by boat. In the fall the water can be very high. In the spring it is very low. It is really hard to get out onto the reservoir. There is a lot of slush.

All the game is only on the islands. The only time we go to our land is just to see what is there. We don't go there that much any more. We just stay around the highway. We only go up on weekends. My father is there year round. He traps close by the camp but he cannot go very far from there.

Sam Cox says that the mink, otter, beaver and other fish-eating animals are being affected by the mercury in the reservoir. A mercury study of mink collapsed when the trappers were only able to catch one in the La Grande area.

I saw a dead otter one time, the carcass was just lying around. I knew it had died from something because nobody hunts in that area. Nobody would have shot it. It was just lying there dead. Beaver are affected a lot. When we send our skins down to be sold they come up with a report "singed." That is caused by the water in the reservoirs so that the quality of the fur is not very good. So far we have no problems with the meat.

In the winter of 1990, Chissasibi hunters took six moose that were not edible. Sam Tapiatic works for the Eeyou Company and is the general manager for the Mitigating Works Fund which was created as part of the La Grande Agreement of 1986. He is also Deputy Chief and a Chissasibi Band Councillor. Sam says, "The intestines of the animals were too dehydrated or the livers or lungs were not normal." Sam wrote to the Hunting, Fishing and Trapping Co-ordinating Committee asking for a study to find out why the moose in the areas of LG-2, LG-3 and LG-4 are sick and dying. "Just in the last couple of years we have been finding moose carcasses in the reservoirs. We don't know what is causing it. It does not seem to be happening elsewhere. It seems to be contracted right in the La Grande Complex." A thorough study will require the co-operation of Hydro-Québec and several provincial government departments. Sam is frustrated as he contemplates the task ahead of him.

Some people think that the moose habitat has been destroyed and is underwater so the moose are finding it hard to find good, suitable wintering grounds. The moose do not have any problem in the summertime. It is in the wintertime when they have to look harder for food that they have a hard time.

The people have been warned not to eat any animal with any deformation of its organs. Sam Cox says, "They even told us that the birds and the rabbits are affected too. Dying off for some reason."

As General Manager of the Mitigating Works Fund, Sam Tapiatic is trying to re-organize the trapping areas to restore the equitable balance that the lines had before the flooding.

They are so used to their own territory that now, when it is broken up and some of it is lost, they have a sense or pride that makes it difficult for them to accept taking other people's territory. The consensus is, from all the trappers, that they want to invite the people whose traplines are fully underwater onto their territories. But the tallymen who are affected do not want to interfere onto other people's territories.

With the loss of fishing in the La Grande, the Chissasibi people have had to identify new sources of fish. Families with land on lakes and rivers upstream from the main river are being asked to catch extra fish to bring back to the community. This solution provides a limited supply for those who do not go out in the bush. It is not a great help for families who head out onto their traplines in the fall and need to catch fish as the easiest food supply while they are setting up camp.

In 1990, the whitefish were declared edible once again. But the pike, lake trout and all the other fish in the La Grande remain toxic. There was only one lake that had non-toxic whitefish. It is now almost fished out. Sam Cox says that the problem of edible fish stocks is compounded by another matter. Under the *Agreement*, Category III lands are open to sport hunting and fishing.

This last summer there were a lot of Americans and people from other parts of Québec fishing that lake. So we didn't go there. Our trapline is in category III lands so we have to share with white people. Everything we do nowadays we have to compete with the white people for our share, for hunting caribou, for fishing. The one thing that they cannot do is to trap beaver.

Last winter when they opened the caribou season there were a lot of problems. The white people were shooting too close to the Native camps. At my father's camp they had to leave because it was too dangerous with the white people shooting anything that moved. If they saw a caribou in the middle of the road they shot it even if there was a car coming.

We're trying to regulate who goes on the land, especially around here. We're trying to get that control over who goes onto the land and what they can do on the land. Right now there is no control. Anyone can go in there. It is quite a mess. Sometimes we find non-Native people setting up cabins. They are not supposed to but there are cabins going up everywhere now.

There are game wardens but there are only four to try to control a vast area from LG-2 to Caniapiscau. That's a big area for only four game wardens. Last year they told us that there were one thousand hunters from the day the season opened in December until it closed on March 31.

The tourism program can only go ahead if the Cree agencies are able to gain the support and co-operation of both Hydro-Québec and the (*Québec Ministère de la Chasse et la Pêcherie*) (Department of Hunting and Fishing). Sam Cox says that a Cree outfitter at LG-2 would be mutually beneficial. His model for such a venture comes from similar Cree efforts on Category II, lands protected for Cree use. "We have three fishing camps and one goose camp now. Any non-resident who wants to hunt or fish in the area of those camps has to pass through our outfitters."

Much of the land that has not been flooded has still been rendered incapable of supporting life. Josie Sam's father had a trapline that ran from the present village site up toward LG-2. What remains of the trapline has been taken over by his brothers and nephews.

> Even though it is not flooded on the inland area the transmission lines run in there. The trees have been cut down, gravel pits dug to build the dikes. So half the land is gone from being of any use. It used to be a very rich land for fur bearing animals.

> Hydro-Québec said that they intended to put things back the way they were but this cannot be done. It takes time to have trees grow and it takes even more time for berries to grow. And that is talking about summer. In the winter, it is the homeland of the ptarmigan. They feed off the white birch and the willows. All those feeding grounds are gone. The ptarmigan have gone somewhere else and the game is not as plentiful as it used to be when the land was untouched.

Josie Sam says that in the 15 years since the gravel pits were dug on his family's lands, the authorities have not made any effort at restoration. Meanwhile, the new growth is "not the same plants that used to be there. There are different types of willows, not the kind on which the ptarmigan feeds in the winter time."

This is why Josie Sam does not think many of his students will have a future in the bush. But despite Josie Sam's admiration for the road as a new-found source of food he also says that "the road is very bad" when he thinks about it as a source of drugs and alcohol. The drug and alcohol influx has been dramatically reduced since the band erected a gate at the outer limit of the Category I or village settlement lands and began to inspect each vehicle coming into the community. Larry House says that the *Agreement* requires such a gate to be erected and maintained by Hydro-Québec. Pointing to the gate at the LG-1 construction site, he says that it controls traffic in the wrong direction.

What the elders miss from the island, where they and their ancestors lived for so many years, is much more than the atmosphere and the scenery. Life on the island was a story about "Man and Nature." Even if, as Josie Sam recalls, the food supply could be irregular at times, there was a belief that this was a matter to be resolved through the community's relationship with Nature, or with their Creator.

Life at the new Chissasibi village site has become less and less "Man and Nature" and more and more "Man versus Frontier Bureaucracy." This, more than any lack of social skills may be why, as Chief Pachanos reflected, people who are self-sufficient in the bush become helpless in the village.

Chief Pachanos says that senior Québec officials have made it clear to her that their co-operation on many of the projects vital to the health and development of Chissasibi depends on her willingness, and that of the other Cree leaders, to put the Great Whale hydro-electric project on the table at the same time.

Chissasibi's solidarity with Whapmagoostui has been expensive. Chissasibi's hospital is the main medical centre for the entire territory served by the Cree Health Board. Chief Pachanos has been trying to up-grade the Chissasibi airstrip, partly for the benefit of the hospital, since she took office in 1989.

> The airstrip we have now is only gravel. There is no shelter and no lights. Only a fuel tank. In the winter, when the days are short and there are snow storms it is quite hazardous for a plane to land here. People waiting for the plane have to sit in a vehicle. Sometimes a plane lands and there is nobody there to meet the passengers.

> When there is a medical evacuation, they refuse to use the Chissasibi air-port. So the patient has to come 75 miles by ambulance from the La Grande Airport. If it is a real emergency, the patient's life is further jeopardized by the extra travel.

At one meeting, Chief Pachanos confronted a Deputy Minister man-dated by the Premier to finalize implementation of the James Bay Agree-ment. "Are you telling me you're just not going to talk about the airport until we sit down and talk about Great Whale?" Chief Pachanos came away from the meeting with the understanding that when the Crees were ready to talk about Great Whale the Deputy Minister would talk about the airstrip.

Until then, her community lives in a quiet crisis. While there appear to be a great many modern, comfortable houses, many of them are home to two or three families. On the other hand, a family which spends most of its time in the bush is expected to pay the same monthly rent as ones who live in town most of the year. Trying to create employment and offer the generation coming of age some sort of future, while also trying to re-tain some part of the traditional economy, presents Chief Pachanos and her Council with an unenviable challenge.

Asked what advice she might offer the Whapmagoostui Council if they were to ask, Viola Pachanos recalls all the surprises which beset her community.

> There is an influx of things that come all at once for which you can never really be ready. It also has a special impact for the trappers when the road goes through their traplines. They can not make a living from what they get for their furs now. When there are other people hunting on the same land it just gets that much harder.
>
> We want people to understand that we want to get away from being told how we should live and how we should be when we have always had our own way of being. We want our young people to understand what it is to live on the land. We don't want them to lose that gift by living in a town like this.
>
> We also face the difficulty of retaining a language that comes from our experience of living on the land. We have to develop our language to accommodate other ways. But the changes are happening so fast that we do not have time to develop the language so that we can use it in all areas of life as they change. To me, keeping our language is a basic element of retaining our identity as a people.

Launching in the Ottawa

The Great Whale people asked the Chissasibi Band Council for help. Chissasibi's contribution was Larry House. Larry was part of a Chissasibi youth movement. He had a strong desire to connect, through the elders, to a traditional spiritual path. That urge can sometimes be more difficult to satisfy in a remote community such as Chissasibi than in a more southerly reserve community. Further south, if young people do not find the elders they are seeking in their own community, there are other communities, within the same culture, not too far away. Larry's role on the *Odeyak* trip afforded him the opportunity to discover that many of the skills and talents he was already developing were just what was needed to bridge the gap between the Cree communities and the outside world.

Larry's task was the transportation of the *Odeyak* between the places where it would actually be paddled on bodies of water. Creeco, a Cree development company in Val d'Or, had agreed to supply a pick-up truck. The *Odeyak* was being delivered to Val d'Or on a flatbed that was dead-heading back from Chissasibi. His first opportunity to show his talents set the trial-and-error tone which would characterize the logistics through the greater part of the *Odeyak* trip.

> When I got to Val d'Or I looked at the frame that they had made to put the *Odeyak* on and saw that there would have to be some modification if it were

going to be strong enough to hold the boat. I told them to add a few more braces. When we picked up the truck we found that there was no muffler, the clutch was almost gone and the differential was leaking.

The first time we tied down the *Odeyak* was just before we left Val d'Or. A few hours later, on the way through La Verendrye Park, when a big transport went by, the *Odeyak* was almost blown off. After that we found a way to tie it down more securely.

Most of the *Odeyak* travellers from the Great Whale villages flew south on an Air Creebec charter from Kuujjuaraapik to Montréal. In Montréal they boarded the bus which would accompany the *Odeyak* and headed for Ottawa. Those who were not paddling would spend the largest part of their days on this bus for the next three weeks. They arrived in Ottawa in time for a Friday evening pot luck supper, the first of many, at St. Alban's, one of the two Anglican churches which would host their Ottawa visit.

Ottawa was chosen as the launching site for two quite unrelated reasons. Most important, it was the first place south of Great Whale at which the *Odeyak* could be launched. Even 20 miles upstream where the Ottawa River broadens to become a mile wide, the ice would not go out until the week before Easter. Downstream from the Chaudière Falls, between Ottawa and Hull, the ice was out early enough that the *Odeyak* could be introduced to the water and the paddlers could get the feel of their unique craft.

The place where the ice opens early is also directly below Parliament Hill, the place where the Crees would renew their demands for a full federal environmental assessment before any part of the construction of the Great Whale hydro-electric project would be allowed to proceed.

Because it is the national capital, Ottawa has a sizable Native population. These are people who come from communities all across the country to work either for the federal government or for the several national Aboriginal organizations. There are also a large number of Cree students from northern Québec and northern Ontario who come to the national capital area to attend high school. For reasons of political expediency the Cree students from the Québec side of James Bay are enrolled in schools in Hull, the city on the Québec side of the river, across from Ottawa, while the ones from the Ontario side are enrolled in Ottawa schools.

The early morning sky was overcast on Saturday, March 24, 1990, when Larry House, with the help of an Ottawa guide, drove the pick-up carrying the *Odeyak* from the church where it had been kept overnight, part way across the inter-provincial bridge to Victoria Island. The Ottawa office of the Grand Council of the Crees had ensured that the event was well advertised among the Ottawa Native community. The *Odeyak* travellers and the local Native community were joined by a crowd of well-wishers and by the several Canadian television network news teams. A few brief words were said by Mayor Sappa Fleming and by Robbie Niquanicappo, the Deputy Chief of Whapmagoostui.

Victoria Island is not the easiest place from which to launch a canoe for its very first run. There was no dock. Large masses of ice were bobbing in the fast-moving water. For Native people and their friends who have lived in Ottawa for any length of time, it is, however, a place with strong memories. Victoria Island has been the site where Indian protests have formed up, and sometimes where they have camped out, in Ottawa, since the abandoned stone buildings on the island were occupied at the end of a March-on-Ottawa in 1974 and it declared the Indian Embassy. Since then it has become the site of summer craft fairs and the annual Ottawa pow-wow. An island named for the Queen in whose name most of Canada's early treaties were signed, in sight of the Parliament Buildings where all of them have been violated, was a good place to test the *Odeyak* in the waters of the spring run-off.

The first group of paddlers hoisted the *Odeyak* and walked it into the icy, flowing water. Seven hundred miles from home, surrounded by towering buildings, Billie Weetaltuk, the builder of half a century's boats, said his prayer for the *Odeyak*. In a voice barely audible to the friends surrounding him, he was heard to say in Inuktituut, "I sure hope it floats."

Float it did. Heavy and wide, the *Odeyak* was in no danger of capsizing. The rounded bottom let it sit in the water with less draft than the flat-bottomed hull used for the motorized canoes Billie usually builds for hunters. The eight experienced paddlers took the *Odeyak* quickly out into the swift current as they headed toward the steep cliffs below the Parliament Buildings. Half-way to the bluffs they turned into the rapids until the bow of the *Odeyak* came around to face the crowd watching on the island. Heading the boat into the current, the crew put it through its paces to see how it would maneuvre. As the *Odeyak* came back to Victoria Island its slow, steady pace was recorded by the TV networks for the first of many times.

Once the boat had been proven seaworthy, the travellers could devote the weekend to gathering their strength for the official events with which the next week would begin. The Crees and Inuit, like many people newly arrived in a city, were eager to do some shopping. Ottawa, where many of the visitors had friends and where most of the shops are strung out along two or three downtown streets, also turned out to be a rare oasis of freedom and a time when the visitors were not faced with constant demands for extemporaneous appearances. A social and cultural evening had been organized for the travellers by Ottawa support groups at St. John's Anglican Church. Sunday morning the devout returned to St. John's where Deputy Chief Robbie Niquanicappo gave an address.

The joy of finally seeing the *Odeyak* afloat and the fun of shopping were seriously dampened, however, when Mina Weetaltuk, Billie's wife, became ill and was rushed to the hospital. Several hours later, after the elderly but usually robust Mina had been thoroughly examined, a major lesson of the trip's first big city stop was learned. Mina, accustomed to the raw fish, frozen seal, dried goose, duck and caribou which form the staples of the Kuujjuaraapik diet, had simply not eaten since she had arrived down south. Once she and the doctors agreed that her illness came from a lack of food, steps were taken to make sure she always had a steady supply of fresh fish throughout the trip.

At eight o'clock Monday morning the *Odeyak* travellers gathered again on Victoria Island. This time they were being greeted by Jean-Maurice Matchewan, Chief of the Algonquin Nation at Barrière Lake. The greeting was particularly appropriate because the Ottawa River is the highway running through the traditional Algonquin lands.

What had brought Chief Matchewan to Ottawa and enabled him to greet the *Odeyak* was, however, a very immediate crisis for his own people. Although the Algonquin lands are quite far south, compared to the Cree or the Inuit, the Barrière Lake people had retained a great part of their traditional lifestyle. They had been able to do so because their village site and their hunting lands lie deep within the very large La Verendrye Provincial Park. Their lives were suddenly and dramatically disrupted in 1989, when the Québec Government began to permit clear cut logging in the provincial park. There had been no consultations and no opportunity for the Algonquin people to say how their lives would be affected by the sudden removal of the forest on which they relied for their livelihood, for shelter and for insulation from the outside world. Tensions between the Algonquin Nation at Barrière Lake and the Québec Government reached a breaking point in the summer of 1989, when an Algonquin roadblock against timber trucks was met by a Sûreté du Québec roadblock against vehicles driven by Algonquins and their friends.

Now, eight months later, a conference had been organized for the Barrière Lake people with the help of other, more urbanized Algonquins, Mohawks from further down the Ottawa River, and allies from across the country. The *Odeyak* was the perfect way to symbolize the conference theme of "First Nations Implementation of Sustainable Development."

When Chief Matchewan invited the travellers to bring the *Odeyak* to the conference in the Chaudière Plaza Hotel, the most exclusive hotel in Hull, he also asked Sappa Fleming and Robbie Niquanicappo to make the opening statements at the conference.

Jeff Wollock from Solidarity, a New York City-based Aboriginal research and support group, first saw the *Odeyak* and realized that it had become a reality when he came to Hull for the Algonquin conference. Three weeks earlier, Jeff had been at a Montréal press conference on the Great Whale Hydro Project at which Matthew Mukash had announced that the communities were in the midst of building a boat which would arrive in New York City for Earth Day. At that time, Jeff simply thought, "Good luck!"

Once he realized that the *Odeyak* had already travelled more than half the distance from Great Whale to New York, Jeff became concerned. Nobody, it appeared, had yet made contact with any of the Indian community groups or the various support groups in New York City. Out of Jeff's chance meeting with the *Odeyak* group at the Algonquin conference, came some of the earliest efforts to create a plan for the arrival of sixty Crees and Inuit in New York City, complete with their 25-foot canoe, a chartered bus and a pick-up truck.

Out of his contact with Matthew Mukash, to whom he had introduced himself and offered help at the Montréal conference and now renewed the acquaintance in Hull, Jeff Wollock received a one-page list of places and events entitled "*Odeyak* Itinerary." Much later, he would learn from Denny Alsop that this was simply a sketch drawn up by Denny and Marie as a model of how the trip might go. On his return from Hull to New York City, Jeff decided the best support he could offer would begin with putting the *Odeyak* itinerary into the widest possible circulation.

Monday was also the day when Stella Masty, the student who had won her place on the trip by writing a prize essay, made her debut as a public speaker. Following lunch, she and Randy Pepabano, another Cree student, went to visit Philemon Wright Secondary, the Hull school attended by most of the Cree students coming south from James Bay. Stella would speak to students at schools all along the way. Randy was willing to visit the schools and talk with the students, but the prospect of addressing an assembly larger than his own village, in English, his second language, was simply too much. Isaac Masty, the school supervisor and Stella's father says that the students "had never in their lives had to use so much English as they did on this journey." The chance to make her first speech to an audience with a number of Cree students helped Stella to get past her initial anxiety. The magic of her speech lay in the simplicity and directness of her presentation.

Good evening brothers and sisters. I would like to share with you my feelings about the proposed Hydro project in our area. But first I would like to introduce myself. My name is Stella Sarah Masty. My real last name is Maseetayapeemeko. But the white man changed it for his own convenience (which in itself is another story). I am 14 years old.

I go to Badabin Eeyou School at Whapmagoostui. I am in Secondary Two and I am proud to say that I am the Student Council Treasurer.

Now brothers and sisters, I am going to share with you my feelings about the proposed Hydro project. The proposed Hydro project makes me feel very unhappy to know that all the peace and quiet that I experience when me and my family go out into the wilderness, to hunt or just to enjoy the beauties that the Creator has provided, may soon be lost.

Imagine brothers and sisters, all the beauty I have described being under polluted, contaminated water. Imagine too, all the beauty in the trees, the flowers, the plants, which are the essence of all living creatures, being under that same water. That's what will happen once the Hydro project is built in our area.

I dedicate this speech to my grandfather who still lives on the land and comes to town only on special occasions such as Christmas.

Stella soon learned that her own strength lay, for the presentations, exactly with the love of the land she had learned from her grandparents. She quickly learned to pass on, to her father or another adult accompanying her, the technical questions raised by the older students. The Cree students in Hull were a more subdued, less responsive audience than ones she would meet in the States, but they did not need the numbers and the scientific data. Even if they were not all as ready to speak publicly in a second language, they were glad that someone was prepared to say the things Stella was saying.

On Tuesday morning, when the *Odeyak* was portaged from Victoria Island to Parliament Hill, one Member of Parliament from each of the three political parties in the House of Commons came out to greet the travellers. (The three appointed Aboriginal senators, Charlie Watt, a Liberal and an Inuk from northern Québec, Len Marchand, a former Liberal cabinet minister from the B.C. interior and Willie Adams, an Inuk from the North West Territories, were all conspicuous by their absence.) Jim Fulton, a New Democratic Member from Skeena, B.C., would continue to ask cabinet ministers all the difficult and embarrassing questions about the Great Whale Project. Charles Caccia, Liberal M.P. from Toronto's Davenport riding, also headed the Centre for Environmentally Sustainable Development. Guy St. Julien was the Conservative who represented the northern Québec riding in which the project would be located. Each of the three joined with the Cree and Inuit carriers to help portage the

Odeyak from the steps of the main Parliament Building down the long walk past the eternal flame and across the street to the National Press Building.

Grand Chief Matthew Coon Come also walked with the *Odeyak* to the press theater where he was the main speaker.

> Just as Noah built and launched a boat to save the living things of Earth from a flood, so we launch a boat, an Indian and Inuit boat, to save ourselves from another flood. . . .
>
> *Odeyak* carries a message to Canadians, to the people of Québec, to Americans: You may think that what happens in the North does not concern you. You just want to flick the switch and turn on the lights. But there are people involved. We Native people are the victims. But we are only the first victims.

During Question Period in the House of Commons following the press conference, Lucien Bouchard, the Conservative Environment Minister, was questioned by Robert Skelly, the New Democratic Party's critic for Native affairs. Bouchard reiterated his earlier promises that the Great Whale Project would not proceed without a full environmental review. "Talks are under way with Québec," the Minister said, "to establish a joint federal-provincial review." But he warned that the federal government would proceed alone "if we must."

Lucien Bouchard's statement on that day, when the Visitors' Gallery was largely occupied by people from Great Whale, was one of those political events which seems completely routine when it happens but would become of increasing importance over time. By the beginning of summer, after the collapse of the Meech Lake Accord, Mr. Bouchard quit the Mulroney Conservative Government to form the Bloc Québécois, a Québec independence movement within the federal House of Commons. Bouchard would be replaced by long-time Tory deal maker, Robert de Cotret. When de Cotret was unable to make a deal satisfactory to the Bourassa Government in Québec, he would simply back down and announce that the Federal Government did not really have any authority to conduct an independent review of the Great Whale Project.

When the Crees sued the Federal Administrator of *The James Bay and Northern Québec Agreement*, Raymond Robinson, Lucien Bouchard's repeated statements that there would be a federal environmental assessment became critical testimony, along with the previous statements of the Administrator. They demonstrated that the government had long held a belief that it did have an obligation to conduct an environmental assessment under section 22 of the *Agreement*.

These statements led Mr. Justice Paul Rouleau of the Federal Court of Canada to describe the position set out by Robert de Cotret and Raymond Robinson eight months after Mr. Bouchard's statement, in November, 1990, as "an abrupt reversal." The federal government would defend their refusal to conduct an environmental assessment by telling the court that the *Agreement* was only a contract and did not have the force of law. When Judge Rouleau ruled, one year less a week after the *Odeyak* passed through Ottawa, that the *Agreement* was, indeed, both a federal and a provincial statute, his decision was later affirmed by the Supreme Court of Canada. The government then told the Judge that section 22 only required an environmental assessment if Hydro-Québec gave the government notice of its intentions. Judge Rouleau characterized this federal argument as "spurious" and "ludicrous."

Even had the people from Whapmagoostui and Kuujjuaraapik, seated in the Visitors' Gallery in the House of Commons that day understood both English and French, they could not have known that what they were hearing would later become evidence in a case brought against the government by their leaders. By the end of Question Period when the House of Commons settled down to debate some other issue, the Cree and Inuit visitors were ready for the Parliamentry tour and some further shopping.

The shopping seemed innocent enough but it presented some challenges to the *Odeyak* trip leaders. Matthew Mukash had been having "a bit of a problem keeping all the people together." The problem had been growing since their arrival in Ottawa. Many had friends in the city and had not been south for a long time. During the weekend, when the agenda was light, it had not made much difference. As the schedule became busier, keeping the people together became more important. The Cree custom of not being highly directive did not give Matthew specific tools for dealing with problems of discipline.

On the last full day in Ottawa, however, Matthew Mukash might have wished that less of the group had been together. Their own Member of Parliament, Guy St. Julien, invited the travellers to lunch in the Parliamentary cafeteria. The visitors met Mr. St. Julien at the West Block cafeteria after spending the morning on a tour of the Museum of Civilization. While the Great Whale people were in the line-up, their MP was mysteriously called away. When Matthew reached the cashier he found himself picking up the tab for more than thirty lunches. By Thursday morning, when the *Odeyak* set off for the Mohawk community of Kanesatake at Oka, Québec, halfway between Ottawa and Montréal, that lunch had become the most symbolic event of their time on Parliament Hill and of the promises of politicians.

Kanesatake — Before the Oka Crisis

Leaving Ottawa, following the highway along the shore of the Ottawa River, the *Odeyak* also left behind the traditional Algonquin lands, which extend roughly from the southern end of Cree country to the lower Ottawa Valley, which is the northern boundary of the Mohawk Nation. Kanesatake, the Mohawk community at Oka, Québec, is on the north shore of the Lake of Two Mountains, where the Ottawa River flows into the St. Lawrence. The Mohawk is the easternmost nation of the Longhouse or Iroquois Confederacy. Traditionally the Mohawks occupied the area south and east of Lake Ontario, as far as Albany, New York, and the upper St. Lawrence Valley. Through the French-English Wars, the American Revolution (sometimes called the War Among the English in Mohawk) and the War of 1812, the Mohawk were allied with the English Crown.

Kanesatake has a complex history. The land was traditionally used by both Iroquois and Algonquin peoples. Aboriginal title to this day has never been superceded by Crown title. There has never been a treaty or sale of the land. During the time of French rule in the 1600s, members of the Sulpician order moved out of the growing city of Montréal and established a monastary at Lake of Two Mountains. The move had the blessing of both French and Mohawk authorities but only French documentation survives. Subsequently, the French missionaries formed a confederacy among various Native peoples. That was done with a fair amount of sensitivity for Native beliefs and by honoring the traditional systems of clan chiefs and clan mothers. Following the American Revolution, however, the Mohawk of Kanesatake became increasingly separated from other elements of the old Longhouse Confederacy.

With the imposition of the 1876 *Act for the gradual civilization of the Indians*, the traditional faction in the community was slowly reduced to inconsequential numbers although the people understood the importance of what they represented. In the 1970s, a group of neo-traditionalists essentially took over the government. All of these factors and forces seemed to merge in the events of 1990.

When the *Odeyak* arrived for lunch at Kanesatake on March 29, 1990, the tension in the Mohawk community had already begun to rise. Hostilities long kept beneath the surface would soon explode into the longest confrontation between Canadian authorities and a First Nation. A proposal to permit the Pines, a sacred grove on the edge of the Mohawk community, to be developed as a golf course had already been approved by the Oka town council. Some Mohawk warriors had begun to carry guns. Over the next five months, barricades to prevent the development would be raised by the Mohawks. In response the community was sealed off by the *Sûreté du Québec* (SQ), the provincial police. Weeks after the barricades went up, on July 11, 1990, a police officer was killed in an exchange of gun-fire. Whether he was shot by a Mohawk or by another police officer would remain unknown. The Québec coroner took more than a year to produce an inconclusive report.

One of the primary points of contention at Oka, and one with which the Great Whale people would become familiar in their own struggle, was who had jurisdiction over Native lands. Tom Siddon, the federal Minister of Indian Affairs during the siege, would declare that Kanesatake was not reserve land. The Minister's interest was to disclaim any federal role in protecting the lands in order to avoid offense to Québec at a time when it wanted to assert jurisdiction over First Nations land. The Minister's view was hard to reconcile with the *Royal Proclamation of 1763*. If these lands had never been surrendered, how and when had Canada ever acquired domain over them? His views were equally difficult to reconcile with the *The British North America Act of 1867*. This backbone of the present Canadian constitution follows the spirit and intent of the *Royal Proclamation* in declaring both "Indians" and "lands reserved for Indians" to be matters within the exclusive jurisdiction of the federal Parliament. The *Indian Act* includes as reserve lands not only tracts received by the First Nations at the time of treaties but also "special reserves" which were either purchased or set aside by religious orders. Kanesatake clearly fell into the catagory of "special reserve." The federal government would deny responsibility for the James Bay lands in the same way they attempted to get out of their obligations at Kanesatake. Denial was to become a major instrument of federal policy.

If there was tension between Ottawa and Québec over who controlled Native land there were also divisions within the Mohawk Nation which further complicated the events of the summer of 1990. It was a faction called the "Warriors' Society," which had begun to conduct armed patrols around the perimeter of the Pines. While the Warriors could claim some historic roots in the tradition of the Great Law of Peace, the central Constitution of the Longhouse Confederacy, it was basically a newly formed entity. Its members were a melange of the most sincere young people dedicated to the defence of their community and a handful of graduates from the security arm of the locally managed gambling houses at Akwesasne, a Mohawk community straddling the St. Lawrence River and the international border near Massena, N.Y., and Cornwall, Ontario. The inability of the band council administration to challenge the municipally initiated, Québec sponsored, federally supported depredation of Mohawk land created the vacuum the Warriors' Society was ready to fill.

As hard as the federal government tried to absolve itself of responsibility in the Oka Crisis, it was the distrust of the SQ, by all the factions of a divided Mohawk people, that eventually led to their replacement in the stand-off by the Canadian Army. That was seen as a first step toward reducing the level of conflict. Even when the last of the Mohawk Warriors were ready to lay down their weapons, the final condition was that the Army would hold the Warriors in custody at a military base and not hand them over to the SQ.

At mid-day on that Thursday, when the *Odeyak* paddlers, with their busload of children and elders, rolled into Kanesatake, Robbie N. remembers that a crowd had gathered to welcome them. The traditional Longhouse chiefs greeted them and accompanied them into the community center. The thick corn soup and bannock were a welcome change from city food. Robbie N. was continuing to substitute for Chief Robbie Dick who was, by this time, recovering from emergency heart surgery in a Montréal hospital.

> I think that was where I delivered my best speech. I was given a very great honor. The Mohawks, I understand, do not clap when someone has made a speech. They never do. But the clan mothers, who are the leaders, stood up after I had completed my speech, and then the chiefs stood up. I was told later that this was a very great honor. I didn't know that at the time. Afterward, someone took me aside and explained that it was a sign of respect and honor for the speech I had given.

After Robbie N. and Sappa Fleming had each spoken, John Cree, a traditional Mohawk chief, rose to speak. He began his address in Mohawk and then moved into English so that he could share his thoughts with the visitors. Standing in the community center, he pointed to the forests that were still standing and to those that used to surround the community. He spoke of the river at whose mouth his community lived. He talked of what it means to his people to live at the junction of the St. Lawrence, which connects the deep interior of the continent to the ocean, and the Ottawa, which joins the whole north below the James Bay basin to the St. Lawrence. He wanted to tell the people from Great Whale that he understood how they felt about their land because his own people were once free to hunt as the Crees and the Inuit continue to do today. But as Chief John Cree told how the culture of the Longhouse Confederacy and particularly the Mohawk Nation at Kanesatake had suffered for the loss of their land he began to cry. "Most of us who understood what was happening to him also had tears in our eyes watching him cry. That is not something that happens every day."

Chief Cree's point was not lost. The Elder, James Kawapit, remembers the visit to Kanesatake in his own way. "That is where we had a feast. The feast itself was in the style of the Mohawk people but they could not give us anything that they had hunted because they can no longer hunt. They talked to us of their ways and also of their stand about the land." Other elders were also surprised to see the two communities, Kanesatake and the other Mohawk village they visited at Kahnawake, almost within the urban area of Montréal. It was there where they could see the impossibility of carrying on the basic routines of their own lives and where hunting was clearly impossible that they began to understand what could happen to future generations in Great Whale. It was very frightening to them.

When the barricades did go up and the tension finally culminated in the firefight of July 11, the elders and the young people from Great Whale who had visited Kanesatake with the *Odeyak* were even more profoundly affected than other Aboriginal people across the country. Stella Masty, who would come back south to spend the early weeks of the summer as a counsellor at a children's camp, remembers being transfixed by the television reports from Oka.

> I just sat there and watched it. I couldn't do anything else. It was like I was in a cage. I just wanted to go down there and help them. I heard that there were a lot of people down there starving and sick and that the army would not let the Red Cross in to bring them food and medicine. I just wanted to be there to help them in any way I could.
>
> I heard that when they surrendered and the army went into the Treatment Centre they were shocked at all the different ceremonies that the Mohawks had done there. They couldn't believe their eyes. I have even heard that some of the soldiers ended up in the mental hospital because they couldn't accept what was going on in there. The [spiritual] powers, they had scared the army but they never used those powers to hurt the army; they just used their powers to make themselves stronger.

The nightmare of Oka unfolded through the summer of 1990 at the same time that Iraq was invading Kuwait and taking North American and European workers in Kuwait as hostages. At the same time that CNN was providing sustained live coverage of the events in Kuwait and Baghdad, Newsworld, the Canadian Broadcasting Corporation's all-news-network, was providing similar coverage of the confrontation at Kanesatake.

Even in the sub-Arctic, the parallels were not lost on First Nations people who could flip back and forth between the two news networks. The television presence became an essential part of both events. At Oka it may have helped to moderate the behavior of the occupying forces. When live coverage brought both battles into people's living rooms, however, a number of the most respected commentators proclaimed that constant coverage, without analysis and interpretation, focussed on Aboriginal resistance to Canadian authorities, was not valid journalism.

The viewers' experience of Kanesatake as an event back-to-back with Kuwait became an important part of the reality for Québec because the dominant French Canadian culture was so preoccupied with asserting itself that it had become unable to hear the Aboriginal peoples voicing their aspirations. Many liberal Quebeckers, who had personally identified with First Nations and Third World issues in the past, would later explain the conduct of their leaders and compatriots by saying that the Warriors had insulted the symbols of Québec statehood. Kanesatake's crisis, coming so closely on the heels of the defeat of the Meech Lake proposals to recognize Québec in the Canadian Constitution as a "distinct society," undoubtedly challenged those symbols at a most sensitive moment. Nationalist fervor prevented Quebeckers from appreciating the aspirations of the First Nations, and recognizing that they, too, see themselves as a distinct society.

The tragedy of Kanesatake was heightened for Native leaders when the Supreme Court of Canada made decisions on two major Aboriginal rights cases, *Sparrow* from British Columbia and *Sioui* from Québec. The court ruled in favor of the Aboriginal person in each case. Indeed, the court went even further. It laid out an entire schema for what it said would be a just and equitable application of Native rights to natural resources such as fishing. The tragedy was that the Supreme Court rulings which might have laid the groundwork for a peaceful recognition of Aboriginal rights within the framework of the Canadian Constitution were ignored by the press and treated with disdain by governments. Canada and Québec had already embarked on a policy of denial as their chief instrument of Aboriginal policy. The inability of the media to relate these major court decisions to the growing hostility between Québec and the Mohawk Nation precluded the possibility of the courts offering an alternative to the army.

The following winter Robbie N. found that he remembered Oka more clearly than he remembered being greeted on the steps of the Parliament Buildings. He remembered the warmth and friendliness of the chiefs and the clan mothers and wondered how each one who had greeted him had survived through the difficult summer when he, too, saw how far they were willing to go to hold on to the last of their ancestral lands.

Matthew Coon Come was in the Cree community of Mistissini the following Halloween. Every second child he saw was dressed up as "Lasagna," the most violent-looking Mohawk Warrior, and reportedly one of the least reputable. The sight of Cree children turning into Lasagna look-alikes was truly frightening for the Grand Chief.

Guns will not advance our cause. I know that! But these young people are not afraid. They're willing to die. They're the same as the young people being sent to Iraq who are willing to die.

Their heroes are not Billie Diamond or Matthew Coon Come. "Those guys signed our rights away," they're saying. "Then the Government does not respect the *Agreement* that they signed. So why should we sign another Agreement? If we can stop it we might as well try. You guys tried everything. You tried the courts. You tried the public media. What's left to do? I've got nothing to lose. My inheritance is underwater."

In the Mohawk Longhouse

After the feast at Kanesatake the *Odeyak* group travelled to Kahnawake, a Mohawk community directly across from Montréal Island on the south shore of the St. Lawrence River. When plans for housing and hospitality in Montréal had fallen through, the traditional Mohawk people offered the Cree and Inuit travellers hospitality at the Kahnawake Longhouse. The Longhouse at Kahnawake is a sizeable, new-looking, handsome, squared timber building set off by two smaller buildings of similar construction, a cook-house and the Mohawk Nation office.

When the Mohawks held a reception for the *Odeyak* travellers on their first evening at Kahnawake, the Cree and Inuit reciprocated the hospitality with a display of some traditional bush skills. It was in the spiritual center of the Mohawk Nation that the Cree elders discovered that they could share something profoundly moving with their hosts. Hunters who develop animal calls and bird calls to a fine art for the sake of survival also compete with one another and entertain their families. Now, in the darkened Longhouse, without needing to speak any language but their own, the visitors found that they possessed a way to re-create the mystery of their land. Kenneth Deer was the Director of the Mohawk Nation Office when he first learned about the *Odeyak* by reading a story in *The Montréal Gazette*.

> We decided we wanted to help these people. It also occurred to us that they would be passing through Mohawk territory to get to New York City, so it would be a good idea to give them safe passage and to escort them. Our intent was to welcome them to our territory. We did that and we gave them safe passage through a ceremony where we asked the waters to transport them safely wherever they were going. This is something that was done in the past when people asked permission to pass through our territory.

> What we wanted to do was to escort them down from the St. Lawrence to Albany, which is our traditional Mohawk territory. In the end, our two paddlers went with them all the way to New York City. Our canoe also stayed with them all the way to New York. It is a large voyageur type of canoe, a 26-foot simulated birch bark. It is a very good-looking canoe.

Kenneth says that it was the development of the Kahnawake Canoe Club following the building of the St. Lawrence Seaway, as a way of re-connecting the community with the river, that allowed the Mohawks to offer to escort the *Odeyak*.

We are river people. Mohawk communities are always attached to their river. When the Seaway came through, it divorced us from the river. It put this big, ugly ditch between us and the river. People used to fish and swim in the river. The next generation of people who were raised here were separated from that river.

In 1972, we decided that there was a still a lot of river and we weren't doing much with it. So we decided to form a canoe club. It happened, by good fortune, that a defunct racing club offered us their racing canoes. That was how it all started.

We developed a generation of young people who had some affinity with the water. It may not have been totally traditional but it gave them a chance to be comfortable with the water, to paddle, to know how to handle a canoe. We even developed an Olympic champion here. Alan Morris is only the third Native American ever to win a Gold Medal. The objective of our club was recreational but it was all built around racing. It put kids on the water, it gave them activities, it gave them goals.

There were some people who would paddle from Ottawa to Montréal on an annual trip. That was our first experience of distance canoeing. Then, in 1986, when we were invited to take part in this trip to Albany, we raised money to buy a canoe and got into distance canoeing. The older paddlers became very interested and have been continuing to do distance.

Kahnawake is the easternmost settlement in the Longhouse Confederacy. It has been the gatekeeper of the Confederacy for hundreds of years. Located on the St. Lawrence, the river that reaches more than halfway into the continent and offers easy portages to the far west and the deep south, the Mohawk Nation has greeted every traveller wanting to penetrate to the heart of their territory.

As the Keepers of the Eastern Gate, the Mohawk people have been portrayed, through several centuries of European literature, as "particularly war-like," especially by those wanting to break their hold on the key to the continent. The actual customs and teachings of the Longhouse are centred in *The Great Law of Peace* (perhaps the world's first federal, democratic constitution), and the revelation on which the Longhouse Confederacy is founded. Probably the earliest version of this caricature of the fierce Mohawk is found in the *Jesuit Relations*, a work written by French missionaries engaged in developing converts among traditional enemies of the Mohawks. When the Mohawks were no longer a potent military ally, it became convenient for the English to adopt the French view of their "savage" style.

Shortly after Canadian Confederation, following the passage of *The Indian Advancement Act*, the Longhouse at Kahnawake was the first of the longhouses to be suppressed by federal Canadian police. It was also the first to be re-built at a time when both First Nation spiritual practices and asserting Aboriginal rights to the land had been declared criminal offences by the Parliament of Canada.

In the summer of 1990, when the barricades of the Mohawk Nation at Kanesatake had been matched by those of the Sûreté du Québec, Kahnawake supporters of Kanesatake closed the Mercier Bridge joining Montréal Island to the south shore of the St. Lawrence. What had been intended as an act of solidarity may have had a major part in turning a great deal of popular Québec opinion against the Mohawks. Commuters, crossing the bridge on their way to work each day, initially expressed sympathy for the Mohawks' blockade against a golf course. When their own livelihoods were threatened, not for an occasional day but for weeks on end, the initial sympathy began to sour. Working class people were becoming ripe for media tirades portraying the Mohawks as Anglophone tools interspersed on the television and radio with political leaders asserting Québec sovereignty, denying federal jurisdiction and certifying Mohawk criminality.

In the early spring, when the *Odeyak* arrived at Kahnawake, Kenneth Deer had just opened a woodworking shop where he planned to produce garden furniture he could sell in the surrounding suburbs. Along with the Mohawk Canoe Club and the Longhouse, the prospect of a livelihood made in his own shop was a dream come true. The hostilities of the coming summer would cost Kenneth his business. But when the *Odeyak* arrived at Kahnawake, his shop was a great blessing.

> It was a nice and sturdy boat. The art work was interesting. But when the boat got here there were no seats in it. So we brought the boat to the shop to repair it. I let the two old men [Billie Weetaltuk and Andrew Natashaquan] have the run of my shop. When they repaired the boat, I noticed that they never used a measuring tape. They used a stick to measure along the sides of the canoe and when they got to the end they turned the stick over. They cut all the wood for the seats that way and the thing worked perfectly. The canoe is curved but the seats had to be straight. And with a little stick they managed to measure and put it in perfectly.

One early task of providing an escort for the *Odeyak* was seeing that the Crees and Inuit continued south a little better equipped than they were when they arrived at Kahnawake.

> When the people came they had brought very little with them. They had not brought any sleeping bags. There were reports that they would have to camp out along the way but they had no tents or sleeping bags or ground

mats. So we raised money locally to buy sleeping bags. We bought about forty sleeping bags. They weren't the best but it was all we could do with the money available.

Kenneth Deer recalls that the Longhouse members were especially intrigued by the visitors from the north. The Crees and the Inuit were similarly intrigued by staying in a Longhouse, a way of living recognizably and comfortably Aboriginal, but quite unlike anything in either of their northern traditions. Gilbert Dick recalled it as a sharp and pleasant contrast to the hotel atmosphere of the YM-YWCA where they had stayed in Ottawa.

Robbie N. recalled a different aspect of staying in the Longhouse. It was the first of many times when most of the travellers would sleep together in one big hall. "The Crees were up by around six or seven in the morning and the Inuit wanted to sleep. They also thought we went to bed too late." When two male Cree elders, among other elders who were put up in individual homes, were invited to stay at the home of a Mohawk widow, the humor that followed did not require translation.

Caroline Weetaltuk gained a strong sense of a traditional First Nation community "trying their best to hang on to their culture and to get their language going." She was impressed that the Longhouse consisted of three woman-centered clans, "Turtles and Wolves and Bear," which provide a strong and effective voice for the women in the affairs of the Mohawk Nation. Another quality which impressed Caroline, and distinguished the Longhouse community from other places they would visit down south was that it was a safe place for their children.

When the kids wanted to play outside they were able to just go out and play. In the city it was not possible for the children just to go out to play because it is dangerous, but in the Mohawk villages it felt quite free for the children.

On the last day of their stay at the Kahnawake Longhouse, the Crees and Inuit reciprocated for the feast which had been given in their honor on the first night. Arrangements had been made for caribou meat, fish and other northern foods to be flown down to Montréal. Kenneth Deer recalls, "We had taken care of them for five days. On the final day they fêted us. They also held some songs and dances in the Longhouse and gave us gifts."

To accommodate the various presentations she was to make in Montréal, Stella Masty stayed at someone's house rather than in the Longhouse. Her recollection centers on a standing ovation she received from an audience of "six or seven hundred students. After, a lot of students came up to talk and exchange addresses." Stella had also missed the reception at the Longhouse when she went to hear the Cree and Inuit leaders make presentations at McGill University.

They also made another presentation in a church. A lot of leaders came to the church from other First Nations. It was almost like a conference. It was really strange when I looked up, during that meeting, and suddenly noticed that right where we were meeting, in that church, the Hydro-Québec Building was towering over us.

Stella's sense of Montréal as a site of achievement for the *Odeyak* travellers was not shared by Matthew Mukash. For Matthew, Montréal was the place where the *Odeyak* held a parade and nobody came. The Montréal City Council had been asked to welcome the *Odeyak*. The Mayor and a majority of city councillors turned down the idea. The minority of councillors who supported the *Odeyak*, however, were adamant in their support and made a point of being there to welcome the *Odeyak* when it was portaged from the Old Port of Montréal and made its way to Place Vauquelin. Later, the *Odeyak* group would join a protest by Montagnais and Naskapi against NATO low-level training flights over Labrador, on the eastern side of the Ungava.

Very little advance publicity had been done in Montréal. Even when Matthew Mukash did do a couple of radio programs a few days before the *Odeyak* arrived, in a city as sharply divided along linguistic lines as Montréal, such an effort would hardly make an impact. Neither the Crees nor the Inuit had speakers who could make presentations in French with anything resembling the fluency with which their younger leaders could speak English. Nor did they have publicists who could function in French or who had contacts among the French media. In the largest French speaking city after Paris, a sizeable turnout in English was not very likely.

The lack of French talent among the Crees and the Inuit was, however, as much a symbolic problem as a real one. An attack on Hydro-Québec, the once revered symbol of Québec's emancipation, would have to outdo Hydro both as a source of jobs and as a nationalist symbol. Quebeckers had been told, time and time again, that the north had been bought and paid for by *The James Bay Agreement*. How many Quebeckers could find Great Whale or any other Cree or Inuit communities on a map was beside the point. What was important was that before the last election, Premier Bourassa had published a book declaring the energy from the rivers of James Bay to be "the engine of our emancipation."

Quebeckers did not necessarily believe their leaders more than English-speaking North Americans believe theirs. But both the Québec Liberal Party and the Parti Québécois were led by economists whose primary disagreement was on the desirability of Québec's secession from Canada. In the spring of 1990 no Québec political leader was about to challenge Robert Bourassa's dream of harnessing the eight major rivers of northern Québec.

The *Odeyak* had also reached Montréal at the time when the final debate was getting under way on a proposal popularly known as "The Meech Lake Accord." Its intent was to amend Canada's *Constitution Act, 1982* to make it acceptable to Québec, the one province which had refused to sign it orginally. The Accord included a declaration of Québec to be "a distinct society."

An attack on Hydro in the name of the Aboriginal rights of Natives who, Quebeckers believed, had already been paid off for their interest in the land, and who did not even speak French, was hardly likely to attract a mass audience on the last Friday of March, 1990. Over the next year, the Québec environmental movement would, indeed, dedicate itself to convincing Quebeckers that Hydro-Québec should not be allowed to dictate to them. The environmental movement would challenge Québec's major mega-corporation on its own ground by declaring that Hydro was a state corporation, but it did not function in the public interest and that, unlike other utilities and state corporations, it was not accountable to the public through public tribunals. Why were Quebeckers being denied these fundamental controls over Hydro-Québec? The Québec environmentalists would also argue that the jobs to be created by Hydro-Québec at James Bay offered only low skilled, dead-end and temporary work many hundreds of miles from the workers' homes. They would charge that, far from financing Québec's sovereignty, the export of energy to the United States, the main use of the Great Whale power for the first twenty years, was simply moving from the Canadian frying pan into the American fire since it would have to be financed by an already debt-burdened provincial treasury. Finally, Québec environmentalists would argue that destroying the remaining rivers of Nouveau Québec would contribute to pollution, would not produce the "clean energy" Hydro claimed and, in the long run, would jeopardize the ecology of Québec.

The objection which would be least heard in Montréal, and which would become harder to make before it became easier, was that the destruction of the Great Whale and the several neighboring rivers would destroy the way of life of the original peoples of that land whose right to continue in their traditional way of life was guaranteed rather than extinguished by *The James Bay Agreement*. Quebeckers, who knew that *The Agreement* required both federal and provincial environmental assessments, were not about to challenge the exclusive authority of Québec over a project so thoroughly wrapped in the fleur-de-lis.

There were two points on which all opponents of the Great Whale Project agreed, in the months following the *Odeyak*. These were that a thorough public environmental assessment would most likely result in the demise or indefinite postponement of the project, and that a public debate on energy policy was essential for the economic, environmental, and political health of all elements of Québec society.

The formation of a Coalition for a Public Debate on Energy Policy would, however, remain muted by the constant need to reconcile Québec's national aspirations with an energy policy seemingly designed to undermine the essential elements of sovereignty.

On Monday, April 2, when the *Odeyak* was launched for its departure from Montréal, the media finally arrived. Matthew Mukash, who had spent most of his adult life there, would recall his first *Odeyak* adventure in Montréal by saying, "Only when we said that we were heading for Vermont did media people in Montréal begin to give the *Odeyak* attention."

Chapter 6:
The Odeyak Discovers Lake Champlain

The Hero Island Schools

As the *Odeyak* approached the bridge between Vermont and Rouse's Point, New York, on Tuesday, April 3, 1990, a paddling song could be heard riding on the tail-wind coming up the Richelieu River onto Lake Champlain. When the boat from Great Whale with its Mohawk companion vessel had set out from St. Jean-sur-le-Richelieu, a few hours earlier, on its first long paddle, Kenneth Deer had asked if they had any paddling songs. Caroline Weetaltuk was paddling in the Mohawk canoe.

> So we mixed the Mohawk paddling song with our song. We just used the words, "Eeyou" and "Inuit." When we were actually crossing the border we used the Mohawk song. Later, when we were in the bus, we figured out how to sing the Mohawk song with our own words.

Weemish Mamiumscum, who had ridden with the *Odeyak* on its dog sled from Great Whale to Chissasibi, and whose grandfather was the first Cree to settle permanently at Whapmagoostui, was apprehensive about going to another country for the first time in his life. He joined in the song as he paddled in the *Odeyak*. "I wondered how the people would be there, whether they would be friendly toward us. As it turned out, we had a better reception in the States than in Canada."

A song that moved the canoes with the rhythm of the water, while announcing the identity of the paddlers, also helped to overcome a number of anxieties as the *Odeyak* headed into United States waters. Like any boat heading for a "Stateside" landing, the *Odeyak* was already past the international border. The point at which the *Odeyak* landed, sometime after one o'clock in the afternoon, was a gravelled turnaround on the Vermont side of the inter-state bridge at the top of Lake Champlain. Rouse's Point, almost directly opposite, is a well known port on the New York side, where U.S. Customs normally receives incoming international marine traffic. The *Odeyak*, however, needed to arrive in Vermont, so that its travellers could be received by Vermont supporters and meet the Vermont press.

One Vermonter who would later develop a closer friendship with Matthew Mukash was Bob Hoffman, the past president of the Vermont Trappers' Association. Bob had come out of pure curiosity.

It was quite exciting to see them coming across the water there. When they got up close to shore we were higher up and could look down into their canoes and see all the junk food wrappers and tin cans. That was kind of a shock. And everybody had these high type tennis shoes.

Arrangements had been made in advance for U.S. Customs officers to clear the *Odeyak* and the Mohawk boat at Vermont's outermost parking lot. The Mohawk paddlers had objected to any acknowledgement of the border. They had said that if the Customs officers questioned them they would not deal with them at all. The Mohawks' position arose from having the border run through their traditional lands, in some places even dividing their villages. Two peace treaties between the United States and Britain, inherited by Canada, guarantee that Indians coming to the border might cross "freely with their personal goods and possessions." Canada had long denied what the Mohawks and other First Nations located along the border call "Jay's Treaty Rights" which promise that "the border would be raised whenever would they go by."

The Crees and Inuit, coming from villages hundreds of miles to the north, had heard of Jay's Treaty Rights without experiencing it as an issue in the day-to-day lives of their communities over many generations. They also needed, as the Mohawks understood, to be seen officially entering the United States of America. And no place would be more appropriate in its simplicity than this tiny turnaround on a peninsula jutting into Lake Champlain between the head of the Richelieu River and Missisquoi Bay, a fragment of Québec terrain penetrating American waters.

The Border Patrol understood the issue as well as the Mohawks. Indeed, the local commander of the Border Patrol attended the arrival of the *Odeyak* himself. He stood back from the crowd, with his officers. When the two boats had landed, he greeted them and said, "We're going to let you folks cross the border. We're not going to check anything."

Once the *Odeyak* had made its official entry into the United States, the travellers from the north were welcomed by a blend of Vermont folk who would all agree that very little besides the *Odeyak* would have assembled them all in one place. Among them were Homer St. Francis, the phlegmatic Chief of the Abenaki Nation at Swanton. The Atlantic Chapter of the Sierra Club was represented by Ray Gonda, a systems engineer and white water canoeist who would spend a week of his annual vacation time co-ordinating the *Odeyak* tour in Vermont.

After Ray Gonda read a statement of support from the Sierra Club, Matthew Mukash made a statement explaining why the people of Great Whale had come to Vermont. He appealed to the people of Vermont to think of the people of the North when they turned on their lights and when they made their decisions about where to buy electricity. Sappa Fleming's statement surprised people with the sting of his anger. The usually soft spoken and gentle Mayor of Kuujjuaraapik said that the project would represent a genocide of his people.

A car pulled up as the press conference was concluding. Matthew Coon Come, the Grand Chief of the Crees of Québec, had driven down to the border-crossing event from Montréal where he had been attending meetings. Chief Robbie Dick, just released from the hospital where he had had heart surgery, was joining the trip and had ridden from Montréal with the Grand Chief. Violet Pachanos, Chief of Chissasibi, who had also been at the Montréal meetings, had also accompanied the Grand Chief to the border.

Matthew Coon Come listened thoughtfully to a journalist's question. Was it true, as Québec's Minister of Energy, Lise Bacon had suggested, that the Crees' strategy was simply to squeeze more benefits from the Government? The Grand Chief said, "We never gave our consent to the Great Whale Project. The *James Bay and Northern Québec Agreement* only provides for negotiations of future projects." At the time not even friendly journalists were prepared to lend much weight to the Crees' interpretation of the *Agreement*. It was not until the Crees began to win the support of the courts, almost a year after the *Odeyak's* first long voyage, that this attitude began to change. What would gain the attention of the American media, who may have been familiar with the lack of durability of Indian treaties in their own country, was the warmth of the rapport which developed between the local people and the northern visitors at almost every stop along the way.

The late arrival of the leaders was the first of a series of challenges for Ray Gonda, Susan Martin and George Webb, the local co-ordinators who were attempting to move the *Odeyak* group around Vermont. After the *Odeyak* had landed and met the press, the bus took the elders and children and others to a restaurant at Rouse's Point on the New York side. No provision had been made for a lunch that could be served along the way. Ray Gonda had grown up hunting and trapping in the mountains of Pennsylvania. He had later learned to bring a "systems approach" to his own long distance canoeing. The previous weekend, when Ray could not find out just how many *Odeyak* travellers needed to be accommodated, he had driven up to Kahnawake and met with them. Only then did he learn that the thirty or forty people of whom he had heard earlier had grown to sixty. "The whole thing had to be done in real time. We did not have any lead time. We did not know in advance how many people were coming." He also learned that the Crees and Inuit "had come almost un-equipped"

and certainly without any of the camping equipment with which they
could readily have made themselves comfortable in rural Vermont.

> We learned those things as we started to ask ourselves such questions as,
> "Where do they stay?" "What do they eat?" "Do they have any money?"
> "Are they sponsored or are they paying their own way?" We only learned
> what the situation actually was as it unfolded.

As things unfolded, however, Vermont hospitality overcame many
problems. When Ray Gonda asked the local sheriff where the *Odeyak* and
the Mohawk canoe could be safely stored to save hauling them around, the
sheriff gave directions to his own house and said, "Just put them out
behind the house. They'll be safe there." When the canoes had been fully
secured in the sheriff's backyard, Larry House and Randy Pepabano set
off to join the rest of the *Odeyak* travellers at Friends' House in Burlington. Arrangements had been made for all of the travellers to spend three
nights in the private homes of supporters in the Burlington area. While
this meant they would be comfortably housed in Vermont, it also meant
re-tracing some steps. The Hero Islands were communities through
which the *Odeyak* travellers had passed half way down the east side of
Lake Champlain between their landing at the bridge and the city of
Burlington. The second day they made the thirty-mile trip back to visit
the schools on the Islands.

The original plan had been to paddle the *Odeyak* the length of Lake
Champlain, stopping at each point where a presentation was to be made
along the way. When the *Odeyak* leaders met with the core group of their
Vermont hosts at George Webb's house on their first night in the state, it
became apparent that the *Odeyak* would best serve as a symbolic show-
piece taken from place to place on the pickup truck. The ice along the
shore at the north end of Lake Champlain was still thick enough to endan-
ger the passage of the boats. Under similar conditions at home, coming
back from Spring Goose Break, for instance, people would simply have
continued to hunt while they waited two or three days for the ice to shift.
In Vermont, there was a new and much more complex situation. There
was an overcrowded schedule of appearances at schools, colleges, town
halls and the statehouse. There was also the need for a timely departure
that would see the *Odeyak* through the Hudson Valley in time to arrive in
New York City for Earth Day.

The enthusiasm of the reception at the Hero Island Schools was typical of what the *Odeyak* would receive both along the Lake Champlain
route and inland in Vermont. What the teachers and parents wanted was
for their children to meet people who could travel great distances by canoe.
The *Odeyak* provided the people living on the islands of Lake Champlain

an opportunity to connect with their own history and to dramatize their own sense of place. Historically, their islands had been major stopping points on the route up to the St. Lawrence. In the earliest days of European settlement, and indeed long before Samuel de Champlain, when the Richelieu River and the Lake were the boundary between the Mohawk and the Abenaki Nations, this waterway connected the area both to the outside world and to the interior of the continent.

During its own fur trading period and in the first era of major settlement, the commerce of this area had followed the natural navigation through Montréal and the St. Lawrence to Europe. The same traders who came south into the Champlain system also went north up the Ottawa, over the divide into the lands of the James Bay Crees. The visit of the *Odeyak* students and the elders, who frequently described their own rivers as highways, dramatically illustrated the historic and natural link between the Lake Champlain area and the rivers of the north. For the Hero Island students, it was an encounter more compelling for the students than television. Ray Gonda, who takes his own sense of local history for granted, described the response in the schools quite simply.

> I think the way that the people in the schools reacted was that the Crees and the Inuit became real people for them. Real Indians. Real Eskimos. People who don't lead the kind of life we live. They still live off the land. Just the image of Indians coming down here from the north in a boat struck people's imaginations in a quite incredible fashion.

Isaac Masty, the Cree school supervisor, and Sarah Bennett, the Inuit teacher, felt an immediate sense of relief when they walked into their first American classrooms. Isaac recalled their feelings.

> At all the schools that we visited we were well received and our fears were all taken away. My biggest fear was that the attitude of the students would be "Who cares? So what?" I was afraid that people would not take the time to try to understand the message our students were carrying. If that would happen the students would pick it up right away.

While one group re-traced the route to the Hero Island schools, another *Odeyak* contingent went to schools in Middleton and Williston, both in the Burlington area. The potluck supper at the Folsom Community Center was followed by speeches by the *Odeyak* leaders and a slide show about the Great Whale communities and the hydro-electric project.

Vermont Welcome

A surprising number of the Vermonters who came to play a leading role in welcoming the *Odeyak* and mounting their own local opposition to the purchase of power from Hydro-Québec by Vermont were, as Kenneth Deer described the Mohawk Nation, "river people." They were people who had a strong personal relationship with the rivers of their own region or who had travelled extensively along the waterways of the Ungava Peninsula.

Later, when the U.S. movement grew strong enough to be worth attacking, Lise Bacon, the Québec Minister of Energy, would attempt to solicit sympathy by saying that she could not gain support by paddling a canoe to New York City. Neither Mme. Bacon nor the *Globe and Mail* "Report on Business" writers who attributed the Crees' success to a "Madison Avenue public relations firm" understood the two critical points on which the *Odeyak's* message depended. The first was that the general absence of anything resembling planning and organization with which the trip began was overcome by the combination of the steady determination of the *Odeyak* travellers themselves and the comparable commitment of the host groups at each stage along the way. Second was that the supporters who came to describe themselves as "river people" developed a devotion to this issue born from years, and sometimes a lifetime, of viewing their own lives in relationship with the rivers' need for stewardship and healing. This devotion came from a personal identification with the world view expressed by the elders from Great Whale. In short, the sense of kinship between the *Odeyak* travellers and their hosts grew from a deep and long-standing connection for which no price could be asked nor offered.

Jim Higgins had worked for six years urging Vermonters to extend the environmental sensitivity that they bring to local decision-making in the Green Mountain State to the sources of power from outside their borders on which they rely. A middle-aged psychiatric social worker, Jim became acquainted with the Ungava through a series of annual month-long canoe trips on a number of the different rivers of the region. "I haven't done the N.B.R. [Nottaway-Broadback-Rupert] but I've done the George River up to Ungava and a lot of rivers going south from Schefferville, like the Moisie and the Manitou. Also the trip from Mistissini to Lac St. Jean."

What began as an annual rite of re-creation took a political turn in the fall of 1984 when Jim read about the drowning of the ten thousand caribou crossing the Caniapiscau River.

> I happened to be in Ungava just before that happened. When I came back the newspaper reports were almost useless but very sensationalist. I know that when I was up there, on the George, people were saying that the river was so low that the salmon had not come up to the fishing camps. Then

suddenly, Hydro-Québec was saying that there had been torrential rains all through September which really was not true. It would have taken many days' rain to raise the river levels because of the retention capability of the ground cover of sphagnum moss. Hydro-Québec had just finished their dikes on the Caniapiscau reservoir.

Perhaps six months later, I read a story in *The Audubon* by Ted Williams that tied together the disaster with the economics of Bourassa. What really got me going was the combination of events. At that point, I started writing a couple of articles. I was probably the only person talking about it in Vermont. Gradually, I started reading things and, as I kept my ears open, I would hear little tidbits.

When Jim first tried to invite Matthew Coon Come to Vermont he called acquaintances at Akwesasne, the Mohawk community which is divided by the Ontario-Quebec-New York border. "I had no idea where to start or who to talk to. I was totally on my own in the dark." After reading *The Plot to Drown the North Woods*, Jim tried to reach the author, Boyce Richardson, only to be told that he had moved back to New Zealand. Through later successful connection with Boyce, Jim received the address of Hélène Connor-Lajambe, an environmentalist who returned to graduate school to study economics to better explain the aberrations she perceived in the development of James Bay power as the engine of Québec's emancipation. Through her, Jim was introduced to people in Montréal who were concerned with what was happening in the North.

When a passionate letter about James Bay appeared in *The Burlington Free Press*, Jim picked up the phone to call the writer, Don Odell. Kim Chase, Don's wife took the call. When Jim told Kim the purpose of his call she said, "Well, I know something about this too." Kim is a Vermonter who celebrated her roots by mastering a fluent Québécois dialect. When she attended a Montréal press conference sponsored by the Audubon Society and the Sierra Club, this Franco-American who could actually speak Québec French was something of a novelty and gained positive coverage. As a teacher, Kim had shown slides of her own canoe trips to many classes. Kim and Don had been canoeing on "the N.B.R.[Nottaway-Broadback-Rupert] area over a ten-year period and become quite familiar with the bush and to some extent with the Cree people."

Don is an electronics engineer who grew up canoeing in the Adirondacks. "As you grow up you look for something more challenging. At least, I did, and the northern Québec rivers were the natural extension of that." He has become involved "in some aspects of the issue that some other people may feel are not very interesting. I am able to deal with some of the power statistics and other details. But it all ties together. The principal arguments are energy efficiency and demand-side management."

When "two or three were gathered together" a variety of opportunities for outreach started to come along. In September, 1989, before the Public Service Board (PSB) hearings got underway, their organization, the New England Coalition for Energy Efficiency and the Environment, together with the Vermont based Arctic to Amazonia Conference, brought Bill Namagoose to Burlington. When Matthew Coon Come first came to Vermont to attend the PSB proceedings, Jim took the opportunity to complete some networking. Higgins had been corresponding for some time with Brian Craik, the Crees' Director of Federal Relations. They arranged a meeting between the Grand Chief Coon Come and Homer St. Francis, the Chief of the Abenaki Nation. "Homer St. Francis is like a backwoods Vermonter. Matthew appeared in his three piece suit. The Abenaki headquarters happens to be in Swanton, one of the towns that would later have a town vote on accepting power from Hydro-Québec."

The *Odeyak* trip became one of the first occasions for Vermont and Québec environmentalists to start sharing a common concern. Although living no more than a two hour drive from one another they belong to different cultures and are not generally comfortable speaking one another's language or reading one another's literature. Kim, Don and Jim stayed in Montréal with Jean-Phillippe Waaub, an environmental researcher at the University of Montréal who also sits on the James Bay Task Force of the Sierra Club.

The Montréal press conference where Kim Chase had surprised the media with her command of French, was the occasion at which Matthew Mukash had announced that the Crees and Inuit of Great Whale would shortly be bringing a boat through Vermont and New York State. The *Odeyak* was in the midst of being built at the time. Like Jeff Wollock from New York City, this was the first time that Jim, Don or Kim had heard of the impending event. Two weeks later, when he had gone to Ottawa for the Barrière Lake Conference, Jim Higgins was able to meet the members of the *Odeyak* group and inform others in the Vermont Coalition to Save James Bay that the Crees and Inuit were actually about to arrive. Meeting them at a reception, Jim had not been able to estimate numbers or assess their equipment as Ray Gonda would do at Kahnawake two weeks later.

Jim Higgins says that the national Sierra Club started to become involved with the James Bay power issue when Harvard Ayers, then head of the Sierra Club's Native Sites Committee, saw some local posters about James Bay power while he was on a cross country skiing trip to Vermont. This first contact eventually led the highly structured Sierra Club to sponsor an international Task Force, an umbrella under which major players from all parts of Québec, New England and New York would meet regularly to compare notes and discuss current developments. Jim Dumont, the Vermont attorney who represented the Grand Council of the Crees before the Vermont Public Service Board and, later, before New York regulatory agencies, had also represented the Sierra Club on environmental interventions over the past ten years.

Jim Higgins emphasizes that "the whole thing started off grass roots, in Maine and in Vermont and, I think, everywhere really." Ray Gonda, the Crees' Vermont guide, works closely with three members of the Vermont Senate Committee on Natural Resources. He takes a less sanguine view of the grass roots approach. "I think the press was fairly accurate in their assessment that it was mostly the fringe groups who were involved." Despite Ray's personal commitment both to the Crees and to the Sierra Club he sees that the press do not consider the Sierra Club "a major environmental organization" in Vermont. He points out that the Sierra Club has only half the membership of the Vermont Natural Resources Council and consequently has no paid staff. Gonda says that from the viewpoint of the statehouse press corps, environmental groups graduate from fringe to mainstream not so much according to policy but by their ability to support professional staff.

Bob Hoffman's deep connection with the Crees came more from his years as a trapper and an advocate for the trappers' way of life, than from being a river person. Bob first began to connect with the issue of Vermont's purchase of James Bay power from Hydro-Québec through one of Jim Higgins' periodic mailings. Until then, he had only "vaguely heard the word 'Cree' and something about the hydro-electric project years ago." When Bob received another mailing, something clicked. He called Jim Higgins who "told me about the *Odeyak* trip which was coming down." When Bob learned that the *Odeyak* was to land at Alburg he took the day off from his antique store. "I just went to see. By then, I was curious but not involved."

Bob started to become involved when he was asked to serve as a guide for Matthew Mukash, who was driving his own car so that he could move ahead of the bus and the boat as the need arose. Linda Corstin, from the Ottawa office of the Grand Council, who had made many of the initial contacts, rode with Matthew and Danielle Mukash and the elder, John Petagumskum. As a guide, Bob is really more comfortable in the area Vermonters call "the North East Kingdom."

> I don't know anything about either Alburg or Burlington, especially Burlington, where it starts to get more congested. We came in there at night and I was driving my car and they were following me in Matthew's. I had a city map but I can't see very well. We got good and lost.

When Bob had been in the Burlington area with the *Odeyak* group for two days he arranged to have Matthew Mukash and a group of Inuit come to Barnet, in the northeast corner of the state, for an afternoon and evening. "We did a presentation in the local elementary school and then in the evening we did the town hall here. We had sixty people come out to meet them. We had worked feverishly and sent out, I think, four hundred invitations."

During the next year, Bob Hoffman wrote ads to run in the local papers and raised the money to pay for the ads. The purpose of the advertisements was to sway voters to reject the proposed Vermont contract for James Bay power. The Vermont contract to buy power from Hydro-Québec was subject to approval by the annual meeting of each of the 19 towns or villages in which an electrical utility was located. The campaign to get out the vote for the town meetings in his part of the state became the major activity in the cubbyhole office above his antique shop. Looking back after he had become immersed in the issue Bob said, "The *Odeyak* is what got me. Luckily, Jim Higgins had sent me one more notice and I made a phone call or I might have missed it."

> One thing that impressed me when I met these people is that they seem to know a helluva lot more about what's going on down here than we know about what's going on up in Canada. Before I met the Crees and Inuit, I couldn't have told you where James Bay was. Mary Mickeyook lives up there on Hudson Bay and she knows what's going on down here.

> Another thing that struck me is that there are at least two languages that most of them speak and I saw some kids speaking three. Samuni Tukatuk, an Inuk, said to me, "Boy, you people are so sophisticated," and I am thinking how they can all speak a number of languages while we are all in this one little space that is the only place where the world exists for us.

Bob's view of his own work over the next year corroborates Ray Gonda's sense that the Vermont Coalition was centred around smaller, grassroots organizations without paid professional staff. "I've spent a lot of time spinning my wheels. I'm not the best office person." This very lack of professionalism may well have contributed to the success both of the *Odeyak* trip and to the movement to swing the town votes against the Vermont contract with Hydro-Québec the following year. It was the grassroots nature of the Coalition which brought the bird watchers, the trappers and a broad range of other interests together to confront a common concern.

Ray Gonda was one of the few Vermont *Odeyak* hosts with a professional political background.

I think it showed that a broad variety of types of people with various interests could work together and get something done. When I went to the various functions in the different cities and saw how many people turned out, I was totally amazed. If anybody had suggested ahead of time that I would be sitting here thinking this, I would have said, "Bullshit."

The *Odeyak* and its Mohawk companion were launched near the Burlington High School at mid-day of Thursday, April 5, 1990. The two small craft set their course for the Boat House, a two-storey floating community centre sitting on top of a very sizeable barge, two miles down the eastern shore of Lake Champlain. A flotilla of canoes headed out into the choppy bay and escorted the visiting boats to the Mayor's official reception at the heart of Burlington Harbor.

Mayor Peter Clavelle's decision to greet the *Odeyak* travellers personally attracted the presence of a wide range of other political figures. It also attracted the networks and wire services. Peter Clavelle was a unique mayor because when he welcomed an unusual group of visitors to his city he also became thoroughly familiar with their issue and its significance for his own people. The next spring, during the town vote on the Vermont-Québec contract, the utilities placed campaign literature in the polling booths. Fourteen months later, when the courts eventually ordered a new vote in Burlington, Mayor Clavelle joined the campaign to reject the purchase of Hydro-Québec power. After the official reception, tea and bannock were served at a teepee which had been erected at City Hall Park. Meanwhile, some of the *Odeyak* travellers became special guests at an inspirational performance about their struggle at the University of Vermont entitled *Beyond the North Wind*.

While one contingent headed up the lake to Middlebury to show the slide presentation *For Our Children*, festivities continued in Burlington at the Boat House with a potluck supper. The turnout of four hundred people was almost equal to the entire population of either Kuujjuaraapik or Whapmagoostui. This show of support undoubtedly helped to convince Stella Masty and Weemish Mamiumscum that there was much more solid support for the Great Whale cause in the United States than in Canada. As important as the good feelings conveyed to the visitors by the turnout, this astounding success on such short notice with a little help from the Burlington Mayor's office may have inspired the grass roots of Vermont to carry on their campaign over the next two years.

Meeting the Governor

A meeting had been arranged with the Governor of Vermont, Madeleine Kunin. Grand Chief Matthew Coon Come flew back to Vermont for the occasion. After Denny Alsop picked up the Grand Chief at the airport they stopped by the hotel to pick up Mayor Sappa Fleming and Chief Robbie Dick. Once they had left Burlington on the forty-minute drive to Montpelier, the capital of Vermont, Denny recalled Matthew taking a very special interest in the landscape. "As we were driving along the Winooski River, Matthew Coon Come kept looking at the river and at the steep sides of the valley and saying, 'Great dam site' ."

When the Grand Chief asked for a briefing on the Governor, Denny said, "Well, she has just announced her decision to resign this morning. The morning papers reported her saying she was resigning to spend the rest of her active political life working for women's issues and the environment. Based on that we should be able to go in there with confidence and with our heads up." What actually happened in the Governor's office came to be regarded as the major rejection of the message of the *Odeyak* and as a personal attack by the Governor, especially on Mayor Sappa Fleming.

Denny Alsop recalls two of the Governor's aides, George Hamilton and George Steresenger, greeting the delegation in the ante-chamber and leading them into a conference room. Denny and a reporter sat at the far end of the table. When George Steresenger began to speak the reporter started taking notes. "Steresenger and Hamilton laid their cards on the table. They told us 'This is what is going to happen.' There is no room for compromise. It is a *fait accompli*. We are just waiting for the decision from the Public Service Board."

The Grand Chief suggested that perhaps they might want to understand the Crees' position which he then proceeded to outline. As he was doing so, the Governor walked in. Everyone stood up. As Governor Kunin walked toward the table, without waiting for introductions she began to speak. "I'm aware of your position. There really isn't anything I can do about it. I'm very sorry." Then she asked, "But what do you have to say?"

Matthew Coon Come looked visibly upset. Denny sensed that Matthew felt dishonored by Kunin's conduct. Matthew started to stand up as if to leave the table. He said, "What's the point? What are we here for? Why are we talking? There is nothing more to say." The Governor asked, "Is there anybody else who would like to speak?" Sappa spoke very briefly. Then Robbie Dick made a statement in which he summarized the entire environmental issue in a few sentences and stressed that the project would be a disaster for his people. Suddenly the Governor noticed the reporter and Denny and demanded to know, "Who are these people? This was supposed to be a private meeting! I had not given my consent for the press to be here."

When Denny and the reporter had left the room, Mayor Sappa Fleming made a closing plea to Governor Madeleine Kunin. He said that he was concerned for the children of his village. "The lives of everyone's children up there are at stake." Governor Kunin replied, "I have to think about *my* children's future." There was not much left to say. Mayor Fleming stood up and walked out. Grand Chief Matthew Coon Come and Chief Robbie Dick followed him. Their meeting with the Governor of Vermont was over.

Denny had waited in the ante-chamber. When Matthew Coon Come left the conference room he spoke briefly to Denny and then walked over to where Sappa Fleming and Robbie Dick were standing. As the three Aboriginal leaders stood talking, the Governor came out of the conference room. She stopped to speak to Denny Alsop. After she introduced herself she said, "This was one of the hardest things I've ever had to do in my life. This is a very sad situation." Denny replied, "You didn't have to do it." Governor Kunin turned and walked out.

Standing on the steps of the statehouse, Matthew Coon Come looked at the hills around Montpelier and said, "All I can think of is that this would make just as great a place to build a dam as the Great Whale River." His remark was not very different from the wry joke on the drive up to Montpelier. The difference was that the laughter was gone from his voice.

The timing of the one *Odeyak* press conference in the Vermont state capital could not have been worse. On almost any other day, the Grand Chief, the Mayor and the Chief would have been serious drawing cards, the more so when their statement to the press was supported by the Vermont Federation of Sportsmen's Clubs, the Trappers' Association and the Sierra Club. But their press conference, scheduled to take place at the teepee immediately following the meeting with the Governor could not compete for the attention of the press with Peter Welsh's press conference announcing his candidacy for Governor on the other side of the statehouse.

The Vermont Public Service Board — Cutting the Goose

The Public Service Board (PSB), from which the Governor's aide, Mr. Steresenger, was awaiting a decision, is the regulatory agency which must grant approval before any Vermont utility can make any large purchase of power. The Vermont Joint Owners (VJO), an umbrella group representing the utilities of Vermont, had applied to the PSB for approval to buy 450 kilowatt hours from Hydro-Québec. The application had been submitted almost a year before the *Odeyak* visited Vermont.

Although the PSB's decision would not actually come down until months after the *Odeyak's* Vermont visit, the PSB and the *Odeyak* became the primary symbols of the two opposing sides in the Vermont debate about buying power from Hydro-Québec. It was the PSB which first provided a forum for both the Crees and Hydro to argue their respective cases in the United States. The hearings had provided the opportunity for the Cree leaders to come to Vermont and meet activists such as Denny Alsop and Jim Higgins. As a quasi-judicial body, the Public Service Board's decisions are subject to a political review by the Governor and also to a judicial review on matters of procedure by the Vermont Supreme Court.

Vermont takes its democracy very seriously and very locally. Under an ancient and peculiarly New England custom, the PSB decision would not simply lead to the Governor's office. It would also lead to the town meeting where the purchase of power by the local utility would be put to a specific vote in 19 different towns. The arguments which were first raised through expert evidence before the quasi-judicial Public Service Board would be heard again and again, in local political forums throughout Vermont over the next year and a half as each town prepared to vote.

The combination of the Public Service Board hearings and the votes in different town meetings provided the "public debate on energy policy" in Vermont that the major coalition of community, labour and environmental groups in Québec were to make their central demand. But under the Bourassa Government's careful manipulation, a thorough public debate always seemed to remain just beyond their grasp. Paradoxically, the Vermont and Cree customs of local control would come to inspire some leading Québec environmentalists to believe that both decentralizing and democratizing Hydro-Québec were essential steps to an authentic sovereignty for the people of Québec.

The *Odeyak* came into Vermont almost six months after the PSB had concluded its hearings but two months before it rendered its decision. More important, by developing personal ties between the Vermonters and the northern Aboriginal peoples, the *Odeyak* set the stage for the town and village meeting debates which took place the following winter. Not only the people who campaigned but a great many of the voters who made the effort to attend their town meetings had shaken hands and shared coffee with the Cree and Inuit visitors the previous spring. Probably no other international issue had been so thoroughly debated at local meetings since 122 Vermont villages voted to become nuclear free zones.

The decision the Public Service Board finally brought down identified the Hydro-Québec contract as something of a golden goose for Vermont electric power users. But it also acknowledged the possibility of some environmental costs. The PSB then aspired to the wisdom of Solomon and proposed to divide the golden goose in proportion to these costs and benefits. Unlike the biblical king, the Board believed its own decision and offered no alternative when the natural mother protested against cutting up her child. The apparent symmetry of a decision to approve three parts of the purchase and reject one part failed to address the fundamental environmental and ethical issues. The PSB decision thus set the stage for a heated debate the following winter at each of the village meetings where the grass roots movement was able to speak on behalf of a broader responsibility for the environment.

The local utilities in Vermont are small local agencies who had banded together to form the Vermont Joint Owners (VJO) in order to have a sizeable body to negotiate with Hydro-Québec. By the time they appeared before the Public Service Board, the VJO not only represented almost all the utilities of Vermont, they also had the full and active participation of Hydro-Québec, the largest financial power in Québec. Opposing the VJO and Hydro were a number of Vermont environmental organizations, most notably the Sierra Club and the Audubon Society, supported by the Grand Council of the Crees and the Village of Kuujjuaraapik.

The argument submitted by the Vermont Joint Owners was that the hydro-electric power it proposed to purchase from Hydro-Québec was both clean and cheap. They argued that it was the cheapest power available to Vermont and that the impact on the environment would be minimal. They also argued that Vermont had had a previous contract with Hydro-Québec for over 300 megawatts and, therefore, this contract represented only a very small increment. The environmental argument focused largely on the readily apparent degradations from fossil fuels emissions and the widely shared fear of radiation damages from nuclear generation. The environmental and Aboriginal interveners attacked the VJO submission from three separate but related arguments.

The first of these asserted that hydro is not clean power. The second argument was that the purchase constituted a greater environmental impact than the difference between the old 300 megawatt contract and the proposed 450 megawatts. Hydro-Québec had previously stated that the sources from which it had supplied Vermont under the expiring contract would now be used for domestic purposes. Even though Hydro-Québec had told the Board that this contract would be filled from what they called "system power" and not depend on any single source, the new contract could only be fulfilled through the building of the Great Whale Project. And the Great Whale Project, the interveners argued, will devastate the environment of a region almost equal to the whole of Vermont. In particular, by changing the seasonal fluctuation of five different rivers, it will change the water quality of Hudson Bay, jeopardizing both beluga whales and marine seals.

Thirdly, the Crees' lawyer, Jim Dumont, told the PSB Vermont has a real interest in the international waters of Hudson Bay because the geese and ducks which pass through Vermont every spring and fall are also threatened by dramatic changes in the salinity of the Bay. Hydro-Québec said that, from their experience at La Grande, a change in the salinity does not affect the eel grass. But when Dumont reviewed everything Hydro's experts had published, it was evident that the change in salinity had only reached the eel grass beds in 1989, the year of the hearings.

Vermont's responsibility for environmental degradation, the interveners asserted, cannot stop at its geographic boundaries when its power purchases play an essential role in financing massive construction projects hundreds of miles beyond its borders. Hydro-Québec had refused to conduct a public environmental assessment and in the absence of proper baseline studies, could not say what the environmental impacts might be. Construction of such a massive project would only be permitted in a territory where the majority of the population were Native people. This, the Crees argued, contituted a form of environmental racism.

Fourthly, the Crees and environmentalists told the PSB, alternative energy sources were available to Vermont at no greater cost than the proposed VJO-Hydro contract. The availability of alternative energy sources is a hard case to sell. It requires a complex calculation to show that power from a large number of small sources will be cheaper than power from a single large source. Part of the calculation rests on the benefits of using the moneys that would go out-of-state to create local jobs instead. It is a calculation that applies differently in a smaller, less industrialized state such as Vermont than in neighboring New York. Procedurally, the argument requires the opponent to show that the public interest is better served by a course different from the proposal before the Board.

Ian Goodman, an energy consultant from Boston, provided the key testimony for alternative energy sources. He identified four possible alternative power supplies for Vermont: Demand Side Management (DSM), arbitrage, co-generation and small local hydro stations.

To begin with, Goodman argued DSM could be pursued much more aggressively by Vermont utilities. DSM is a strategy through which utilities provide consumers with incentives and even subsidies to use energy more efficiently. DSM effectively allows the utility to buy back the energy saved within its own system. This is often called "negawatts." The energy acquired when customers install more efficient electric motors or light bulbs is clearly far less expensive than imported power. Vermont could achieve a large proportion of its projected power needs internally through efficiency.

In addition to energy efficiency within Vermont, a system of arbitrage was proposed, under which, instead of helping to finance the Great Whale Project, Vermont would invest in energy efficiency in Québec, the place of highest per capita energy consumption in the world. Known sources of wastage within Hydro-Québec's system would readily exceed the new power to be generated at Great Whale.

Co-generation is the production of electricity using the excess steam produced by various manufacturing processes. Don Odell, an environmentally-minded electrical engineer, points to studies suggesting that existing facilities could produce 50% to 70% more power with the development of presently available efficiencies. Local production makes more efficient use of scarce resources while avoiding both the cost of transportation and the need to export money outside the state. Odell says that electrical generation from fossil fuels or most other heat sources, including wood, converts energy at a rate of 30% to 40%. "With co-generation it is the rest of the heat that is captured for use in industrial projects from cheese production to classroom heating. It is the capturing of energy which would otherwise be lost which is sometimes called 'negawatts'." Don says that there are three cheese factories in Vermont each, producing about thirty megawatts through co-generation. "Power from this source could be dramatically increased beyond the handful of present operations in Vermont. Wood gasification is another example of co-generation. It allows the clean, local production of power from sawdust and scrap wood, which is an otherwise unused source of energy in timber areas."

The Independent Power Producers of Vermont, an association of owners of renovated small local hydro-electric plants, argued that they could greatly increase their potential contribution to the state's power consumption, especially if they were paid at the same rate as Hydro-Québec proposed. They also pointed out the advantages of local, run-of-the-river hydro which, unlike the forty-storey-high Great Whale dam, would not cause massive flooding or reverse the seasonal flows of rivers.

The essential argument was that the sum of all these potential sources greatly exceeded the needs of Vermont. The Public Service Board was asked to direct the Public Service Department to develop a plan to ensure an adequate supply of power to the people of Vermont from least cost sources with all costs, including environmental impacts, included in the calculation.

All these arguments had been made at hearings before Christmas in 1989. Months after the *Odeyak* had brought together both long-standing and new-found friends of the Crees and Inuit in Vermont, the PSB brought in a decision. Had Canadian scholars read this decision they might have noticed the hand of William Lyon Mackenzie King, Canada's wartime prime minister, of whom it was said that he would never do by halves what could be done by quarters. Like Mackenzie King, the Board concealed procrastination by obfuscation, invoking noble sentiments in the aid of inaction.

The PSB decided to grant the request for 340 megawatts while denying a request for an additional 110 megawatts. The PSB made its approval of the 340 megawatts purchase subject to Hydro-Québec completing the environmental assessments which the National Energy Board of Canada (NEB) had already required as a condition of its export permits.

The Board was emphatic in the credence which it lent to the environmental issues which had been raised by the Crees and the Sierra Club. However, after an extended lamentation, the Board decided that the environmental impact occurring outside Vermont's boundaries was beyond its jurisdiction. Only if the impact was shown to flow into Vermont would the Board feel confident in asserting jurisdiction on behalf of the State. On the basis of a direct impact in Vermont, the Board did demonstrate a Vermont interest in the geese and ducks which fly through Vermont each fall and spring. Vermont, the Board said, had a real interest in these waterfowl and could, therefore, impose some environmental requirements. Accordingly, the PSB reduced the total volume of the contract by 110 megawatts and made the whole contract subject to the environmental assessment required by the NEB. The PSB justified approval of the 340 megawatts on the basis of necessity. Vermont would come to need that power over the twenty-year life of the contract. The PSB said that while it was inspired by the proposals for energy efficiency and co-generation it was not convinced that these would provide reliable power during the time period of the contract.

Jim Dumont and Ian Goodman found two conspicuous problems with the PSB's decision to buy the VJO argument from necessity. First, the PSB expressed scepticism about the actual potential from alternative energy sources based on current technology, but it did not direct either its own staff or the Vermont Department of Public Service to conduct independent studies of utilities in other states making major use of alternative energy sources. Secondly, the PSB accepted arguments on the issue of necessity from the utilities after the public hearings were concluded, contrary to all the requirements of due process.

The decision to accept 340 megawatts while refusing 110 was the Board's way of nodding simultaneously in both directions. It agreed with the utilities that the power was needed while acknowledging the reality of the threat to the environment. The failure to gain independent verification of the reliability of alternative energy sources allowed the PSB to collaborate in the utilities' appeal to popular fears of impending power shortages.

Doubtless, the Board believed that it was doing more than dividing the golden goose down the three-quarter line. By making its approval conditional on the National Energy Board's granting of export permits for which the Canadian regulator had already required environmental assessments, the PSB may have been convinced that it was indirectly requiring an environmental assessment. Such perfect solutions often turn out to have flaws. Both the Crees and Hydro-Québec had already launched appeals of the NEB decision. Hydro insisted that the federal Board had invaded a provincial jurisdiction. Lise Bacon, the Québec Minister of Energy, had attacked the quasi-judicial NEB as a tool of federal intrusion. The PSB, in its search for the perfect solution, had clearly not been sensitive to the political volatility underlying the contract it was approving. A year later, the Federal Court of Appeal of Canada would decide that the NEB had exceeded its jurisdiction in requiring an environmental assessment.

In drawing the line on directly requiring environmental assessments at the Vermont state boundary, the PSB emphatically expressed concern that, as a Vermont State agency, it should not make judgments on behalf of other jurisdictions lest it appear "chauvinist." As a statement of Board policy, the concern to avoid the appearance of chauvinism was the most flawed and problematic statement in its decision. This concern misunderstood the central argument of Vermont environmentalists. They were not asking their Board to make judgments on behalf of Québec, they would respond. They were asking their Board to be the agency through which Vermonters would decide which energy sources they would choose to consume and whether the environmental impact would be a part of that decision.

Only one group, without a direct financial interest, shared the PSB's fear that Vermont might be painted with the brush of chauvinism. Bernard Landry, the Vice-President of the independentist Parti Québécois (PQ) referred to a New York legislative proposal which would require consideration of environmental impacts outside the state as "an old American imperialist dream of extra-territoriality." He saw such proposals as a direct assault on Québec's sovereignty. Like the Liberal Government the PQ nominally opposes, Mr. Landry took the view that there was no serious competition to Hydro-Québec in the northeastern states. "If they prefer to burn hydrocarbons they are in a sovereign state."

Marc Chenier, co-ordinator of the Coalition for a Public Debate on an Energy Policy in Québec and a world-travelled geologist, heard a different tune. His reply to Bernard Landry suggests that an essential aspect of local autonomy is to be a good neighbor.

> The environment has no political boundaries. Of course, Quebeckers don't want to be told what to do by outsiders. We, in Québec, have been pushing for the United States to pass a law on acid rain, to limit the sulphur content of emissions so I don't see why the reverse shouldn't happen.

Nobody, it appears, wants to be "told what to do" while everybody would like to benefit from the resources of the neighboring territory. Ian Goodman described this as "the problem of the Global Commons. "

> If each area of the globe pursues what it views, narrowly defined, as its own self-interest, I think our future is in tremendous danger.

Some years ago a Canadian Senate Committee was hearing testimony on ways to export natural gas from the western Arctic. One witness recommended submarine tankers to travel down the Greenland coast. A Newfoundland senator asked, "But I thought we objected when the Americans proposed to send tankers down our west coast." "Senator," the witness replied, "that was their tanker and our coast."

There were times during the *Odeyak* tour and the campaign which followed when such blunt talk might have helped the Crees' cause. Eric van Lennep, an anthropologist and organizer of the Arctic to Amazonia Conference, observed that Vermonters appreciated "the incredible courtesy, openness and warmth" of both the Crees and the Inuit. These same qualities, however, led their speakers from the kind of stinging invective which typically characterizes political debate. The leaders were, for example, unprepared to reply to Governor Kunin's inhospitable remarks. Although Cree speakers would tour Vermont for the next year and a half, through the village votes and thereafter, only very late in their campaign did the Cree speakers begin to question the security of supply from Hydro-Québec or to remind Vermonters that Québec's claim to Great

Whale depended on the continuing force of the *James Bay Agreement*. Only when Québec had mounted a massive advertising campaign in Vermont, together with a general movement to discredit the integrity of the Cree leaders, did the Crees begin to raise such issues. Throughout the *Odeyak* trip and for most of the first year, Cree speakers avoided statements which might cause Québec to lose face.

The Towns Vote

Many analyses of the Vermont town votes hold that the *Odeyak* visit played an essential role in establishing a relationship which led Vermonters to see the Crees and Inuit as real people and, therefore, made the human rights issue a reality. The most remote and rural towns, where trapping and a relationship with the land remain an important part of the Vermont culture, rejected the Hydro proposal as strongly as college towns or the City of Burlington. The town votes on the Vermont Joint Owners contract with Hydro-Québec took place in 16 different Vermont villages between February and April, 1991. The question local voters were asked to decide was whether they approved of their local utility's participation in the contract.

The most practical comment on the PSB's fear of appearing chauvinist comes from the Vermonters who monitored the village votes. Burlington held a second vote in September, 1991 after the courts disqualified the first vote. In more than one smaller town, when the local utility lost, the clerk attempted to hold a second vote without giving due notice. Two one-industry villages dominated by the ski resort industry reportedly pressed their workers to vote in favor of the Hydro contract.

Hydro-Québec agents were visibly present at each town meeting. They played a role in preparing the literature for the small local utilities. Hydro-Québec did not share the PSB's concern about chauvinism in its interventions in the Vermont town meetings. Hydro-Québec was represented both by their own executive officers and by a local public relations firm. Hydro-Québec representatives suggested that there was no connection between the Vermont contract and the Great Whale Project, even though they had told the PSB that the sources used in the previous Hydro-Vermont contract would now be committed to domestic use. On other occasions they told the public meetings that the rivers which would be dammed by the Great Whale project were not fertile.

Prevarication was, no doubt, an important debating tactic in town meetings long before Hydro-Québec decided to participate in Vermont politics. When the subject was the local river, every farmer and miller might be something of an authority. However, when the local utility brings the largest provincial agency in Québec to provide misinformation about rivers a thousand miles away, it is surely the Québec state corporation which might be said to lack respect for the sovereignty of Vermont.

When the final vote was counted in Burlington in September, eight of the sixteen towns voting, and far more than 50% of the population, voted no. One observer noted that it was often the poorest villages, places where hunting, fishing and trapping continued to be an important supplement to family incomes, that most strongly rejected the contract and voted with the Crees. In some cases, however, there seemed to be more of a town-gown split. In most of the towns where the contract was approved, the grass roots movement simply appears to have lacked a local presence.

Hydro-Québec's other activities in Vermont deserve closer examination. The free trips it has provided to civic and utility officials must represent one of the major tourist bonanzas in the history of northern Québec. At least three to four officials in each town or village with an electric department involved in Hydro's Vermont contract were invited on an all-expense paid tour. The tours, however, always ended at the LG-2 site at Radisson. They did not include the communities on the Great Whale. Neither Cree nor Inuit leaders were invited to any of the lavish dinners.

Hydro-Québec has also become a major patron of the arts in Vermont. It has supported the local symphony, public television and public radio. It has also, through its full page advertising, become a significant patron of the daily press where a series of advertisements were run beginning with Richard Drouin, Chairman of the Board of Hydro-Québec, congratulating Vermont on its 200th anniversary. All this, of course, is a charge on the public purse of Québec, where the Government has continued to avoid a public debate on energy policy.

Hydro-Québec was also very fortunate in its choice of Kimball and Sherman as their lobbying firms in Vermont. On the death of Richard Snelling, who had replaced Madeleine Kunin, Howard Dean became Governor. Mr. Sherman, of Kimball and Sherman, headed Governor Dean's transition team while his firm continued to lobby for Hydro-Québec. Clearly, the Public Service Board's stated concern about intervening in another state's affairs is restricted to the Board's own members.

The Vermont leg of the *Odeyak* trip opened a dialogue between the Crees, the Inuit and environmentalists. Vermonters' own attachment to their land, to a tradition of human rights and to a highly decentralized democracy, made Vermont an opportune place. The dialogue was fundamentally a discourse on responsibility. In his statement when the *Odeyak* landed in Vermont, Matthew Mukash had said that he wanted Vermonters to know the real costs of the power they used and to think about those costs each time they flipped a switch, in effect to accept responsibility for their own way of life. Far more than the interdisciplinary blending of different kinds of expertise, environmental commitment consists of accepting that responsibility.

This is why Cree speakers increasingly came to describe those who were prepared to build forty-storey dams on Cree lands while refusing the most modest increase in the price of power in their own locale as "environmental racists." Vermonters, like Quebeckers, had been in the forefront of the demand for a strong federal U.S. *Clean Air Act*. The acid rain that originates with the burning of coal in the mid-western United States falls on Québec and on Vermont. But evidence before the Vermont Public Service Board and the National Energy Board of Canada demonstrated that hydro-electric megaprojects were not any cleaner than hydrocarbons. The choice offered to Vermonters by Hydro-Québec was to pass on to the Crees and the Inuit damage they were resisting from their own southern neighbors. The alternative was to accept responsibility both in their own state and in the adjacent areas for the effects of their lifestyle.

The dialogue which began in Vermont had a slow, halting but quite perceptible ripple effect into the rest of New England, New York State and, despite such obvious obstacles as the language barrier, into Québec. It was this ripple effect which was the most far-reaching and long lasting consequence of the voyage of the *Odeyak*. It took different forms. In Québec, it stimulated the realization that Sovereignty-Association without local autonomy and decentralization of massive state corporations would do little to democratize Québec or to ensure an economic base for its children. Quebeckers of good will were also prompted to break through their stereotype of "*les sauvages*" and begin to recognize the diversity of First Nations within Québec. The ripple that the *Odeyak's* challenging navigation had begun would grow to a wave as it gathered crowds in towns along the Hudson in its progress toward New York City. Ironically, the *New York Times* would be the last newspaper to continue describing the Inuit as "Eskimos," a highly derogatory racial epithet. In spite of coming to understand the true meaning of the word Eskimo other papers would continue to refer to "Cree and Inuit Indians." That, presumably so their readers would know that Crees and Inuit were First Nations peoples.

On Saturday, April 7, the *Odeyak* headed south from Burlington toward Middlebury. Jim Higgins was able to make arrangements for the whole group to stay at Camp Keewatin, a vacant children's camp. Jim and Seth Gibson, who runs canoe trips from Camp Keewatin, had met on the

George River in Ungava. "At some point I contacted Seth and suggested that maybe they could stay at the camp. It is that kind of networking that was at work here."

Camp Keewatin was a particularly special time for the *Odeyak* travellers. It was a weekend in the bush, a genuine rest from the city and from the road. If the hills were different from favorite camping places back home, the quiet felt much the same. Families were able to stay together, each in their own cabin. After a potluck dinner on Saturday evening and a presentation of the play *Beyond the North Wind* at the Isley Theater, most of the travellers had an entire Sunday to walk in the woods. Children could play without their parents worrying about traffic. Weemish Mamiumscum, and other elders, were able to walk in the woods and look at the trees and flowers they had seen on the road from a distance.

The most striking difference was the many types of trees. We have only three types of trees. And the trees were also much taller. It was the time of year when the flowers were blooming. From time to time, I saw animals on the land. I liked these things very much.

Chapter 7:
The Clearwater's Blanket

North River Friends

It was Palm Sunday, seven days before Easter. The place was Crown Point, the New York side of the bridge from Chimney Point, Vermont. This is where Lake Champlain narrows dramatically from a vast expanse of inland water into a mere channel. When the *Odeyak* travellers rolled into Crown Point, Dale Rice and Nancy Papish were there to meet the bus, the boat and the rest of the entourage. Crown Point would be the place where the *Odeyak* would begin to travel substantial distances on the water.

The plan for the early part of the *Odeyak's* New York State trip was to travel down the south channel of Lake Champlain, stopping at Ticonderoga on the first evening and at Whitehall near the top of the New York State Barge Canal on the second. The Canal connects Lake Champlain to Ft. Edwards on the Hudson River above Albany. The *Odeyak* would reach Albany, the state capitol, on Thursday, the day before Good Friday.

This itinerary had been worked out in hurried phone calls beginning with the arrival of the Great Whale people in Kahnawake, but only culminating in more concrete plans during the *Odeyak's* week in Vermont. It started with Kenneth Deer, then director of the Mohawk Nation Office and a leading member of the Kahnawake Canoe Club, calling Nancy Papish in Schenectady. When the traditional Longhouse people at Kahnawake had heard that a Cree and Inuit canoe was on its way to New York there had been a strong sense that providing an escort, at least to the traditional southern boundary of Mohawk land at Albany, was an essential courtesy. Kenneth had developed a strong friendship with Nancy Papish and Dale Rice in 1986 when he and several other Mohawks from Kahnawake made the trip to Albany by canoe, with members of the North River Friends' Historical Brigade.

The North River Friends are the most northern or upstream branch of the *Clearwater* network. Nancy describes the sailing sloop *Clearwater* as "the flagship of an environmental movement in the Hudson River Valley." Because the vessel has a very tall mast, however, it cannot go above the lift bridge in Albany. The North River Friends carry the work of the *Clearwater* Sloop Clubs upstream onto the Mohawk River and its canal extensions to Lake Erie and Lake Ontario, as well as up into Lake Champlain with its connection to the St. Lawrence.

Nancy Papish explains that one major function of North River Friends and the other sloop clubs associated with the *Clearwater* is to provide hospitality to crew members when either their flagship or other boats come to their area to do public relations or conduct educational programs.

> We meet the boat and find out who needs to get to a train, who needs to go shopping, how much ice does the boat need, what engine repairs does it need. When we're canoeing or sailing and we come into Poughkeepsie or into Beacon we can call up and say, "Hi, I need a shower," or "I came in on a boat. Can you come and get me?" We do this for one another.

When Kenneth called Nancy in mid-March he still believed that the *Odeyak* people would already have made their own plans for accommodations in New York State. He was calling simply to ask if Nancy could arrange hospitality for his own club members from Kahnawake. Kenneth gave Nancy a jovial description of the trip,

> You always chew me out when we come and we don't call. So we're coming and I'm calling and I don't have all the details but another group of Natives are canoeing from Montréal to New York City for Earth Day. They're protesting the building of a power plant on their lands. We're going to put a boatload of Mohawk men on the river to go through our territory with them.

Kenneth said that he did not have any further information at that point. Nancy and two other North River Friends each called three of the other *Clearwater* sloop clubs to make arrangements for the arrival of half a dozen Mohawk canoeists.

About the same time, Doris Delaney, then vice-president of an environmental action group called PROTECT, based near Newburgh on the Hudson below Albany, received a call from Jeff Wollock. When he got home following the Montréal conference where Matthew Mukash had announced the Great Whale peoples' intention to send the *Odeyak* to New York City, Jeff began to put out the word. On health and safety grounds PROTECT had been challenging the huge power line coming through New York State from James Bay One. Doris had been a key activist from PROTECT's earliest days in 1982. Doris brings a full range of organizational skills to community activism. In February of 1990 Doris had helped Jean Jones, who was then president of PROTECT, write a letter of comment for submission to the National Energy Board of Canada's hearings on Hydro's application for a permit to export power to New York State under its new contract with the New York Power Authority (NYPA).

Jeff called Doris to say that a group of Crees and Inuit were going to be coming down by boat to appeal to the world for help in New York City on Earth Day. A few days later, Doris received an item in the mail about the *Odeyak* trip. Although the New York part had thirteen stops, the itinerary did not have a great deal of substance when examined at close range. "After we had been using it for some time," Jeff recalls, "we learned from Denny [Alsop] that this itinerary was just drawn up as a sketch by Marie [Symes-Grehan] and him. It was their initial idea of how the trip might be put together."

Toshi Seeger — Grandmother of the Hudson

Doris was miffed when she thought that Pete and Toshi Seeger were hosting the *Odeyak* at the Beacon Sloop Club while PROTECT, which had written a brief to the NEB on behalf of the Crees, had not been invited to participate. Neither Doris nor Jeff Wollock from whom she had received the itinerary knew at that point that items such as "Rendezvous with *CLEARWATER*" reflected only Denny's and Marie's intentions. Such items were not necessarily confirmed invitations.

When Doris phoned Toshi to say that her group had been left out, Toshi, after a moment's silence said, "I don't know what you're talking about." Toshi said she had been to a meeting early that day to discuss the *Clearwater* Club's calendar. "If there's a group of Natives coming down from Canada we have to find out about it. We can't leave them stranded. You find out more and I'll see what I can find out." When Doris got back to Toshi several days later, Toshi had reached Nancy Papish. By that time Nancy had received a further call from Kenneth. This time he was no longer as jovial. He told Nancy, "We're in trouble. I can't find anybody who's in charge. I can't find anybody who knows where they are staying or how they are being fed." Nancy assured Kenneth his people would have food and lodging. By the time the *Odeyak* arrived at Kahnawake without sleeping bags or life jackets Kenneth had become the main contact with the more upstate New York support groups.

Toshi put Doris in touch with Nancy. She also provided Doris with the name and number of every sloop club president along the length of the Hudson River. Doris describes Toshi as the grandmother of the environmental movement in the Hudson region, "Toshi stayed in touch with it the whole way. She didn't actually do the organizing but she was always there to help."

The itinerary that emerged in time for the arrival of the *Odeyak* grew out of Toshi Seeger's making the match between Doris Delaney and Nancy Papish. Well before either of them had heard from the *Odeyak* organizers, Matthew Mukash, Marie Symes-Grehan or Denny Alsop, Nancy and Doris were both in contact with Kenneth Deer. Doris and Nancy had no way to reach the *Odeyak* organizers except by leaving messages with Jeff Wollock's Solidarity office in New York City. Jeff describes himself as a researcher and emphasizes that he is not an organizer. When the *Odeyak* first arrived at Kahnawake, Kenneth's report sounded "pretty frantic." He told Doris, "They don't have life preservers. They don't have lights to carry on the boat. They don't have sleeping bags. They're packed like sardines in a bus." Life preservers and running lights are basic safety equipment required by law.

Nancy focussed initially on contacts north of Albany while Doris worked on the southern part of the route. In addition to the sloop clubs Doris found Native American organizations, canoeing clubs, church groups and Red Cross Societies, each of whom had some kind of support to offer in their own vicinity. Doris and Nancy looked for facilities in small town New York State that more or less replicated the Longhouse facilities when she had heard that the *Odeyak* people had enjoyed their stay at Kahnawake. Doris recalls that gradually, they were able to put together a variety of alternative accommodations. "They may not have always been great but they were cost free alternatives for the Natives who were coming down. Free is kind of scary to arrange for sixty people."

When Doris finally heard from Marie Symes-Grehan, two or three days after Kenneth's report on the *Odeyak's* arrival at Kahnawake, she was horrified by what she learned.

They had no money. Two elders had landed in the hospital in Ottawa because they could not adjust to the changes from the Native diet. Most of the people on the trip had never left their own village from the picture she gave me. The weather was terrible. People were homesick. They were tired. They had already been on the move for a long, long time.

"What would it take for you to turn back?"

"We're not turning back. Under no circumstances. The future of this people depend on getting to New York City. We are not turning back."

I hung up the phone and I cried. I didn't know what to do for these people. Then I got myself together and called the attorney who had represented PROTECT because he is well connected. I told David Sive, "I don't know what to do. They're insisting on coming. Nothing is going to stop them. What are we going to do?"

After Doris talked to Attorney Sive she received a phone call from the Commissioner of Parks, Recreation and Historic Preservation of New York State asking, "What can we do for you?" Another call came from the Deputy Commissioner of Environmental Conservation. Even though no direct use was made of their help, the offers led Doris to realize, "It would be a terrible embarrassment for New York State if anything went wrong for these people." This sense of responsibility applied at the official level of state commissioners. It also became "a drumbeat up and down the river. 'We have to make this thing work'."

A Springtime Route

Meanwhile, Nancy "started to get calls from people I did not know and had never heard of. My calls and Doris Delaney's got crossed. We still had not gotten an itinerary." Shortly after the *Odeyak* came into Vermont, Nancy had a call from Denny Alsop. He told her that the *Odeyak* was her responsibility from Crown Point to Kingston, New York. He also said that that distance had to be covered in two days. "We could provide hospitality. About that distance by canoe I simply said, 'Not possible.' He said, 'Do what you can'."

The time pressure eased up somewhat when ice and wind conditions at the north end of Lake Champlain had prevented the *Odeyak* from doing long distances on the water.

> We knew that we could get them down the south end of Lake Champlain if the ice was out. The real problem became that the canal would not be open or operable. We did not know what to do about that. I thought possibly we could take them down Lake George. Lake George had been a traditional route before the canal was opened. It would require a motor portage there and back. I asked Denny. He said, "You're in charge." Then Dale and I went to Lake George and saw that it was ice bound. I called Denny back and said, "This is not possible. We can drive along the river but there is no way to paddle." He insisted it was possible and I insisted that it was not.

The itinerary presented to the *Odeyak* travellers on Palm Sunday started to come together when Nancy and Dale made some decisions about what could realistically happen north of Albany.

> We knew that from Albany south we were in ice free water and that with Robert Hanson navigating they would be alright even without the buoys being out yet. When Dale asked how he could help I told him to take Lake Champlain off of my hands. I was teaching. I had a full time job. This was becoming a nightmare. I don't know when this was planned. If we had known even one month in advance there would have been no problem. There was no need for it to be dropped in our laps that way. We did not like

the kind of planning that we were having to do. We felt that the people were not being properly considered. This made us very uncomfortable.

When Dale and Nancy met the *Odeyak* on Palm Sunday, they had brought their own canoe, a 26-foot freighter made of Kevlar ®material in a traditional birch bark design. It was a twin of the Mohawk escort. Dale would serve as a water guide, paddling his own canoe, with the *Odeyak* and the Mohawk escort following along. Dale assumed that Crees from the north woods must all naturally be experienced canoeists.

The name "Cree" might conjure up somebody who was born in a canoe. Cree, Ojibway and Chippewa are known to canoeists as the canoe Indians. Well, it turned out that this was the first day that they had actually had the *Odeyak* on the water for a real long paddle.

Dale's first day's trip from Crown Point to Ticonderoga was to be 18 miles, "a decent day's paddle that went very well."

We didn't know anything about the *Odeyak* itself, like how fast it went. Frequently, in a big canoe, no matter how many people there are in it, or how light it is loaded, or how strong the canoeists, the boat will only move along at a certain speed. Most of them peak out at around four to four-and-a-half miles an hour just because of the hull shape. The *Odeyak* was considerably slower because of the design and because it is really a work boat and so it had much more beam than our big canoes. Obviously being shaped to be half-kayak, half-canoe it was pretty unique.

There were four adults in Dale's boats when the three canoes left Crown Point. An experienced canoeist from North River Friends was in the bow. Number two and three thwarts were each occupied by older Cree men. Dale was sterning. After spending time on the same waters with many urban groups, Dale found his time with the *Odeyak* people a unique experience.

The things that I started to notice about the people was that they were very, very interested in every rock formation, every kind of vegetation, bushes and trees even though it was early spring and not much had started to sprout as far as greenery or leaves. They noticed all sorts of things about the birds, both waterfowl that were starting to come north and the songbirds. They were just incredibly tuned into the environment. They taxed my knowledge asking about every bird that we saw.

The Crees didn't have a distrust of us but they wanted to find out who they were with. They had no way of interviewing me, no way of really questioning me closely. I was tested for about an hour or an hour and a half. It was very interesting to see how this happened. We would be paddling along. There would be conversation, in Cree, between number two and number three. Suddenly they would be doing draw strokes which took the canoe off course. I would do a counter-stroke, a cross-draw or a rudder to stay on course. They would draw harder. I would take a further counter-stroke. They would stop drawing, do a regular forward stroke and we would pick up the rhythm for another couple of minutes. Then someone would look at me. I would look up the gunwale and say, "Hi."

This went on for awhile and I began to appreciate what they were doing. I imagined how it might be if the tables were turned. "If I went to Ungava and got into a boat with someone I didn't know, with whom I couldn't really have much of a conversation, after weeks of confusion and upheaval, how would I feel?" I would have to find a way to test them.

Half an hour later they decided to do some more testing. Then when they decided that I passed the test there were no more draw-strokes and the canoe just moved along quite smoothly. To me, these people were really very committed to their trip. They just didn't want to put it in the hands of someone they didn't know or trust. I was impressed with that approach. I also thought it was a lot of fun.

James Kawapit recalls the view from the *Odeyak* as they paddled down the shores of Lake Champlain.

The land that I have seen from the water has very different trees and vegetation than what we have around Whapmagoostui. I didn't see much in the way of rocky beaches like ours here. The land is more rolling than the rocky land that we have.

The things that I had never seen that amazed me were the bridges across the rivers and the braces and pillars going into the rivers. I was also struck by the way the roads go so high up into the mountains and seem to climb the cliffs. I also saw very old ships from a hundred years ago beached along the shore. These were all things that I had never seen before.

In Ticonderoga the Knights of Columbus hosted the *Odeyak* travellers. The K. of C. Hall provided an interesting setting for the *Odeyak* people and the North River Friends to have a chance to get properly acquainted. Jim Higgins travelled with the *Odeyak* to Ticonderoga. He found the up-state New York town presented a sharp contrast with Vermont where many of the *Odeyak* people had just spent their first week in the United States.

The culture of New York State is different from Vermont. It seems a lot more deprived economically. Ticonderoga has the aura of an old town that has really slowed down. I became intrigued by these places. At the dock in Ticonderoga there are older people who drive their cars down and spend the day hanging out with their friends. I happened to be there when an old man drove up and parked. He had a beard and seemed to drink a good deal. He began to tell me a whole history of Native people in that area. He seemed to be really well versed. What is so fascinating to me is never knowing who might come along with something to tell.

Jim's impression was that the Knights of Columbus of Ticonderoga "had agreed to put this thing on without really knowing who these people were. Somebody had told them it was a good idea. There was this one old man who was on the advisory committee for the New York Power Authority so I spent time talking with him and giving him our propaganda." This was the setting in which Nancy Papish finally met Marie Symes-Grehan and Denny Alsop. Nancy was instantly taken with Marie.

> She was one of the most amazing people I have ever met. Incredibly well organized, extremely sensitive to human beings, aware of the two different groups for whom she was providing. I have never met anybody with her abilities. I can not imagine that that trip would have come off without her.

> When we met in Ticonderoga the main question was what would happen after they reached Whitehall the next day. Denny was very insistent that they go on the canal. I had to point out that it was not open and it was not operable. "You will be arrested. The boat will be impounded."

> When we met at Ticonderoga there was nobody to go with them on the river for the next stage of the trip. Denny said that he was not going with them. I told Denny, "I want you personally to go to the lockmaster and get permission and call me tomorrow morning at six o'clock. Let me know if you have permission to go on the canal, where they are to go on and where they are to get out."

> The next morning he called me to say that it was cleared and there was permission to go on the canal. He said that the locks were operating. He did not say where to get on.

When Nancy found that there was still a shortage of life jackets she visualized the *Odeyak* being cited for a violation as it went through the canal under the supervision of a state lockmaster. At the army surplus, Nancy picked out the four biggest life jackets.

> On David Masty it looked like a child's jacket. It wouldn't close in the front. There were two men and two women for whom we could not provide jackets. That meant that they could not be part of the paddling rotation.

By mid-morning, the *Odeyak* finally left Ticonderoga for Whitehall. The distance of 23 miles would be the longest paddle of the trip. Although the interest in the flora and fauna continued, and the weather was no worse than usual, Dale gained a strong sense that the Crees and the Inuit missed the motor power to which they were accustomed and were not happy about paddling so many hours into a sloppy spring wind.

Two of the younger Crees were paddling in the middle of Dale's canoe on the second day in place of the elders.

> Every time there was a site along the river where a power plant could be installed they would point it out to me, "You could have a station here." I'm

as backwards as it comes about this stuff. I found out later that each of the places to which she pointed was a site where there had been an old generating station which had been let go for some reason or another. They were into the issue on a much more knowledgeable scale than most of the people to whom they talked. They knew more about it technically.

While the *Odeyak* was ploughing southward on Lake Champlain, Nancy drove down to the main lock in Whitehall. When she barged into the office, Nancy vaguely remembered Herb Esswein, one of the two men sitting there, from the 1986 trip. She greeted him with great warmth and introduced herself. Then she added, "I hear we're paddling here tomorrow."

Herb Esswein looked at Nancy very strangely and asked, "What are you talking about?"

"I've been told that arrangements have been made and that we are to paddle on the canal tomorrow."

"The locks are not open and nobody is paddling and I don't know who told you that."

Nancy recalls feeling very foolish and thinking unkind thoughts about Denny's sense of determination. But her years as an English teacher had taught her something about just such situations. "Can you call the other locks and see if he talked to them? He told me that he went and got permission. He checked that there is no ice and that the river is open."

"Sure I'll check for you."

Nancy had worked with canal operators since 1959. "I have learned that they are a very independent group. They also have orders which they must follow. Pressure was not likely to move them." She sat and talked with the two lockmen. She learned that the lock at Whitehall is managed all year long, 24 hours a day, for flood control. Herb Esswein phoned each of the other locks. Nancy became convinced that no one from the trip had talked to any of the lock keepers. After she had chatted with the two lockmen for two and a half hours, Herb Esswein said, "The locks operate. Some of them. We test them once a week. Otherwise we can't open in the middle of May. This lock works. The next one doesn't. Its completely pumped out. The next below that one works too. Would you like me to see if it is possible to operate one lock for you?"

"I would like that very much. These people have never seen a lock operate. They don't really have a clear picture of what it is that a lock does."

"I can't make a promise. Don't you promise anybody. This is absolutely not allowed and I'm not about to lose my job even though I appreciate what you're trying to do. If I can get permission we'll do something."

About four o'clock Herb Esswein started to call up and down the canal system for the head engineer who would have to approve the opening. When the night shift came on Herb briefed the new crew chief who continued to call around in search of one of the two men with authority to give them permission to open the locks. Nancy finally left him to his telephone sleuthing when the *Odeyak* arrived in Whitehall.

The *Odeyak* travellers were the guests of the Adirondack Northeastern Woodsmen who served a beef stew in the Gainsboro Emergency Rescue Building. After the slide show about the Great Whale River, Nancy returned to Whitehall to check with the lock crew. No word yet. About one o'clock in the morning, before her insomnia ran out, Nancy checked again. They assured Nancy that they would keep trying all night. In the morning, before she joined the others for breakfast, Nancy checked in at the lock house once more. Herb Esswein was back on duty.

> He told me that we were cleared for the first lock. He also said that we had to pull out before the next lock because it was not operating. Then he stressed once again the importance of staying away from the dams downstream from Ft. Edwards.

The low head dams further downstream are especially dangerous. A low head dam is a concrete wall that is made so that there is a smooth, uniform stream of water going over it and a lock over at one side. The dams are especially dangerous because they are not visible until the boat is so close that it gets sucked into the falls. During the boating season there are buoys and markers setting out the channel. Between the two upstream locks the *Odeyak* would not be in danger because where the lock was shutting down for repairs the water was flowing the other way. There was no chance of going over a low head dam on that stretch. Herb told Nancy that two days earlier he could not have let them through no matter what. The lake had been so high with the spring run-off that the water was coming over the height of the lock and there was no way to open the gates.

Nancy went off to search for Larry House, the *Odeyak's* truck driver and Mike Canoe, the Kahnawake paddler who was taking care of the Mohawk escort. She asked Larry to move the canoes back to the locks. They had already been moved around to the other side of town in the expectation that they were off the water for the next two days. Nancy developed a special respect for Larry's hard work.

At this point Larry's was the only truck and by this point there were three boats. Larry found himself delivering the *Odeyak*, returning for the Mohawk boat and then coming back for ours. Larry was a gentle, patient man who saw the boats through an endless maze of changes in plan and route. Until Ticonderoga, I don't think anyone had actually handed him a map with a route drawn on it. I gave Marie my set of maps and went and bought Larry a new set of maps.

Mike Canoe and I spent an hour and a half in the lock house with the lockman. He offered to draw us the channel as best he could. He reminded us that there would be no buoy markers for the main channel and no markers for the side cuts. "If you know what you're looking for you'll see the dams before you're even near them. Show your drivers where to be on the road and please get out of the water before you're even near the dams."

Nancy and Mike returned to the church in time for the last breakfast call. Nancy was still excited when she told Matthew Mukash and Marie Symes-Grehan that they had received permission to go through the locks. Then she told David Masty that there was a need for two crews to go through the locks. David went off to talk with the paddlers. A few minutes later he came back and said, "Nobody will paddle today."

"What's the problem, Dave?" Nancy asked.

"It's cold and it's raining and both crews paddled yesterday. They won't paddle."

Mike Canoe, a cool fountain of enthusiasm, announced, "I am paddling. I have my boat here. I took all this time to come down here to paddle. I am going to paddle." Nancy told Mike that she would paddle with him. Then she asked David Masty whether there were some people who are not paddling regularly who wanted to paddle. Jeffrey Fleming, Sappa's 14-year-old son volunteered. So did Caroline Weetaltuk and Heather Tukatuk. Sappa had gone back to Vermont for the day, and had taken Billie and Mina Weetaltuk with him. Caroline had the day free from helping her mother. Jeffrey had a day without parental supervision. That was enough to fill Mike's boat.

Nancy turned back to David, "I'm not a fast paddler. I'm not a killer paddler. But I got the locks to open for you. Can you fill the *Odeyak* with anybody?" David went back and found a crew who were prepared to paddle.

Everyone who was not paddling came down to the lock to watch the *Odeyak* and its escort pass through. Herb Esswein came out of the lock house to meet the travellers. Herb gave a very careful explanation of the lock's working so that the translators could take his precise information into Cree and Inuktituut. The dampened spirits picked up once the canoes were launched. Nancy was in the bow of Mike's canoe. Mike yelled at her to pick up the pace. The *Odeyak* paddling song which Mike had started on the Richelieu now had Cree and Inuit words. The Crees and the Inuit did animal calls and told the names of different animals in their own languages. Caroline found the Mohawk boat with its high gloss finish and narrow beam, "very tippy . . . when you move, it moves." Going through the locks was quite frightening at first. "I thought it was going to turn us over. I thought it might go very fast but it went gently."

As the *Odeyak* paddled toward the second lock, Larry and his helper Randy Pepabano found the road running beside the river. They honked and waved from the warmth of the truck's cab as they looked for a safe, public landing to take the boats out of the water well before they reached the closed lock. Denny had arranged for a television crew to meet them on the far side of the next locks at one o'clock. When they finally flagged the canoes to come off the water, they landed at a rather nondescript spot. The crews of both boats immediately scurried under the nearest trees to shake the chill of the river out of their bones and find some warmth. The reporter was prepared to interview whoever stood still, and so when Mike and Nancy did not run into the bush they found themselves facing a television camera. Despite "being in the middle of nowhere" this was not the television crew for which Denny had arranged. When Mike Canoe told the reporter that the people he wanted to interview were all in the woods the reporter was content to take some pictures of the boats being tied up.

Randy and Larry managed to get coffee and the lunches for the paddlers but the bus was yet to be found. The boats and paddlers needed to be moved down below the next locks to the place where Denny had arranged for the other television crew to meet them. The boats could be moved but the crews were stuck waiting for the bus. Finally, Nancy walked to the lock where she said hello to her old friend Herb. She asked if he had seen a television crew. "Yeah," he said, "They were here an hour ago. They got tired of waiting. They're gone." When the *Odeyak* had not shown up promptly at one o'clock the television crew had left. Larry and Randy found the bus waiting below the lock, right where the television crew had been looking for the *Odeyak*.

Crisis At Glens Falls

When everybody had boarded the bus, Nancy handed the trip over to Charles Moore. Charles had been the *Odeyak's* land guide from Crown Point to Whitehall. Now he would take the *Odeyak* travellers to be the guests of his own home group, the Feeder Canal Alliance at Glens Falls.

Glens Falls is an old mill town on the Mohawk River system just above the Hudson, twenty miles from Whitehall. The Alliance is a community and advocate group who want to convert the canal into a public space now that it is no longer used commercially. Lodging would be at the Church of the Messiah. Dinner would be provided by the local Red Cross and Civil Defense.

Three months earlier, in January, 1990, Charles and Gaynell Moore had called to ask if the Historical Brigade of the North River Friends would be willing to paddle in full costume in the Feeder Canal Festival. When Nancy Papish recruited Dale Rice as the *Odeyak's* water guide from Crown Point to Whitehall she had also recruited Charles Moore as the land guide for the same stretch. He, in turn, had arranged hospitality for the *Odeyak* in Glens Falls. Nancy had met Charles for the first time when everyone arrived at the landing site at Crown Point on the Sunday morning. Leaving the travellers with Charles and Gaynell, Nancy was able to head home to Schenectady, on the outskirts of Albany and make final preparations for their arrival in the state capitol. Mike Canoe took a break from his role as Mohawk guide to the *Odeyak* and visited with the Boy Scout troop who had come with Nancy to canoe near Kahnawake each summer.

Tension had been growing among the *Odeyak* travellers for some time. Some of it came simply from the difficulty of being constantly on display. Crees and Inuit were both accustomed to the hardships of the bush and tundra. But neither were accustomed to sleeping in church basements or in civil defense facilities. Robbie Niquanicappo recalls that the tension finally reached a breaking point at Glens Falls.

> There were some uncomfortable times. One of the main difficulties which became a cause for concern was that the Inuit did not have the support of their regional government. They did not have financial resources. On some of the stops the Cree stayed at hotels and the Inuit didn't. So relations were becoming strained.

> But all that changed when we reached Glens Falls in New York. One of the Inuit women started ranting about how the Crees were making themselves comfortable at hotels while the Inuit had to sleep on mattresses on the floor. It started a big argument. It was very uncomfortable.

> At one point, everyone had become so disgusted that it felt like we were just waiting for someone to say let's go home. We were all sitting around the table wondering what to do. There were arguments going back and forth. The two leaders were conferring with their people. I was running between the leaders and the others. Finally, Caroline Weetaltuk got up and said, "What's the matter with you people? We're fighting for something here. I'm not doing it for me. I'm doing it for my child."

She continued on in this way until she started crying. It was a very moving and very emotional speech of not more than two or three minutes. Everybody shut up. Next thing we knew, everyone was crying.

We all went over to the young lady who had made the speech. We all gave her a hug and a kiss and thanked her. We joined hands in a circle, the symbol of Native unity, and we all said a prayer together. Then we all trooped off to the hotel. That's when the decision was made that everyone was going to sleep in the hotel at Cree expense. It didn't matter who might complain about the expense back home later. There were the few odd personal differences, but by the end of the trip we were united in spirit, in friendship.

Part of the underlying pressure was relieved when Bill Namagoose, Executive Director of the Grand Council of the Crees, contacted Makivik, the Inuit regional association. He was told that Makivik had, in fact, voted $8,000 in support of the Inuit contingent on the *Odeyak* trip. Some miscommunication had prevented the Kuujjuaraapik people from receiving either the news or the money. When Bill Namagoose went down to take some money to the Crees he also arranged to bring some of the money voted by Makivik to the Inuit.

The official arrival in Albany was scheduled for twelve o'clock on Thursday, April 12. The *Odeyak*, accompanied by both its escorts, the twin craft from Mohawk Canoe Club at Kahnawake and the North River Friends', after launching at a safe place some distance up river they came around Green Island. Dale Rice had re-joined the group to guide them into Albany. As they headed toward their landing at Corning Preserve, local canoeists came out to meet them.

After they had launched, a short distance below Watervliet, on a stretch of the river surrounded by industry and wrapped in cement walls, two wild turkeys flew right in front of the boats. One of the *Odeyak* women in Dale's boat drew a bead with her finger on the lead turkey. "Look at the size of those ptarmigans." Dale realized only then that while the *Odeyak* people knew all the waterfowl and game birds of their own northern region they were totally unfamiliar with the most distinctive indigenous game bird of his area.

When I first got out of college I helped to re-stock those birds in a game management area near Albany. Those turkeys had been extinct in this area for many, many years. Since then, they have come back in a fantastic way. The *Odeyak* people became very interested in the idea of re-stocking. They were moved, I think, by the idea that people in our area had cared enough to restore the original wildlife to this region.

The crisis at Glens Falls had passed with a long night's sleep. Wednesday had been a time to rest and find the laundromat before the short bus ride into Albany, where the *Odeyak* inspired a highly ecumenical supper. Nancy Papish had recruited Jack Sissman to do something for supper that evening. Jack arranged for the Jewish congregation, *Beth Emeth*, to provide dinner for the *Odeyak* travellers at the main Episcopal centre, All Saints Cathedral.

By the time the *Odeyak* was coming into Corning Preserve Nancy was looking for the simplest way to move the *Odeyak* and the travellers from the landing to a press conference on the steps of the New York State Capitol. Portaging the heavy boat on a march up a steep hill through a warehouse district, with 56 northern Native people, including children and elderly people seemed, as one publicist had suggested, like "a dog and pony show." Nancy was also concerned that Robbie Dick would feel obliged to lead such a march despite his heart condition. The lack of a parade permit and police escort foreclosed the prospect of an extended debate. When Larry House asked Nancy for directions for taking the *Odeyak* to the capitol, Nancy directed him to Academy Park and told him to make sure that the truck did not get towed away.

Larry, who had never been to the United States before he became official trucker to the *Odeyak*, "had a stereotype image of everything in the States being big, with big cities all over the place." The experience of pleasant, small towns where people were friendly and interested enough to ask questions about his curious cargo gave him a new sense of confidence. "I'm sure we got more interest expressed than we did in Canada. In Québec or Canada you don't get that kind of reaction. Only from ethnic minorities, such as the Greeks." Larry was surprised and delighted at the helpful attitude of the officials at the capitol buildings. "They let me park on the lawn of the capitol building. We carried it from there right onto the steps of the Legislature."

At The New York State Capitol

There were statements and short speeches and then, as the ceremony on the steps was ending, Nancy Papish was told they had received permission for the *Odeyak* to be brought into the Concourse. The Concourse is the walkway connecting the various buildings of the state complex with the legislature and the ideal place to display the *Odeyak*. People walking by could stop and talk about the boat and its message for New York State, the largest prospective buyer of the power to be produced on the Great Whale River.

Larry House certainly did not know how to drive a truck into the Legislative Concourse. Neither did any of the North River Friends.

Nancy finally told Larry to take the truck behind the complex to the double doors where the busses park.

The stress was beginning to show on a number of people. Robbie Dick actually complained. "My kid is freezing. I'm tired. Get me inside where I can sit down, where it's not cold and my family can eat." In order to meet the noon hour crowd, no lunch had been planned. Nor did anyone realize that the eateries along the Concourse close in mid-afternoon. Doris Delaney found a place that would stay open long enough to serve sandwiches to the visitors. As Nancy was sitting down with Robbie Dick's family a state building official came to say that the truck had to move because the space was needed for the busses coming to pick up the mass exodus of workers. Larry, who had been patiently carting the *Odeyak* and often one or two other boats at every stop, reached his breaking point at the request to move the truck one more time. A restaurant was found down the street where he could enjoy a steak in the quiet company of another hungry Cree traveller before hauling the *Odeyak* the length of the Concourse.

Randy Lu, a North River Friend with a strong network in the Albany area, had arranged dinner at the Albany Free School. Nancy had recruited several friends to roast turkeys and bring them to the school for supper. Kathie Winter, an Albany folk singer, had recruited a number of local Native people to host *Odeyak* travellers and to cook for the feast at the Free School. The hosts, like the travellers, came in families and there was an extraordinary turnout at the Free School dinner. The biggest challenge in going back to the buffet for seconds was the lack of space to walk between the tables.

A slide show and presentations were planned for the evening. North River Friends' hospitality network had arranged for all the travellers to stay in family homes. By the end of the heavy meal most of the *Odeyak* leaders, elders and speakers were falling asleep on their feet. Some of the hosts were disappointed to miss the show when they took their guests home early. Some of the younger or more tireless *Odeyak* people stayed with Nancy Papish and Marie Symes-Grehan to help run the slide show. The second string were able to bring their own experiences and perspectives to spicing up the leaders' and elders' presentations that were by now as familiar as the recounting of the favorite family story-teller.

On Good Friday the *Odeyak* finally left Albany and met the tide waters of the Hudson River. Bob Hanson replaced Dale Rice in the stern of the North River Friends canoe and became the local guide for the *Odeyak*. Bob, an electrical engineer by training, a sailor and canoeist by devotion, has paddled with North River Friends for many years. When Bob sat down with David Masty, Matthew Mukash and Marie Symes-Grehan to plan the first day's paddle, it was agreed to portage the canoes to a point about 16 miles downstream from Albany.

When the *Odeyak* and its two escorts launched at Coxsackie, the weather was clear and the winds were mild. There was no hint of Good Friday in the air. The aim was to arrive in Hudson, New York, in a timely fashion to meet the press and the people of the area who might want to come out to see the *Odeyak*. The tides travel up the Hudson the full 160 miles from the mouth of the river below Manhattan Island to Albany.

Before the three canoes left, Nancy pulled up in her station wagon, opened the tail gate and presented lunch. A great deal of food had been left over the previous night. Knowing what happened when there was no food available in the middle of an arduous day, Nancy had packed the food into her station wagon where it would remain cool overnight. For the next two days, wherever the boat stopped, there was a wagonload of turkey, cider, cheese, fruit and bread.

The 12-mile paddle took the *Odeyak* on a stretch where the rising tide is strong enough at its peak to offset the downstream current. The *Odeyak* with its broad beam and heavy frame found a real advantage being on the water when the tide was on its way out. It was also a delight to be below Albany where the vista of the Hudson Valley takes on a real breadth and the Catskills begin to dominate the view to the west of the river.

When Walter Blank had called Nancy he had asked, "How can I help?"

"Where are you from?'"

"From Ghent, down the river."

"Find a way to feed these people and to sleep them in the City of Hudson. I don't know anybody."

And so Walter Blank made contact with the Elks Lodge, which hosted the *Odeyak* in Hudson. Walter's help was especially valuable because earlier efforts in the Hudson area had resulted in a firm rebuff from a resident who had told an organizer, "Nobody wants to help because they're saying 'The Indians are shooting at helicopters and they don't want to get involved. They don't want them in their homes'."

Doris called Kenneth Deer and explained the situation to him and asked for his advice. Kenneth told Doris what had happened recently at Ganienge from the Mohawk perspective. Shortly before the *Odeyak* had arrived at Kahnawake, a helicopter had flown over Ganienge, the Mohawk encampment in Adirondack Park. Then it had landed. The pilot asked for help getting an ambulance for his passenger who he said was having an urgent medical problem, perhaps a heart attack. After the ambulance left the Mohawks at Ganienge were told that the passenger had been shot while the helicopter was flying over the encampment. The State Troopers then demanded access to the encampment to investigate the incident. The Troopers had been trying to gain access to the encampment for several years without success. When Doris called Kenneth the standoff between the Mohawks of Ganienge and the Troopers was still in progress. Kenneth said he would see what he could do.

> The next morning on the news it was announced that the Mohawks had accepted the State Police list of inspectors. I was very touched. I knew that that had been done by the Mohawks for the safe passage of the Crees. I thought it was a tremendous thing for them to have done that.

The phone rang at the Elks Hall not long after the travellers arrived in Hudson. When someone answered the phone Jeff Wollock asked, "Are there a bunch of Indians and Inuit there?" When we was told there were he said, "Can I please speak to Marie?" Jeff had been working on arrangements for their arrival in New York City without being able to make contact with the *Odeyak* organizers. This was the first time that Jeff had succeeded in contacting the *Odeyak* since it had crossed the border into the United States. "They were due in New York City in less than a week and we had not so much as chatted about what was going to happen down here."

Bob Hanson met with David Masty after the festivities at the Elks Hall to plan the trip from Hudson to Kingston. David thought the crew was ready for a longer paddle. Bob planned a four hour trip that he hoped would bring them into Kingston at about five o'clock on the Saturday afternoon.

The next morning, the bus and the pick-up carrying the *Odeyak* followed Bob's car out of Hudson across the Rip Van Winkle Bridge to the west side of the Hudson, down Route 9W toward Saugerties. Just below Catskill, Route 9W turns off towards the river. A couple of miles down Route 9W Bob recalled that the road goes through a railroad underpass with a very low clearance.

> This is the way I am regularly accustomed to going to Saugerties but I do not usually do the route with a full scale highway bus in tow. I stopped the car and went back to tell the bus driver that I was not sure if he would be able to take his bus under the bridge. He just said, "We'll go there and we'll find out."

When Bob drove through the underpass he got out of his car to watch the bus. From his vantage point, the bus did not have a full hand to spare.

Lynch's Marine, where the *Clearwater* docks in the winter, is owned by Connie Lynch, an older man who values his independence. Bob had made no advance arrangements for the launching. When Connie saw a fleet of four vehicles, including a truck with two canoes he came out to greet them. The alert that Toshi Seeger had sent up and down the river announcing the impending arrival of the *Odeyak* had been heard by Connie Lynch. The man who hosts the *Clearwater* for its winter storage was also pleased to host the launching of the *Odeyak* at Saugerties.

As the *Odeyak* fleet paddled out of Soapus Creek and around the point into the Hudson, Bob Hanson became a little concerned about the wind. The slight breeze inland had given little indication of the wind force on the broad, open Hudson River. A south wind meant paddling steadily into a wind which would more than offset the tide. Whenever there is a current running against the wind the waves become steeper, choppier, more frequent. Although it was going to be a bit rough, Bob decided that none of the early signs suggested giving up the run on the river.

> The *Odeyak* and the Mohawk canoe started to pull out far ahead of the canoe I was sterning. I really did not understand why the others were pulling ahead. We were having a little trouble making it against the wind but I could not see why we should have more trouble than anyone else. At one point I became concerned for the people in my canoe who seemed to be getting very tired.

> About two miles below Saugerties, I was ready to pull the canoes out of the water, but the other two canoes were so far ahead that I could not get their attention.

Bob's canoe had a signal cannon strapped to the bow. The cannon fired ten-gauge shotgun blanks. A couple of shots were fired to get the attention of the other canoes.

> The wind was so strong that not even the sound of the cannon firing would carry upwind the quarter mile distance between our boats. I thought that they were just ignoring us but it was obvious to me that we were having enough trouble in our canoe that we were unlikely to make the distance to Kingston.

When they found a small construction company dock at Glasgo, the North River escort pulled out of the water. One of the people from the construction company drove Bob's crew back to his car. When Bob had a moment to rest it became clear that he was running a high fever. While there had, indeed, been a strong headwind, it was the fevered state of Bob and others in his crew which had caused the North River escort to drop so far behind both its Mohawk twin and the *Odeyak*. Once they were able to view the two other canoes from the shore, Bob saw that the *Odeyak* actually handled the waves better than the lighter Mohawk canoe.

The chance to sight the other boats ploughing down the river came as Bob and his crew drove south from Glasgo looking for shoreline access. Along that stretch of the Hudson there is a lot of private property and not much public access to the water.

> Once, when we drove down a road just upstream from the Kingston-Rhinecliff Bridge, we came to the shack of a shad fisherman. He came out of his house when he saw us drive up. We asked him if he had seen a couple of canoes go by. He had, indeed, seen two canoes. They had just gone into the next cove south to get out of the wind.

> We stayed with the shad fisherman for about 15 minutes until we saw the canoes come out of that cove and head for the next. When we knew that they would make out alright we headed down to Kingston Point where we found a group of about thirty people assembled on the beach watching the canoes come down the Hudson River.

A group of local canoeists from Kingston were heading out to greet the *Odeyak* and the Mohawk escort as the two larger canoes headed out around Kingston Point. Going around the point meant that they had to go further out into the river where the wind was kicking up waves, which were more of a problem than the wind itself.

The local canoeists who went out to meet them wanted to guide our canoes onto a safer course between the point and the breakwater so that they could come into calm water much more quickly. The only problem was that the breakwater was submerged just below the surface at high tide. This shortcut required that the paddlers get out of the canoes and, while they were standing in the ankle-deep, ice-cold water on the slippery rocks of the submerged breakwater, pull the *Odeyak* and the escort over the breakwater.

Once *Odeyak* and its escort were past the point, they proceeded into Kingston Bay on the Roundout Creek. In an earlier day, the City of Kingston was on the hill overlooking the River. The port at the mouth of the Creek was called Roundout Town. The expansion of the city has brought the towns together. The Hudson River Maritime Center at the mouth of Roundout Creek was the safe harbor for which the *Odeyak* and its escort headed as they came off the Hudson that chilly day.

The crowd of six or seven hundred people in the park behind the Maritime Center appeared to be standing shoulder-to-shoulder. Large numbers of hands emerged from the throng to lift the *Odeyak* and the other canoes out of the water. The Grand Chief of the Algonquins,

Richard Kistabish, had come down to meet the Crees and the Inuit. Black Bear, an Iroquois man who runs a trading post near Kingston, came out to dance for the arrival of the *Odeyak*, resplendent in a costume of his own unique design. The *Odeyak* crew did their chant in appreciation of the tremendous turnout on a windy Saturday afternoon in Kingston.

Doris Delaney also came to meet the group in Kingston. She had been in constant touch with Nancy Papish, organizing support along the way. Doris had also spent time with the travellers in Albany. She had already received an anonymous phone call saying that the Mohawk Warriors were going to show up with assault rifles as the *Odeyak* arrived at Battery Park. At first she simply disregarded this report on account of its sheer silliness. When she heard a reference to the same rumor during the brief reception in Kingston, Doris decided that the it could not be disregarded. The concern she shared with Kenneth Deer was that someone would stage an incident, at the expense of the Crees and Inuit, in order to discredit the Mohawks. Kenneth assured her that the Mohawk Warriors would not do anything which might jeopardize the *Odeyak*. He also made plans, at that point, to be in New York for Earth Day, and decided he would be in Battery Park when the *Odeyak* landed.

After the reception at the Maritime Center, the *Odeyak* travellers boarded their bus once again. Half an hour later they arrived at the Wittenberg Center. Jim Davis, the Center's Director describes it as "an alternative learning facility where people from all walks of life can experience indigenous teachers from around the world, particularly Native American teachers." One of the main features of the Wittenberg Center is the *kiva*, or sound chamber, a round, largely subterranean structure with a low dome roof. The kiva, based on a Pueblo design, is a place of healing. As a Native American outreach center, the Wittenberg Center was an ideal resting site for the *Odeyak* travellers at a point when they were reaching a new level of exhaustion. Some of the travellers were showing signs of fever, colds and other minor ailments which might well undermine the remaining five days to New York City. Betsy Stang, the Center's founder and leading light, arranged for a homeopathic healer to come to the Center. He prescribed some homeopathic medicines which the local pharmacy was able to fill.

Easter on the Hudson

The good ship *Clearwater* may be the only large vessel which does not acknowledge a home base. The *Clearwater* sloop club people feel so strongly that their boat belongs to the whole river that it does not sit well with them to think of their flag ship being registered at a single port. Still and for all, the Beacon Sloop Club may sometimes be thought of as a kind of spiritual home if only because of its long standing connection with Pete and Toshi Seeger, the inspirational founders of the *Clearwater* network.

It was fitting that the *Odeyak* would arrive at the Beacon Sloop Club on Easter Sunday, a week after coming into New York State, and a month after the boat had left Cree territory when it headed south from Val d'Or to Ottawa. The *Odeyak* travellers had been looking forward to reaching Beacon as a place of rest and the last country place before they pushed on for the enormity of New York City. It was also the place they would share a feast on Easter day.

Josh Gordon, a Beacon Sloop Club member, had met the *Odeyak* when it arrived in Kingston late on the Saturday afternoon. He had spent the evening with the travellers at the Wittenberg Center to be available the next morning. Josh Gordon was the first guide to paddle in the *Odeyak*.

> I was somewhere midships on the port side. I was able to talk directly to the person in the stern to let him know about the pile of rocks on the Beacon side of the river and to exchange views on the current.

The challenge of the upwind paddle into Kingston had excited a number of the paddlers. People in the alternate crew wanted their chance at an heroic experience in the *Odeyak*. Saturday evening, after the slide show, there was a meeting to plan the next day. Some paddlers wanted to set out the next morning as early and as far upstream as possible while still arriving at Beacon in the mid-afternoon. Easter Sunday seemed to be in some danger of being pre-empted. "All that got resolved when we just didn't have time because people wanted to go to Mass."

> There are not that many choices as to where you can launch a boat on the west shore of the Hudson in this neck of the woods. The Hudson is unique in that the shoreline is fairly well cut off from access by the railroads. There is a railroad track on either side of the Hudson right along the water's edge. Public access is limited on both sides to relatively few places. So we had to decide whether we were going to paddle five miles, ten miles or 15 miles.

The difficulties of launching, the priorities of Easter and the recovery of the travellers who had been ill the night before, all pointed to a short paddle. The drive from the Wittenberg Center to Newburgh, on the eastern shore of the widening river was a two-hour journey which could only begin when those who had gone to church in Woodstock had returned. The sun had come out before the *Odeyak* was launched and heading across the river.

The Beacon Sloop Club dock could not be seen across the river but the smoke rising from John Mylod's cooking fire outside the club house presented a good point for which to head the *Odeyak*. After the landing and the reception by the dock, as people milled about, John's cooking fire became the center of attention for the Crees and the Inuit.

John, the executive director of the *Clearwater*, was preparing a shad bake. "On the Hudson, there is a rich tradition around the shad season." Shad, the largest fish in the herring family, together with the striped bass and Atlantic sturgeon, John explains, are the "fisheries which have been used by people along the river for ten thousand years. When the Crees and Inuit came we tried to share that history through the shad bake. It was a great deal of fun because the *Odeyak* people were very interested in it."

They may have recognized John as a fellow fisherman. During the spring months when the shad head downstream on the Hudson, John and his partner celebrate the river in a time-worn fashion. They fish for shad the last two hours of the incoming tide and the first two hours of the outgoing tide. That way their 20-foot row boat can drift upstream for a time and then come back down for about the same period. It is a time that uses the river's own power both to move the boat and to set the drift net. "You try to get the slow part of the tide so that the net hangs in the water right and it fishes correctly."

Shad are currently out of fashion, John will tell a visitor. He will also point out that the fish that spawn in the Hudson have been threatened by a Canadian hydro-electric power project. Shad are out of fashion because they are "very bony and have quite a bit of oil. People who are used to effortless eating do not enjoy shad. Most people these days like the shad roe." When the Hudson shad go out to sea they head as far north as the Bay of Fundy before going to Florida for the winter. This annual migration was threatened when New Brunswick proposed to dam the Bay of Fundy to harness its enormous tidal power to generate electrical power. The threat faced by his own fishery gave John all the more reason to share the secrets of the shad with the Cree and Inuit visitors. One such secret is called planking.

It is a cooking method that was done on the Hudson long before any of us came around. You attach the fish to an oak board which is placed standing vertically near an open fire. It is a way to cook outdoors without cooking on a grill. The way you do it now is to nail the fish right to the board. In the old days, folks would have attached it some other way, driving pegs into the cracks in the wood. It provides an ability to cook the fish and have the oil run out.

The Hudson shad bake touched a very deep place, a place deep enough that it felt safe and good to share differences among the various kinds of river people who gathered to celebrate their rivers that Easter afternoon. A couple of Inuit asked John if he would give them some un-cooked shad. Another told him that his mother was very fond of eating her fish frozen. The next day, when a second potluck supper was served, John brought some shad he had put into his freezer the night before.

The Beacon Sloop Club potluck suppers usually lean heavily toward the vegetarian with such highly varied dishes as beans, lentils and tofu. But when the membership put out word about Cree and Inuit visitors from the far north, the group was able to locate an amazing amount of red game meat. Robbie Niquanicappo had been having increasing difficulty showing enthusiasm for beef stew night after night. When he saw the two different venison stews his capacity for profound delight was fully re-stored. And the sight of caribou raised his enthusiasm to new heights.

Most of the *Odeyak* travellers had been billeted with local families. For the fourth time in as many weeks, the Crees and Inuit would have the chance to visit and spend time in the actual homes of their hosts. Stella Masty, and her father Isaac stayed with Jay Armour's family.

> We stayed up quite late that night because he brought a big album of pic-tures of what his land is actually like up there. It was very interesting sitting down with him, my wife and I, and looking through the pictures while his daughter was in the other room doing her homework. She had to do her homework. Even though she was on the trip she still had to keep up with her school work.

> The next day probably two dozen of them came over to the house and did their laundry, basically hung out around the yard and stuff. Later in the afternoon we took about ten of them up to the malls. We left that group up there and came back down while others did their laundry.

The Crees' and Inuit's interest in shopping malls was something of a surprise, even a disappointment to some of their hosts. There was a similar jarring of ideals and reality at the frequency of ATVs (all terrain vehicles) and snowmobiles in the photo albums the travellers displayed. The dissonance may have helped some of the hosts sort out issues, such as the family car, in their own lives. Most of the Beacon people could not have known that the malls, for which the sloop club devotees may have had an understandable disdain, to the *Odeyak* people represented a safe haven. While the malls were an attraction, the streets of Manhattan were a threat that loomed ahead of the northern Natives. The technology which everyone felt comfortable sharing was the camera. Jay Armour's family have a small farm. When the visitors saw a turkey strutting around the yard they wanted a picture of themselves holding the large bird.

The Sloop Club offered a special opportunity for the elders and others who had shown their appreciation for many of their host groups in ways which freed both groups from the constraints of language. When the bird calls were done out of doors, beside the river, they took on a whole different character. John Mylod described it.

Our folks were just enthralled when some *Odeyak* people did their goose calls as some geese were going over and the geese turned around and landed. When people here saw that the calls really worked they tried to learn to do it.

The music that is so much a part of the Sloop Club tradition had a different flavor to Josh Gordon on the evenings of the *Odeyak* visit.

At the Beacon Sloop Club, we always play music. When the *Odeyak* people were there we traded songs. We would do a song and then they would do a song. We sort of performed for each other. That was a very good feeling.

There was a real community aspect to it. Although people were tired and they had been on the road and were kind of displaced, they were also happy to be making the trip. I didn't see anybody who was full of regret. People were doing it because they really believed that it would make a difference. Everyone, even the people on the bus who never paddled, were a part of the travelling community. It was a good community feeling.

Last Stop — Yonkers

After a pancake breakfast cooked over an outdoor fire at the Beacon Sloop Club on Tuesday morning the Great Whale people set off once again. Coming down the Hudson, Yonkers, New York, is the last city before the great metropolis. If Manhattan has the shape of a fountain pen nib, Yonkers is the base of the pen, just where the forefinger sits. The nib is a peninsula, bounded by the Hudson River on one side and Long Island Sound on the other.

Yonkers neighbours New York City, but it is an independent municipality beyond the subway line. It is one of the oldest cities in the Hudson River Valley. Yonkers was the natural staging ground for the *Odeyak's* final paddle down the Hudson River into the harbor of New York City. The welcome and hospitality organized by the Ferry Sloop Club, an independent affiliate of the *Clearwater* network, enjoyed surprisingly warm support from the City of Yonkers.

The Ferry Sloop Club, according to Gretchen McHugh, is a group originally founded to build boats as a strategy for cleaning up their own river. When Pete Seeger and a friend built the *Clearwater*, part of Seeger's vision was that smaller boats, built by the people themselves, would join the *Clearwater* in its work of making the Hudson River the pride of the people who live by it. The hosting of the *Odeyak* by the *Clearwater* network lies in the commonality of the dreams of the *Clearwater* people and the *Odeyak* people.

Bob Walters was president of Ferry Sloops when Doris Delaney first called him to ask about tide charts for the lower river. He lives in New Rochelle, directly across the peninsula from Yonkers, on the Long Island Sound side where he runs the Energy Saver Store. He is putting together a history of the Hudson River from a collection of turn-of-the-century postcards. Bob recalled some of his efforts to co-ordinate the *Odeyak* visit to the area.

> It was interesting trying to persuade Yonkers officials to let us use their building. One of the things that seemed to influence them was when I pointed out that right next door to that building was the site of one of the major villages of the Napinack, the original people of this area. The mouth of the Nepperhan River was a traditional Native American encampment. That seemed to persuade city officials that it was right for the Crees and the Inuit to camp there in the shelter of the Youth Center. Once they were convinced that there was a tie between the history of Yonkers and Native Americans they became very receptive to sharing their building.

Gretchen McHugh, a photographer for the *Riverside Press* and a devoted member of Ferry Sloops, first heard about the *Odeyak* from Bob Hansen, the *Odeyak's* guide from Albany to Kingston. Bob is a captain of the *Sojourner Truth*, the Ferry Club's own sloop. Gretchen would become so absorbed in the struggle of the Crees and the Inuit to preserve their river that, although she was also working on her captain's ticket on the *Sojourner Truth*, she would get out sailing only once during the next year. Later she would travel twice to Whapmagoostui and Kuujjuaraapik to do photo stories, once in the summer and once in the winter.

Mid-afternoon, on Tuesday, April 17, 1990, the *Odeyak* travellers arrived at the Yonkers Youth Center. A rising wind and a threatening storm had persuaded them not to put the *Odeyak* in the water that day. The more so since the official arrival at Yonkers would not take place until the following day. Bob or Gretchen or someone from Ferry Sloops had been inspired to create a banner reading, "WELCOME TO YONKERS" in Cree and Inuit syllabics. When Ferry Sloop people had asked Jeff Wollock to find out how to make the syllabic figures the request was answered by a fax from the Whapmagoostui Band Council office spelling out the message in the figures from the two different syllabaries.

Doug Maas had arrived at the Beacon Sloop Club pancake breakfast expecting to be the *Odeyak's* guide on the water. When river conditions seemed prohibitive he had led the *Odeyak* caravan as slowly as he could down toward Yonkers. The wind and tides had not discouraged Richard Kistabish and Roland Chamberlain. When they woke at first light, Richard and Roland, who had slept in the park beside the river, had launched their Grumman while the river was still calm and quiet. Several hours later, they realized that the *Odeyak* would not be joining them. With the incoming tide and rising wind behind them, Richard and Roland headed upstream. They got back to the Beacon Sloop Club about eight o'clock only to be told that the *Odeyak* caravan had just left. The Grand Chief of the Algonquins would not meet up with the *Odeyak* until the following evening, at the second supper in Yonkers.

Finding the extra time available, the Crees and Inuit had happily accepted the suggestion of visiting the Jefferson Mall along the way. In a stroke of diplomatic genius, Doug Maas made a point of introducing the *Odeyak* leaders to the manager of the mall, with whom he was acquainted. She expressed great delight in welcoming people from such a distance to her mall. She also advised her security staff to welcome them. The Yonkers area was, in 1990, in the process of becoming more racially diversified as upwardly mobile Afro-Americans moved to the suburbs. The Crees and Inuit were dressed more for camping or canoeing than for a suburban shopping mall. Doug's pre-emptive introduction ensured their welcome. But even the delights of Jefferson Mall could only stretch the one-hour drive from Beacon to Yonkers until mid-afternoon.

The arrival of the *Odeyak* in mid-afternoon was, at first, a source of some concern to Bob Walters as the key organizer. He had hoped they would not arrive until several hours later when a full scale barbecue would be in progress behind the Youth Center. Their early arrival had Bob wondering just how to cope with the need to provide a lunch to a group of hungry campers waiting for supper.

Almost as soon as the problem had presented itself, the solution appeared. A young Black man from New Jersey, Arnold Davenport, hitchhiking back from visiting a cousin had managed — through a process no one could later re-construct — to attach himself to the *Odeyak* bus. Nancy Papish says that throughout the trip down the Hudson, Arnold was always careful to disappear whenever the *Odeyak* people were eating or engaged in a presentation. He never imposed himself on the group for food or shelter. But he always managed to arrive just as the bus was ready to pull out each day. He had also consistently made himself useful whenever he was around and anyone had asked for help. Marie had persistently encouraged Arnold to find his own way to New York for the first three days that he was around. Finally, it became apparent that neither the Inuit nor the Crees were going to turn their backs on a fellow traveller who did not get in their way.

Now, shortly after the *Odeyak* caravan had arrived at the Yonkers Youth Center, a car with New Jersey plates pulled in. The young man had kept in touch with his parents, telling them of his progress and asking them to meet him when he got close to home. His parents and sister arrived with Arnold's birthday dinner: two turkeys and enough trimmings to feed the busload. Sometime during the feast that followed, Mrs. Davenport told Marie a little about growing up Black and Cherokee on a southern farm and coming north with her husband many years ago. Two years later, Bob Walters remembered the gratitude felt when the Davenport's miraculous meal appeared to tide everyone over until his barbecue was ready. He also wished he had taken down their names and phone number.

Although the barbecue organized by the Ferry Sloop Club grew out of the necessity of offering a meal to guests, a series of surprisingly generous donations elevated the event to a festivity that remained in the minds of everyone who was there. The time to put out the word and receive the donations was, no doubt, also an important factor. A sense of friendly competition with the Beacon Club may also have played a part.

Bob had been in touch with Doris Delaney as the *Odeyak* had progressed down the Hudson River. He had heard the stories of beef stew in one church basement or community hall after another. Ferry Sloop had succeeded in finding hospitality in the homes of members and friends for most of the travellers. Only a very few would actually sleep in the Youth Center. Bob also ensured that beef stew would not be on the menu in Yonkers. "Caribou meat is a little hard to come by in Westchester County," is the way Bob begins to tell how he managed to do it. "As it turned out a local hunter had caribou meat stored in his freezer which he was pleased to bring to the barbecue."

Two gifts of shad, one fresh and one frozen, competed with the delight of caribou from their own home region. More frozen shad had been sent down from Beacon when John Mylod found a car heading toward Yonkers. He knew that Mina Weetaltuk and other Inuit elders had particularly enjoyed the fresh frozen uncooked shad he had been able to bring to their second supper at Beacon. The fresh shad came from Ron Ingold. Bob often fishes with Ron during shad season. Ron Ingold is a fishing man whose family had been taking their livelihood from the Hudson since before the American Revolution. Ingold could not get away from his nets to go to a barbecue at the height of the shad run, so instead he sent a hundred pounds of fresh-caught fish.

Father Tom Martin, the Anglican priest from Great Whale who had just flown down from Québec, walked into the Solidarity Foundation office on West 52nd Street in Manhattan carrying 45 pounds of caribou under his arm. Matthew Mukash and Denny Alsop walked into Jeff Wollock's office about the same time.

> They said that they wanted to get up to Yonkers as fast as possible. I said that the fastest way would be to take the train. It was rush hour. ... We ran down the street to the 50th Street subway stop, went down to 42nd Street, Times Square. There was a long series of tunnels down which they ran to get to the shuttle to Grand Central Station. At Grand Central Station they ran up stairs, bought tickets and just caught the train that was about to leave. And we were off to Yonkers.

Jeff recalls the trip to Yonkers as a "dreamlike experience." He had had to suddenly guide three people who had never been on a New York subway through the crush of rush hour traffic and onto the Metro North commuter rain.

> Tom is a very big guy and was carrying 45 pounds of caribou. I remember Denny talking on the train about how horrible New York is. I was really insulted. I'm a New Yorker.

The place where the people were staying was right on the river by the train station. The whole trip took us 45 minutes from New York to Yonkers. Everybody was there and it was amazing.

When Gretchen McHugh arrived, "It was overwhelming to walk in and see so many people and the kids galloping up and down. It was really kind of exciting." Mina Weetaltuk frequently coped with the crowds and the concrete by finding a quiet place at the edge of the crowd where she could gaze out on the hills or the river or the sky as she sat smoking a cigarette. Gretchen began her own year-long photo coverage of the *Odeyak* story trying to capture the deeply etched beauty of Mina's face. "Every time she would see the camera she would smile." Besides the photo story, an enduring friendship grew out of the smiles exchanged between Mina and Gretchen.

The simple urge to offer hospitality broke through the kind of stereotypes that continue, in Gretchen's experience, to haunt many southern adults from their school books.

> There was a big area where they could have all slept in sleeping bags on the floor but we found out pretty fast that they much preferred to sleep in people's houses and have showers and stuff.

We just didn't know how primitively they lived. All I could think of were Inuit in igloos and stuff. So it was all very interesting to see that they lived pretty much like us.

Quite late that night, a few of the more adventurous travellers had a small taste of a New York scene, made familiar to them in the distant north through television and which fulfilled some of their worst stereotypes of the Big City. Well after the barbecue, when most of the travellers had gone to their billets, Bob Walters decided to go shopping for some food for the next morning.

A few of the Cree people came with me when I went to the Shop-Rite Supermarket. We went down to see the *Clearwater* which had come in and was tied up at the Yonkers City Pier. But the pier is in an old and sort of eerie section of town. The Crees did not feel very good walking around that section. They wanted to get back to the comfort and security of the building.

The official welcome in Yonkers, as in Burlington and Albany, came the day after the actual arrival. Wednesday morning, the caravan went back up the river the 12 miles from Yonkers to Tarrytown. Meanwhile, elders who were not paddling and the students, Stella and Randy, did a presentation at a school in the Riverdale section of the Bronx. Parents with young children had a much needed quiet day in the homes where they were billeted before they went on to New York.

The quiet time also provided an opportunity for a celebration which had been missed on Easter Sunday. Although some of the travellers had gone to church in Woodstock there had been no opportunity for a service in their own language. So Father Martin, with the co-operation of the Episcopal Church in Yonkers, conducted a joint Inuit-Cree communion service. At home he conducts separate services in each language, so this was an innovation inspired by the challenges of travel. Father Martin is emphatic that his linguistic dexterity consists primarily of a "sufficient command of the prayer book that I can switch back and forth between languages from one section to the next."

The *Odeyak* and Mohawk escort crews travelled in the van. Larry House trucked the *Odeyak* and the Mohawk escort. Bob Walters led the caravan.

We launched at Tarrytown from the Washington Irving Boat Club. It is really a working man's club. It's what they call a member club. It is more blue collar workers. It's not one of these yacht clubs. They have quite big boats but everybody participates in the maintenance of the place. That gives it a little bit of a different atmosphere from some clubs where there is a staff to wait on the members.

Normally, there is a big sign at the boat launch "$25 to launch your boat." When I got hold of the commodore of the boat club I was concerned that he might be a stickler for the rules. So when we all showed up that morning, I went over to speak to him. Just out of courtesy, I asked him, "How much do we owe you for putting the boats in the water on your launch?"

"Well, I kind of understand what these people are doing and I'd never charge them."

Ralph Childers was to be the guide from Tarrytown to Yonkers. Ralph "is a kayaker who has done some paddling in Alaska. He is not a great expert on that stretch of the river but it is a pretty straight run." Gilbert Dick has a vivid recollection of the river on that last leg before Manhattan.

The rivers were almost the same as ours but the water was different. There were such dirty waters! Especially when the canoe was lifted out of the water and you could see the line from the oil in the river. You could even smell it. That's what we want to protect. Our clean waters.

The oil from the river's surface may have provided the extra finish that Caroline Weetaltuk felt the *Odeyak* needed to improve its glide. Gretchen recalls that when the *Odeyak* and the Mohawk escort arrived at the Yonkers Boys' Canoe Club, "they came thundering in," with a strong tail wind pushing them. The Mohawk escort, designed to move along fast, missed one strong turn and capsized as it approached the dock.

"When the *Odeyak* landed, Ralph made a point of landing his kayak off to the side out of the way." Later, Bob Walters went over to Ralph to thank him for guiding the *Odeyak* down the river. "What do you mean," Ralph asked Bob, "I have to thank you for letting me be the guide. How often does a white man get to be the guide for a group of Native American explorers?"

Once the City of Yonkers had been persuaded that welcoming the *Odeyak* connected Yonkers with its own historical roots as a site of Aboriginal settlement, it seemed quite natural that Mayor Hank Stallone would want to come by the Youth Center to welcome his City's visitors from the Far North. Only when the festivities were well past would some of the local people reflect that Mayor Stallone had not previously been "known for embracing liberal causes." Indeed, he had been elected, according to Bob Walters, "on an anti-housing campaign."

On Wednesday afternoon what was important was that Mayor Stallone "was quite wonderful in his greeting to the Crees and the Inuit." The Mayor not only greeted the *Odeyak* as it landed, he or his staff had considered what he might give the visitors as a present.

The only thing they could find that was appropriate was the large bronze medals which Yonkers presents to everyone who enters their annual marathon. He made a big ceremony of draping the big medal a with a red, white and blue ribbon, over the head of a member of each family. The *Odeyak* travellers certainly were, when they reached Yonkers, on the verge of completing a marathon.

After each *Odeyak* family had received a medal there was one medal left. [The master of ceremonies] looked around the room, spotted Bob Walters and said, "Oh, give Bob Walters a medal."

So Chief Robbie Dick was deputized to present Bob Walters with a marathon medal on behalf of the Mayor of Yonkers. For Bob, receiving the medal from Chief Robbie Dick was a very special thing. Sarah Bennett, the Inuit town councillor and elementary school teacher who had helped supervise the Inuit children throughout the trip, moved the Ferry Sloop people with the simplicity and sincerity of her statement during the official welcome. Gretchen, who lives in the Riverside section of the Bronx adjacent to Yonkers, works for a local newspaper and edits the Ferry Sloop newsletter, had been pleased and delighted at the presence of Mayor Stallone. "Then later I read that Yonkers was one of the communities that accepted $50,000 from the New York Power Authority to allow the Marcy South line to come through to Long Island."

The official greetings and the barbecue were followed by an evening of singing and story telling. Kenneth Deer had arrived from Kahnawake to join Mike Canoe in the Mohawk escort for the final day's paddle into New York City. Richard Kistabish, Grand Chief of the Algonquins, had arrived in Yonkers late Tuesday night. He had spent Wednesday exploring the Hudson in his pollution-proof Grumman aluminum canoe and joined the festivities at the Canoe Club. Grand Chief Matthew Coon Come and Bill Namagoose, the Executive Director of the Grand Council of the Crees (Québec), had also re-joined the trip.

When the last song was sung and the last story told, Crees from Whapmagoostui and Inuit from Kuujjuaraapik went to sleep in Yonkers in the company of their spiritual teachers, their priest, and their political leaders. Tomorrow they would leave the hospitality of the sloop clubs to paddle their small craft into New York Harbor.

Chapter 8:
River Talk, Legal Talk

Flyways and Byways

As their bus came into Dorval on the last leg of the drive from New York, one thought was uppermost in the minds of the *Odeyak* travellers: Goose Break. They could certainly not have known, when they stored the *Odeyak* at Kahnawake in anticipation of further trips down south that both Kahnawake and Kanesatake, the two Mohawk communities near Montréal, would be under siege for much of the summer. In the fall, when hostilities between Québec and the Mohawk Nation had subsided, the Great Whale communities did take the *Odeyak* to Québec City.

Like most adventures the voyage of the *Odeyak* had also been an ordeal. Robbie Niquanicappo, Whapmagoostui's Deputy Chief who frequently travels down south, described it as "the experience of a lifetime." But now it was time to be home. The best possible way to shake off the dust of the road and the dirtiness of the southern waters was to be out on their own river and the islands along Hudson Bay. Goose Break celebrates both the arrival of the birds in the late spring and their departure in the early fall. For the Crees of Whapmagoostui and the Inuit of Kuujjuaraapik, the coming and going of the geese are the surest signs of the changing seasons in the near Arctic.

Now that many of North America's rivers are wrapped in concrete and are difficult to find even on a map, it is hard for us to remember how much we need the rivers to sustain us. In some cities residents think of the rivers only when their sewers back up or when they overflow during sudden late summer storms. Vine Deloria, a Sioux philosopher and lawyer, invited to speak in Cleveland, Ohio, wanted to remind his audience that the Cuyahoga River was once a source of sustenance and pleasure. He congratulated the white people who had made the river flammable. Indians, he said, would have lacked the imagination to make a river go up in flames.

The willingness to ignore such gentle prodding spans the time from well before the start of James Bay One in 1971 and continues three years after the first voyage of the *Odeyak* when the Crees and Inuit of Great

Whale are still waiting for a proper environmental assessment. News reports recently identified places in the St. Lawrence River where seagoing ships take care to avoid plumes of waste water from aluminum smelters so as not to damage their steel hulls. The humor of the *Odeyak* travellers about coating their boat with floating contaminants to make it go faster has become the daily news of the great river of Québec. Fortunately, the seven states with which Canada shares the immense St. Lawrence-Great Lakes waterway are all upstream. Unfortunately, many of those states tolerate pollution that is no less abusive of this shared but uncommon waterway.

One way to begin to change the quality of our own relationship with the land is to visualize the continent through the rivers that are its veins and arteries. The rivers of this vast area flow in every direction as they bathe and drain the mountains, plains and lowlands. Before they were made flammable, toxic and acidic, these rivers and their countless tributaries made the land fertile and habitable. They were also the highways and byways which brought peoples together.

The Goose Break to which the *Odeyak* travellers returned also represented a connection with the river systems down the entire length of the continent. The flocks of water fowl that come to Great Whale are among the ones that migrate from Hudson Bay and James Bay to spend the winters along other waterways and inland seas far to the south. Along Chesapeake Bay people are accustomed to saying goodbye to the geese which winter in their area two or three weeks before the same flocks are greeted by the Crees and Inuit. Great Canada geese spend the summer teaching their young to fly near the eel grass at the mouth of the Great Whale River. The goslings must be ready for flight by the time of the early frost when they will join vast flocks for the flight of fifteen hundred miles or more to the southern home their parents left in the spring. Along the way they will spend time in the lakes of southern Ontario and Québec, New York and New England, recovering their strength until the frosted air of winter pushes them on their southern flight once again.

The future of the eel grass where the geese and ducks make their nests along the shore of Hudson and James Bay is no less important to those who still depend, to any significant extent, on wild or country food, whether they live in Vermont, Virginia or Ungava. In late 20th century North America, however, few of us still depend on wild food. Our basic survival needs do not connect us viscerally with the land around us so it is hard to appreciate how much the rivers of this continent sustain the land.

The Moral Equivalent of Famine

A century ago, William James talked of the need for "the moral equivalent of war." He had in mind something which would provide all the rigorous experience without the death and destruction that have periodically ravaged our civilization. If the loss of immediate dependence on the land around us leads to a lack of appreciation for the rivers that sustain that land, then we may also need the moral equivalent of drought and famine. We may need an occasion when we learn that the capacity to haul fruit and vegetables and meat from distant corners of the world is not a license to annihilate the land and rivers on which we live.

The "moral equivalent" of famine would also be an occasion to move past the puerile environmental debate as to whether the land and its rivers are to be appreciated for their own sake or to be valued as resources. There is an essential partnership between a land and the people who live on the land. As in any healthy intimate relationship, there is no line between common economic activity and exchanging energies of a higher order. The greater issue for middle America, including that great strip along the border where the bulk of Canadians live, is not the resolution of such an ethereal debate. It is the apparent license to exhaust their own region and then make up for the self-inflicted deficits by outbidding the local people for the produce from poorer areas of the world. Hydro and its dependents can not imagine that there are people who do not want to participate in this process. In this imaginative failure they are no different from those great Americans and Canadians who have paved their fruit lands and wrapped their rivers in concrete. A moral equivalent of famine may restore the imaginations in which we visualize, depending primarily on the resources in our own locale and region, and our nearest neighbors for our survival.

At the very least we may come to appreciate that such self-sufficiency may be a most sensible choice for the peoples of the North. One of the minor lessons the peoples of the Great Whale have learned, shopping in Chissasibi, is that the ample food supplies ensured by the road from the south are not at all equivalent to their natural or country food counterparts. The frozen steak, chicken and fish that appear in the local store, compared to caribou, goose or the fish of the La Grande, have three serious deficiencies. First, they simply do not taste the same. Secondly, they do not have the same nutritional ingredients. Thirdly, they are not affordable for most Crees or Inuit. Extending the road to the Great Whale will not solve any of these problems.

The *Odeyak* offered both her travellers and those who came out to meet them something of William James' moral equivalent. At the very least, it provided an opportunity to renew the sense of connection with their own river and to develop a neighborly connection between river peoples. The thought of harnessing a river for its power so far north of the places the power would actually be used — the same thought that so excited Robert Bourassa — created a debate in New York and New England because *it was seen as a threat to their own regions as well as to the peoples of Ungava.* For the Crees of Whapmagoostui and the Inuit of Kuujjuaraapik, the first voyage of the *Odeyak* was an opportunity to experience the animals and trees that find their habitat along rivers not very different from their own except for being much farther south. Travelling on a river from which it was unsafe to drink a cup of water was a foretaste of the disaster threatening their own waterways. Meeting people of many cultures who value their rivers no less than the Northerners value theirs, inspired the travellers and gave them messages of encouragement to sustain their communities through the battles which lay ahead. In short, the *Odeyak* provided the Crees and Inuit a glimpse of their own future, at its worst and also at its best.

The Plea for Peace

The Crees' reaction to this glimpse into their own future became an important factor in the discussions at their annual General Assembly the summer after Oka, Meech Lake and the *Odeyak*. The Assembly brings together people, chiefs and leaders from all nine Cree communities in Québec. The Assembly held at Great Whale allowed the Inuit of Kuujjuaraapik to gain a sense of what the other Cree communities were saying. It was the first gathering at which the Aboriginal people were able to respond to Hydro's announcement that their imminent intention to proceed with the project did not include time for an environmental assessment.

The Cree elders had several concerns. The young people from all the Cree communities were quite vocal in expressing their anger. Some young people blamed the elders for signing an *Agreement* that they felt neither Canada nor Québec had any intention of honoring. Other people felt that their Assembly needed to stake out a distinct Cree policy and clarify positions, real or imputed, which had emerged during the collapse of the Meech Lake Accord and the summer-long crisis at Kanesatake. There was some fear that the model of the Mohawk Warrior Society might spread and that young people might direct their hatred of the project against individual Hydro-Québec workers.

John Petagumskum, the leading elder of Whapmagoostui, under-stood what the young people were feeling. As a delegate to the Assembly, he spoke, as he would continue to speak in less formal surroundings, to the sentiments growing among the most dedicated and committed young Crees.

> I asked them to make a resolution that it is not Cree, even if we are unhappy about something, to pick up a gun to fight. As Cree people, we don't even have time to think that way. First of all, we never learned to be warriors or military people. We were not taught anything like this. So even if we are angry it is not given to us to think, "I am going to take up arms to destroy another person." We were given two things. First of all, we were given our physical bodies; then we were also given our souls. If we take up arms in this way we have killed our own souls.

Petagumskum's address was one of the memorable events of the Assembly. It was important that the resolution, though it was not a change in Cree policy, was adopted. Matthew Mukash says that the inter-pretation of John's statement is very complex. "What he is saying is 'Don't kill. The person is being pushed into his actions by the corporation itself, by something that is not real. It is not the person that you hate but the corporation.' He is telling us that this battle can only be won with our minds."

The Campaign to Save Great Whale, 1990-1992

John Petagumskum's resolution voiced the consensus of the General As-sembly of the Cree nation at a moment when the campaign to save the Great Whale River was about to rapidly escalate. Over the next two years this campaign would surface on many fronts, all of them non-violent, most centering on an appeal to public opinion either in Québec or in the North-eastern States. Parallel to the public appeals, the Crees embarked on a series of legal challenges in the Québec Superior Court and the Federal Court. Legal challenges were also made to Hydro's export contracts in Vermont and in New York. Scattered through the challenges in the courts and quasi-judicial tribunals such as the National Energy Board of Canada and the Vermont Public Service Board were submissions to committees of the Québec National Assembly and the Parliament of Canada.

The campaign to save the Great Whale River had, in fact, been going on for some time before the *Odeyak*. Hydro-Québec's announcement, in May, 1989, that it was prepared to proceed with the Great Whale hydro-electric project was not the first time, nor indeed the last time the project would be announced. Earlier intentions to proceed with the Great Whale had been postponed in favor of other developments within the La Grande

Basin, the area of James Bay One. There is a an ambiguous and passing reference to Great Whale in the *James Bay and Northern Québec Agreement*. Québec authorities take the provision to mean that the *Agreement* includes provision for them to proceed with Great Whale. The Grand Council says that the reference in the *Agreement* provides only that there will be discussions. Québec's lawyers have not raised the province's claim that the *Agreement* confers a legal right to proceed in any of the many court challenges between the Crees and Québec.

Matthew Mukash and Marie Symes-Grehan had begun to develop an anti-project task force in December of 1989, two months before Denny Alsop presented the Great Whale councils with the idea of building a special canoe with which to travel to New York City in time for Earth Day, 1990.

From April, 1990, when the *Odeyak* arrived in New York, and for the next two years, the campaign to save the Great Whale became an all-encompassing preoccupation for a much larger body than the two Great Whale communities. Almost everything done by the leaders or senior officials of the Grand Council of the Crees (of Québec) during that time was shaped or informed by the Great Whale campaign. The Cree School Board developed a curriculum which, in turn, was integrated with a public awareness campaign in every Cree community. Southern support groups sprang up throughout New York and New England.

The small group of organizations which might be called a grass roots network but only in the original and loosest sense of that phrase, included at various times, the Vermont Coalition for Peace and Justice and the Vermont Coalition to Save James Bay, PROTECT (a long-standing opponent of the Marcy Power Line from James Bay One in central New York), the James Bay Defense Coalition and the James Bay Action Team in New York City, and in Massachusetts the North East Alliance, the Massachusetts Coalition to Save James Bay and Stewardship. The Student Environmental Action Coalition on campuses throughout New York and New England took up the cause of the Great Whale River. Their efforts together with the newsletters and tabloids published with the help of other local grass roots groups may have provided more Canadian geography and Native history than many of their readers had received in all their years of formal education.

There was also periodic support from some of the major environmental organizations in the United States whose assistance for specific major events was often crucial. The Sierra Club's support for the development of the James Bay Task Force, which met monthly for over a year, helped bring many of the grass roots people together periodically. The

Natural Resources Defence Council came to develop a major interest in the environmental impact of the Great Whale project, both as it would affect the local environment and in its continental implications.

The local and regional public appeal campaigns had a life of their own. Very often they happened when the local community was able to organize a special event or when an annual event was able to include a Great Whale focus. But these public appeal campaigns also had a number of connections with the legal challenges brought by the Crees in one forum after another. The first and strongest connection was the simple need of the Cree leadership to spread their energies over several different fronts.

Secondly, the courts made a series of imaginative and sometimes surprising decisions at strategic moments in the larger political campaign. Whether the Canadian and Québec governments would comply with the court rulings was often a question of real concern both to the Crees and to Canadian court watchers. Indeed, what would become the most important single case came to center on the denial by Canada and Québec that they had binding legal obligations under the *Agreement* particularly in regard to an environmental assessment.

Thirdly, the Cree fight came to focus on the demand for an environmental assessment. The Crees had consistently said that if a proper and thorough assessment were held the project would never go ahead. An assessment is, itself, a quasi-judicial process. In the absence of any recognition by the various governments of an obligation to conduct an environmental assessment, the Crees were obliged to turn simultaneously to public appeals and to the courts.

The public appeals were often made through their supporters in the Northeastern States. Through the winter of 1991 much of the appeal was tied in to the town meetings in Vermont. Most of the legal battles during the same time were in Canada. This meant there was a real need for American supporters to try to understand events unfolding in Canadian courts.

The story of the Cree challenges to Québec and Canada in the Canadian courts deserves to be told here because it is arguably the critical piece to a number of puzzles. First, the decisions of the courts are what have moved the governments to finally agree to an environmental assessment. Secondly, the Crees have had to function in an environment in which it was acceptable for the Deputy Premier of Québec to accuse them of disloyalty to the Québec State because they repudiated her policies. If the U.S. Vice-President, Dan Quayle, had talked about minority groups in the terms Lise Bacon applied to the Crees, he would have been impeached. In this atmosphere, the recognition by the courts that these policies were illegal did more than lend credibility to the Crees' case. The Federal Court of Canada ruling that the Canada-Quebec agreement of November 15, 1990, consituted an illegal conspiracy by the Canadian and Québec governments to violate the *James Bay and Northern Québec Agreement* was one of the most damning indictments of the federal Indian policy.

The Battle for James Bay in the Courts

Any attempt to outline the legal battles over the Great Whale River must begin by acknowledging the earliest court challenge brought by the James Bay Crees. In the early 1970s, the first word that the Crees heard of Québec's plans to bulldoze their lands for the original James Bay Project was from the newspaper reports of Premier Bourassa's announcement. The Grand Council of the Crees (of Québec) was founded, at that time, in order to provide a unified voice for the nine Cree communities. Earlier efforts had demonstrated that the distinct interests of the Crees could not be represented through the southern-based but nominally province-wide Indians of Québec Association.

One of the first major acts of the Grand Council of the Crees was to bring a motion in Québec Superior Court seeking an interlocutory or temporary injunction against the work which had already begun on James Bay One. This case, brought in the names of the chiefs and councillors of the nine Cree and fifteen Inuit communities, became known as *Kanatewat et al.* It went on for more than six months and became the longest trial, up to that time, in the history of Québec. Trappers who had never been in a court before described their way of life in order to establish their claim to an Aboriginal title to their land. At that time the courts in Canada had not yet recognized the principle of an Aboriginal right. Scientists who had toured the river system under the guidance of the elders testified on the likely impact of the construction on the natural ecology and on the way of life of the Crees. In his book, *Strangers Devour the Land*, Boyce Richardson, who sat through more of the proceedings than anyone except possibly the judge, substantially captures both the experience and substance of the long hearings.

At the end, Mr. Justice Albert Malouf brought down his decision granting an injunction. The judgment carefully elaborated the harm to the Cree and Inuit ways of life which could be anticipated if the project were allowed in the form in which it had been proposed.

The Québec and Ontario *Northern Boundary Extension Acts* of 1912 each contained identical provisions requiring the two provinces, as a condition of their acquiring lands being transferred to them, to negotiate treaties on behalf of the federal government. Although the Crees on the Ontario side of James Bay would later say that Treaty Nine was "an unconscionable transaction," Ontario had made at least a nominal effort to comply with its constitutional obligations. Québec, sixty years after agreeing to the terms under which it acquired the land, continued to deny that either the Crees or the Inuit had the fundamental rights of human beings.

If the trial was one of the longest, the appeal was one of the shortest. After a three day hearing the Québec Court of Appeal overturned Judge Malouf's decision. After a hearing in which the burden of proof for maintaining the judgment was largely put on the Crees and the Inuit, the Appeal Court made a ruling focussed on "the balance of convenience," which simply did not address the Aboriginal rights of the Native peoples or the threat posed to their way of life. On any less politically loaded issue the reversal in the Appeal Court would have meant that the Native peoples had lost. Two factors worked to make this case different.

Shortly after the decision of the Québec Court of Appeal in *Kanatewat*, the Supreme Court of Canada recognized the principle of Aboriginal title in the *Calder* case brought by the Nishga nation from the north coast of British Columbia. A seven judge panel of the Supreme Court had divided 3-3 on the question of whether the Aboriginal title of the Nishga Nation had ever been extinguished. Three judges said it had been extinguished by provincial regulation. Three judges said such a matter was beyond the power of provincial regulation. The seventh judge did not deal with the issue. All the judges agreed that Aboriginal title was a principle enshrined in the *Royal Proclamation* of 1763.

The *Royal Proclamation* was an early constitutional document regulating the relations of the British Imperial authorities with "the several Indian nations," as well as with the settlers, following the fall of New France. It has the legal force of a statute and has never been repealed. The *Proclamation*'s provisions recognizing and protecting Aboriginal rights were maintained in the U.S., after the Revolution, in the *North West Ordinances*. In a judgment which repudiated many nineteenth century judicial attitudes, including U.S. Supreme Court Chief Justice Marshall's characterization of Indians as "savages," Mr. Justice Emmett Hall of the Supreme Court of Canada said that the *Royal Proclamation* followed the flag and was not restricted to the territory held by Britain on October 7, 1763.

The significance of the *Calder* case for the James Bay Cree was three-fold. First, Prime Minister Trudeau met with the Nishga leaders and apologized for earlier statements that Aboriginal rights did not have any legal basis. Pierre Trudeau's statement that the Nishgas had "more rights than I thought you had" instilled a confidence in the First Nations all across Canada. Secondly, it lent the support of both the Supreme Court and the Prime Minister to the efforts of the federal Minister of Indian Affairs to bring Québec, the Crees and the Inuit to the bargaining table. Thirdly, the support of the Supreme Court meant that the blatantly political decision of the Québec Court of Appeal might well be reversed if the Crees and Inuit went to the Supreme Court.

The James Bay and Northern Québec Agreement came into being in 1975 because such an agreement was the lesser of evils from everyone's point of view. The Québec Government of Robert Bourassa came close to refusing to ratify the *Agreement*. The notion of recognizing Aboriginal rights, even for the purpose of extinguishing them, was seen by some as both an unnecessary expense and an implicit acceptance of English legal principles. The federal government, which had the constitutional responsibility both for Indians and for Indian lands had, only a few years earlier, brought in a policy statement calling for assimilation as the road to equality for Indians in Canada. Transfer of Indian administration to provincial control was the way to accomplish that assimilation. On the other hand, the federal government was no less obligated than the province to obtain an agreement under the *Royal Proclamation*.

The Inuit had very little to lose at that point since their communities would only be threatened when development moved much further north. However, the Québec Court of Appeal had gone out of their way to say that there was no obligation to sign a treaty with the Inuit since no government had ever made a treaty with Inuit in the past. The Québec Court of Appeal apparently felt itself able to rank some Native peoples as more sub-human than others.

The Cree leaders of the day would later say that they had been forced to negotiate with a gun to their heads. There is no doubt that they found themselves forced into a game of Russian (or at least Canadian) roulette. If they won an appeal to the Supreme Court they might gain more. But years might be required for a Supreme Court decision. If there were no injunction halting construction in the meantime, the devastation of their lands would have been largely complete. Accepting a settlement meant the possibility of limiting the devastation.

Two things distinguish the *James Bay and Northern Québec Agreement* from earlier Indian treaties. First, it is over four hundred pages long and makes quite detailed provision about a great many matters. Secondly, the *Agreement* in its entirety was ratified by both the federal Parliament of Canada and the Québec National Assembly. Both these issues would be vital to the legal battles for the Great Whale River.

Any attempt to summarize or highlight the *Agreement* serves also to underscore the areas of contention and the differences in the Cree and government interpretation of its text. It is generally agreed that the Inuit and Crees surrendered a substantial part of their Aboriginal title in exchange for benefits set out in the *Agreement*. Among the apparent benefits are provision for three categories of land. Within their respective territories, the Crees and Inuit would retain hunting rights throughout the area. But hunting rights would be shared with non-Natives in lands designated under Category III. Hunting rights in Category II would be exclusive to the Cree or Inuit communities. Category I lands would be community sites, federal reserves for the Crees and Québec municipal lands for the Inuit.

The Crees and Inuit each received a sum of money. The actual figures have frequently been reported at several times the actual amounts, particularly in reports claiming that Hydro-Québec played a key role in negotiating the *Agreement*. The inflated figures often represent the sum of the original amounts plus all subsequent grants whether given to the Crees or to the Inuit. Hydro-Québec publicity consistently fails to mention that the original amounts were not in cash but in bonds which were scheduled to mature many years later. Also not mentioned, the subsequent grants received by the Cree communities are often payments intended to offset environmental devastation unforeseen at the time of the original *Agreement*, such as the contamination of the La Grande by mercury.

Most of the subsequent moneys are subsidies for ordinary municipal services. Inclusion of these figures in materials distributed internationally by Hydro distorts the actual value of the land claims settlement in the *Agreement*. It also suggests that supporting services such as health, education or sanitation in Cree and Inuit communities, at a level comparable to other Canadian communities, resulted from the surrender of their land base rather than from being part of the larger community of Québec or of Canada. Until their land was wanted, Québec showed little interest in the welfare of the Crees or the Inuit of the Ungava. Following the *Agreement* every possible opportunity to avoid implementation has been taken both by the federal Canadian and the Québec governments. Sanitation and drainage programs were postponed for lack of funds in several Cree communities until several children died as the result of typhoid.

The *Agreement*, plus the *Cree-Naskapi Act* of the 1980s, appear at first glance to provide at least a limited measure of self-government to the Crees. Self-rule is a major goal of First Nations communities across Canada. That might seem to be a significant gain except that in almost every aspect of environmental protection, industrial development and control of natural resources, Cree community decision-making is superseded by ordinary federal and provincial legislation. Furthermore, band council by-laws are subject to ratification by the community. This democratic impulse, a feature unknown to Québec or to the rest of Canada, is clearly a limitation on the powers of the band council. The Cree Regional Authority holds only the authority given to it by the Cree communities. Its powers do not resemble the high degree of autonomy identified with the term "Authority" in New England or in New York State. The Cree School Board and the Cree Health Board are both subject to regulation and scrutiny by the Québec authorities.

One important test of whether the *Agreement* plus the *Cree-Naskapi Act* actually conveyed significant authority to Cree institutions centered on whether band councils could make decisions which discriminated in favour of their own members. Given that, under Québec's *Cree Villages Act*, ordinary provincial legislation such as the *Cities and Towns Act* was to apply to Cree communities, this was a very real question. The answer came not from the government but from the courts.

In the case of *Eastmain Band v. Gilpin* the court gave to the *Cree-Naskapi Act* an intention that the government and the bureaucrats had not been prepared to allow. The Agreement drew a clear distinction between the guardianship regime under the *Indian Act* and the *Cree-Naskapi Act*. Based on the difference of tenor between the century-old regime of the *Indian Act* and the relatively empowering and innovative *Cree-Naskapi Act*, the court found that the *Cree-Naskapi Act* "must be interpreted, by necessary implication, as conferring on the Cree bands full power to legislate within specified fields, according to community needs identified by themselves."

If the Québec Government had seen the law as it was seen by both the Eastmain Band and by the courts, the case would never have been argued. In real terms, such self-government as has been achieved by the Cree communities has come more from the courts than from the Canadian or Québec governments.

Perhaps the best known recent decision affecting the Great Whale project was the decision of the National Energy Board of Canada in August, 1990. Several factors brought this decision attention that NEB decisions do not usually receive. To begin with, it was the first forum in which the Crees and Hydro joined battle. A Board accustomed to dealing with relatively technical questions related to the calculation of surplus power supplies and reasonableness of prices, found itself hearing evidence about the threat of the Great Whale project to the homeland and economy of the Crees and the Inuit.

Secondly, the powers of the Board in this kind of hearing had been modified by a bill which went through Parliament while the application was before the Board. The esoteric legal question of the Board's powers became a major battle-ground for the Crees and Hydro to argue their case. The Board resolved the issue by deciding that, "the Applicant [Hydro-Québec] is still required to obtain the Board's authorization to export electricity; it is only the criteria that the Board must consider in deciding whether to authorize this export which have been modified by Bill C-23." In the post-Meech, mid-Oka atmosphere, such a judicious and balanced decision was bound to provoke hostility.

Thirdly, the NEB stipulated that the export permits it was otherwise prepared to grant to Hydro-Québec were conditional upon completion of the required environmental assessments. This requirement was also sure to invite appeals from all sides. By August, 1990, Hydro-Québec had reason to think it would never have to comply with a federal environmental assessment review. The Crees, on the other hand, objected to the granting of export permits when Hydro-Québec had already demonstrated such poor faith.

The conditional granting of a permit was cited as an assurance both to the Crees and to American environmentalists by the Vermont Public Service Board. They made their own approval of the application by the Vermont Joint Owners subject to this decision of the NEB. Perhaps the Vermont PSB received independent legal advice before relying on the NEB decision. The political acumen underlying the PSB's decision to take cover behind a Canadian decision was, however, less than prescient.

What the PSB may have thought was their ideal escape hatch in August, 1990, undoubtedly looked less ideal on July 5, 1991, when the Canadian Federal Court of Appeal found that the NEB had exceeded its authority in making the export permits conditional on an environmental assessment. The Appeal Court's ruling was based on its own previous decision in the major case relating to the Great Whale project. Whether the Federal Court of Appeal focussed on one particular legal principle without adequately balancing it against other considerations is a question the Supreme Court of Canada agreed to hear in June, 1992.

The James Bay and Northern Québec Agreement provided that the responsibilities of the federal Canadian government were to be carried out under the direction of the federal Administrator. Raymond Robinson held the office of federal Administrator for several years after 1988. Matters under the *Agreement* relating to any aspect of federal jurisdiction, including navigable waters, fisheries and Indians or lands reserved for the Indians, were subject to his scrutiny. Robinson had another claim to fame in this area. He was also the author of the book, *The Federal Role in Environmental Assessment*. From the time that the Great Whale project was announced until November, 1990, the federal Ministers of the Environment had made repeated statements in the House of Commons and before parliamentary committees that the Great Whale project could not proceed without satisfying a federal environmental assessment. Raymond Robinson, in the nominally independent capacity of federal Administrator, had echoed these statements not only before parliamentary committees but also in correspondence with his Québec counterpart and Hydro-Québec's Vice-President for Environment.

Throughout the spring and summer of 1990, Ottawa and Québec had attempted to negotiate terms for a joint environmental assessment. These negotiations were a matter of life and death to the Crees of Whapmagoostui and the Inuit of Kuujjuaraapik. Further south the matter was not considered of urgent national significance. In fact, the negotiations faced severe competition. They were going on during the period when the Meech Lake Accord had just collapsed and the limited attention span of the Canadian public was divided between the crisis at Kanesatake, running live on Newsworld, the Canadian all-news channel, and the Iraqi invasion of Kuwait, running back-to-back on CNN.

A joint environmental assessment review process would have meant that federally and provincially appointed reviewers could, in principle, be very efficient and also very thorough. Federally and provincially appointed reviewers could have held joint hearings. Each witness group could have made an intervention in which they addressed their concerns as a whole. The reviewers could have taken from each submission the evidence which addressed either federal or provincial areas of jurisdiction.

The problem with a joint environmental review was that it required co-operation between Canada and Québec. For reasons which had nothing to do with either the Crees or the Inuit, Québec was in no mood to co-operate with the federal government. The failure of the Meech Lake Accord created a mood of hostility in which the Bourassa Government could best save face with its own electorate by denouncing any possible public co-operation with the Ottawa. At a time when "the rest of Canada" had supposedly refused to ratify a constitutional amendment recognizing Québec as a "distinct society," the crisis at Kanesatake appeared to some Québec nationalists to be part of an Anglo plot to discredit Québec. Quebeckers share with other Euro-Americans a difficulty believing that Indians might act on their own initiative.

In this atmosphere, if Québec argued that Ottawa had no jurisdiction over the Great Whale project, the only challenge would come from a handful of northern Natives. The one federal Minister of the Environment who appeared to have had a strong commitment to a federal environmental assessment of Great Whale, Lucien Bouchard, left the Mulroney Cabinet and the Conservative Party to form the Bloc Québécois, an independentist faction in the federal House of Commons. His successor, Robert de Cotret, was never suspected of strong environmental convictions.

By the fall of 1990, nothing could better have suited Ottawa's need to mollify Québec than to yield to the demands of the Bourassa government for complete control of the Great Whale issue. On November 15, 1990, Ottawa and Québec entered into an agreement in which Ottawa would abide by an entirely Québec environmental assessment. Québec had already announced that it would split its environmental assessment of the project, dealing with the roads and the three airports in a ninety day assessment to be completed by February, 1991, and a separate assessment of the dams and dikes making up the actual hydro-electric project in the months following. In the absence of any base line studies portraying the flora and fauna of the region, the scientific advisers for the Cree Regional Authority estimated that a competent environmental assessment would require no less than four to five years.

In November, 1990, the federal Administrator, Raymond Robinson told the Crees that he had no mandate to require a federal environmental impact assessment review under the *Agreement*. The Crees sued. More precisely, they sought an order of mandamus in the Federal Court of Canada, an order compelling the federal Administrator to fulfil his statutory obligations.

By that time the Grand Council of the Crees (of Québec), in the name of one or another of its officers, had numerous other suits pending against Québec, Canada, their Attorneys General and Ministers of the Environment. These cases were before the Federal Court, the Québec Superior Court and the Federal Court of Appeal, which had been asked for a ruling on the NEB decision. But it was *Cree Regional Authority and Namagoose v. Raymond Robinson* which would break the legal log jam.

The difficulty with a motion compelling an official to fulfil his statutory obligations is that the court requires the plaintiff to demonstrate that there is a statutory responsibility. It can be far easier to demonstrate that the official is not doing a certain act than it is to demonstrate that he has a statutory obligation to do it. That was the difficulty facing the Crees' lawyers, James O'Reilly and Robert Mainville, when they walked into Federal Court in Montréal in March, 1991. It was not very difficult to prove that Raymond Robinson, the federal Administrator, had not instituted an environmental assessment of Hydro-Québec's proposed Great Whale hydro-electric project. The challenge was to prove that he was, in law, obliged to do so. To prove that the federal Administrator had such an obligation meant proving two quite distinct and different points. First, that the *James Bay and Northern Québec Agreement* was binding federal law and, secondly, that the provisions in sections 22 and 23 of the *JBNQA* applied to the situation of the Great Whale project.

The first question was decided by Mr. Justice Paul Rouleau of the Trial Division of the Federal Court of Canada on March 13, 1991. The second question was decided by Judge Rouleau on September 10, 1991. What happened in between was that the March 13 decision was appealed first to the Federal Court of Appeal and then to the Supreme Court of Canada. Only when the Supreme Court of Canada refused to hear the appeal from the Appeal Court could Judge Rouleau hear arguments on the main question of an order of mandamus.

If the *James Bay and Northern Québec Agreement* were not binding federal law but some lesser category of agreement then, arguably, there may not be a legal obligation on the part of the federal Administrator to do the things which the Agreement requires him to do. At the very least, even if he could be obliged to do them, an injunction or an order of mandamus in the Federal Court might not be the way to compel him to carry out his obligation. If, for instance, the *James Bay and Northern Québec Agreement* were "a mere contract," then there would be no statutory obligation to fulfil.

This was the line of the federal government's argument. It was an especially important argument for two reasons. First, the entire text of the *JBNQA* had been enacted by the federal Parliament of Canada as well as by the National Assembly of Québec. The federal statute embodying the complete *James Bay and Northern Québec Agreement* is entitled the *James Bay and Northern Québec Native Claims Settlement Act* and appears in the books as S.C.1976-77, chapter 32.

Secondly, under section 35(1) of the *Constitution Act, 1982*, treaty rights are specifically recognized and affirmed. The only successful amendment to the 1982 *Constitution Act* was one promoted by the Grand Council of the Crees in 1983, with the blessing of the Québec Premier of that time, René Lévèsque. Section 35(3) provided that modern land claims agreements, such as the *James Bay and Northern Québec Agreement*, are treaties within the meaning of the constitutional provision recognizing and affirming both Aboriginal and treaty rights.

Proving that the *Agreement* was an Indian treaty would not necessarily win much more than recognition of another milestone on the trail of broken treaties. Granted, there was a constitutional provision promising recognition and affirmation of treaty rights in Canada. But there was also a government determined to discount these rights or, in more judicious language, to "read them down." To argue that it was constitutionally protected would not necessarily evoke respect from the government in Ottawa. More important, at that point in time, there were no prior cases from which to determine what legal force was contained in the recognition of a treaty right. The simpler and more efficient route for judicial enforcement of the provisions for an environmental assessment would be to gain the court's recognition that the *Agreement* was, in fact, a federal statute.

The federal government argued that the *James Bay and Northern Québec Agreement* was not a federal law. Since, the government told the court, the *Agreement* was a mere contract, the government was not obliged to honor its terms. This argument deserves careful attention. Ordinary citizens, facing a prosecutor or a civil complainant, may feel that they are entitled to enter any defense that will get them off the hook. But are governments, whether Canadian, American, federal, state or provincial, entitled to invoke the most scurrilous and improbable defenses in order to avoid their obligations?

The Supreme Court of Canada has described the obligation of government to the First Nations as being "trust-like." When the government sold Indian lands at a fraction of their commercial value the court described it as "equitable fraud." In another instance, the Court said that both treaties and statutes relating to Aboriginal peoples were to be interpreted according to their "spirit and intent." Doubts were to be interpreted in favor of the First Nations. In its most recent pronouncement on the matter before *Namagoose v. Robinson* the Supreme Court, in the *Sparrow* case, reiterated all these admonitions and said that "the honour of the Crown" was at stake in the need to fulfil these obligations.

The willingness of the government to invoke arguments better suited to traders in a marketplace is a question which needs to concern us all. It is the very heart of the need for the Crees to expend so much energy fighting to protect their rights in court.

On March 13, 1991, Mr. Justice Rouleau decided that the passage of the *JBNQCS Act* meant that Parliament intended the *Agreement* to operate as part of a statute, a law of Canada. Robinson, Judge Rouleau found, was appointed under sub-section 3(5) of the *JBNQCS Act*. As a result, the Judge said, the Federal Court has jurisdiction to review his decisions. The federal Administrator was a "federal board, commission or other tribunal" within the meaning of the *Federal Court Act*.

On May 14, 1991, the Federal Court of Appeal upheld Judge Rouleau's decision. Mr. Justice MacGuigan, on behalf of the three-judge panel, said that the contract element could only have applied during a transitional period of two years. The intention of Parliament was that the *Agreement* be legislated into effect. It was to have a legislative and not merely a contractual character. The Appeal Court reiterated Judge Rouleau's decision that the place to argue the meaning of the *Agreement*, as a federal law, was in the Federal Court.

What does this mean? It means that the *Agreement* is part of the law of the land. It also means that its provisions extend to everyone acting on the land in question and not only to the immediate parties to the original agreement.

The significance of the Supreme Court decision lay not with any pronouncement made by the Court but with the public response. The decision of the Federal Court of Appeal had been unanimous. Although the immediate parties to the case were the Cree Regional Authority and Bill Namagoose, the Executive Director of the Grand Council of the Crees and Raymond Robinson, federal Administrator of the *James Bay and Northern Québec Agreement*, the appeal to the Supreme Court of Canada was not brought by any of those parties. In a matter that was fundamentally about federal jurisdiction the Attorney General of Canada chose not to intervene. Robinson did not find it necessary or appropriate to appeal from the original trial decision in the Federal Court.

On July 5, 1991, the Supreme Court of Canada heard arguments on a motion for leave to appeal by the Attorney General of Québec and Hydro-Québec. After a ten minute recess, the Supreme Court justices hearing the motion for leave returned to the Chamber and refused the motion. Although the decision had been perfunctory, the Supreme Court had, effectively, upheld the March decision of Mr. Justice Rouleau subject to the slight revisions to his decision by the May decision of the Federal Court of Appeal.

The Globe and Mail, the Toronto-based paper which calls itself "Canada's National Newspaper," carried a brief notice with no subsequent discussion either in news articles or in commentaries. *Le Devoir* had an item of about the same size. Most of the print media took no notice of the Supreme Court decision. This almost complete inattention of the press to the Supreme Court decision was in total contrast to the media response to two other Great Whale events the following week.

On July 9, four days after the Supreme Court decision, the Federal Court of Appeal ruled that the National Energy Board had no right to require a federal environmental review of the Great Whale project as a condition for granting export permits to Hydro-Québec for its electricity sales to New York State and Vermont.

The Federal Court's reversal of the NEB ruling received widespread coverage in Vermont and New York State. The Vermont Public Service Board had relied on the NEB requirement for an environmental assessment in framing its own approval of the Vermont Joint Owners contract with Hydro-Québec. Efforts were being made to tie final approval of the New York Power Authority contract to an environmental assessment. By removing the requirement for an environmental assessment, the appeal court appeared to have granted Hydro-Québec the export permits it was seeking. Hydro, in the flush of victory, impressed some Vermont and New York papers with its American can-do ability to get past those pesky Indians and their environmentalist friends.

A more careful reading of the actual judgment might have prompted an experienced court reporter not to see the decision as a green light but as an orange one. Mr. Justice Louis Marceau ruled that the powers of the Board were limited to considerations such as availability of power and the reasonableness of price and did not extend to environmental impact. Speaking for the three-member Appeal Court, Judge Marceau acknowledged the gravity of the issue at hand, and pointed to a likely solution.

> It is clear that the construction of the energy production facilities raises serious environmental questions which must be considered and resolved. But *those questions are the responsibility of other authorities besides the NEB*, and those authorities have no need of the NEB's support in order to act, nor is it the board's function to lend such support. (emphasis added)

On July 10, the federal Minister of the Environment, Jean Charest, announced a non-binding, purely discretionary and very short-term environmental assessment of the federal aspects of the Great Whale hydroelectric project. "Charest's charade," as the proposal was dubbed at the time, appealed to no one except the most devoted supporters of the Mulroney Government. However silly and contradictory, Québec's position was that there was no federal jurisdiction and that clearly precluded any federal role. Lise Bacon, Québec's Minister of Energy and Pierre Paradis, Québec's Minister of the Environment, roundly attacked the federal Minister in a joint statement. Mme. Bacon threatened to take Charest to court if he proceeded with the federal review. She also said that the province would speed up its own environmental review to allow construction to begin in the fall.

"An environmental assessment must be done globally, not piece by

piece," Charest said. On that pious note he then broke the assessment
into stages to permit road construction to begin before hearings could have
been held on the dams. Mr. Charest invited the accusation of a charade
when he refused to declare a moratorium on construction, saying that he
did not have the legal power to do so. Instead, he said "common sense
requires that hearings be completed before construction begins."

Charest's proposal drew brickbats from the leading voices in two
usually opposing camps; environmentalists, including Bernard Cantin of
Greenpeace Québec, Brian Back of Earthroots, and Toby Vigod of the Environmental Law Association, objected to the farcical nature of the proposal while Ghislain Dufour of the Conseil du Patronat, Québec's largest
employer group, denounced Charest for capitulating to Natives and environmentalists. Jean Charest had not had such a bad day since the time he
tabled a report of a Commons Committee on constitutional reform.

The next day the Grand Council of the Crees (of Québec) announced
that they would boycott the Charest process. "The mandate given by Mr.
Charest to the new commission is flawed and not binding," was the reason
offered by James O'Reilly, senior legal adviser to the Grand Council. "We
want the federal Government to make an evaluation under the *James Bay
and Northern Québec Agreement* which gives the Government the right to
block the project or to require important modifications."

When Matthew Coon Come, the Grand Chief of the Crees, in an
interview on CBC Radio's *As It Happens* was asked why he opposed
Charest's proposal, he used the opportunity to educate the audience about
the basic nature of government in Canada. He asked why he would support an assessment which had no legal force when his people were facing
a life-and-death struggle with a government which had failed to fulfil so
many other obligations under the *Agreement*.

On July 16 — eleven days after the Supreme Court effectively upheld Mr. Justice Rouleau's decision, six days after the federal Minister
offered a toothless federal process — the Crees were back before Judge
Rouleau. Their application for a writ of mandamus could now be argued
on its merits. Did the Great Whale hydro-electric project, as proposed,
include matters which would affect the environment in which the Crees of
Whapmagoostui and the Inuit of Kuujjuaraapik live and on which they
depend for their livelihood and their way of life? Did sections 22 and 23 of
the *Agreement* require an environmental assessment?

For most of two days, James O'Reilly reviewed the Great Whale project, the threat it poses to the Crees and the protections afforded the Crees
under the constitutionally entrenched Agreement. O'Reilly once again, as

he had in the Crees' brief to the Supreme Court, quoted from Raymond Robinson's own book, *The Federal Role in Environmental Assessment.* In his scholarly mode Robinson had said that there was a need to implement the Environmental Assessment Review Process (EARP) "at the conceptual or earliest planning stage." Jean-Marc Aubry, attorney for the federal Administrator, argued that the project is an entirely provincial matter. When he said that there is no federal jurisdiction in regard to the project, Judge Rouleau described his argument as "incomprehensible."

After the chance to review the arguments Judge Rouleau no longer found the federal argument incomprehensible. The federal attorney had argued that the Administrator had no duty to act until the proponent submitted a description of the project to him. Now that the judge understood the nature of the federal argument he described it as "entirely spurious." The federal attorney had told the court that section 22 did not mean what it plainly said. In characterizing the federal interpretation Judge Rouleau said, "Such a conception is ludicrous."

Now that he had mastered the federal position, it was the attitude of Québec which continued to mystify the judge.

> I find it incomprehensible that on the one hand the interveners, the Attorney General for Québec and Hydro-Québec, declare themselves bound to abide by the *JBNQ Agreement*, but on the other hand other signatories to the same agreement are excluded.

Returning to the federal posture, Judge Rouleau cited the leading Supreme Court precedents on Aboriginal rights, the cases of *Guerin* and *Sparrow*. He was quite clear that these same rights applied no less in Québec than in the rest of Canada.

> It is now well established that the federal government has a fiduciary [trust-like] obligation towards the Aboriginal peoples of Canada. Furthermore, ". . . treaties and statutes relating to Indians should be liberally construed and doubtful expressions resolved in favour of the Indians."
>
> . . . where an Indian Band surrenders its interest in land . . . the federal government assumes a fiduciary obligation towards the Indian Band in question.
>
> . . . if it did not already have an existing fiduciary obligation towards the Crees, [the federal government] incurred such when it extinguished their Native rights pursuant to section 3(3) of the *James Bay and Northern Québec Native Claims Settlement Act.*

Judge Rouleau affirmed a lower court ruling that the rights of the Eastmain Band under the *Agreement* were treaty rights protected by section 35(1) of the *Constitution Act, 1982.*

How did the judge account for Robinson's sudden turnaround in late November, 1990? Robinson had claimed that he had received legal advice which prevented him from applying the federal review procedure under the *JBNQA*. Judge Rouleau offered another explanation.

> Counsel for the applicants referred me to an Agreement, entitled "Entente Fédérale-Provinciale — Evaluation Environmental Conjointe-Complexe Grande Baleine," dated November 15, 1990. . . . It was suggested that perhaps this new arrangement may have been persuasive in deterring Mr. Robinson from any further active participation.

In other words, when Ottawa and Québec politicians entered into an agreement under which Ottawa would delegate its authority for an environmental assessment under the *Agreement* to Québec, the federal Administrator reached the supposedly independent decision that he lacked the authority he had repeatedly asserted in the past that his office possessed.

The agreement of November 15, 1990, was, Judge Rouleau found, illegal on several different grounds. First, the purpose of this agreement was to displace the competing provisions in sections 22 and 23 of the *JBNQA*. Unlike the *JBNQA*, the November Agreement lacked any legal authority. The two governments had, the Judge found, collaborated to set aside obligations under an agreement legislated sixteen years earlier, both by the Parliament of Canada and the National Assembly of Québec.

Secondly, the *JBNQA* contemplated the possibility of a joint federal-provincial environmental assessment. Section 22.6.7 of the *JBNQA* allows such a combined review "provided that such combination shall be without prejudice to the rights and guarantees in favour of the Crees established by and in accordance with this section." Section 23.7.5 makes an identical provision in respect of the Inuit.

But the rights of the Crees and the Inuit had been severely prejudiced. Sections 22 and 23 contemplate an environmental assessment involving all the parties to the *JBNQA*. What was being put in its place was a non-binding substitute in which the Crees and the Inuit would not play a significant role.

> The federal-provincial agreement entered into some 16 years subsequent to *The James Bay and Northern Québec Agreement* purports to substitute the federal environmental review process and to proceed with an assessment in according with the Environmental Assessment Review Process Guidelines. It is apparent that this agreement was intended both *to appease and circumvent* the Native population who desired to have a separate federal review of matters within federal competence.

Thirdly, the delegation of authority contemplated in the November

15 Agreement was not constitutionally valid and, therefore, illegal. ". . . the 1975 *JBNQ Agreement* does not and can not delegate any of the federal assessment authority to the provincial administrator; there is, therefore, no power in the provincial administrator to deal with any impact of the project in areas of federal competence."

Lastly, the Supreme Court, in interpreting the recognition and affirmation of Aboriginal and treaty rights in the *Constitution Act, 1982,* had repeatedly affirmed a decision, which said, "the onus of proving that the Sovereign intended to extinguish the Indian title" lies with the Government, who must make their intention "clear and plain." What this means is that "the federal government could not extinguish the rights of the Crees, including their right . . . to the environmental procedures contained in sections 22 and 23 [of the *JBNQA*] without expressly doing so." Even had they gone to Parliament, the Government could not take away the rights of the Crees unless they bluntly stated that that was their intention. *The Government could not do by the back door what they would not do by the front door.* In effect, Judge Rouleau found that these two governments set out, in their agreement of November, 1990, to disregard a process enshrined in both federal and provincial law and to put in its place a process more convenient to the two of them. Although he stopped short of using the term that the law applies to individuals and corporations who plan together to disadvantage a third party, he did declare that the fruit of their conspiracy, the November 15 Agreement, was illegal, null and void.

On September 11, 1991, Judge Rouleau, having earlier determined that the federal Administrator's decision not to carry out an environmental assessment was founded on an effort to comply with the illegal November 15 Agreement, found for the Crees and granted the Grand Council an order of mandamus. He ordered the federal Administrator to comply with the law and to do the job set for him by Parliament.

> I conclude that, under the terms of sections 22 and 23 of the *JBNQ Agreement* . . . the federal Administrator has a public, non-discretionary duty to carry out an independent federal environmental review of the Great Whale Project.

Chapter 9:
The Power and the Glory

Disregard of the Law — Contempt for the First Nations

"Why are we so surprised?" is a question that might well be asked when we hear that government policy is made in disregard, if not in actual contempt of the law. Far from being surprised by Judge Rouleau's descriptions of Ottawa's and Québec's attitudes we should be greatly relieved that a judge of a superior court was willing to put frank and incisive observations about government actions into a written judgment.

If a Cree political leader or a writer with obvious Cree sympathies were to say that a federal government legal argument was "ludicrous" or that a Québec government position was "incomprehensible," such statements would be regarded as reckless. If, at a time when the primary effort in Canada is supposedly devoted to reconciliation between the two founding cultures, a Native person were to say, on his or her own authority, that the governments of Canada and Québec conspired to violate federal and provincial statutes, these charges would be described as inflammatory and provocative.

The *Robinson* decisions illustrate the greatest single difficulty with the *James Bay and Northern Québec Agreement*. Whether or not the Crees and the Inuit were essentially forced into signing the *Agreement* in 1975, or whether Québec evaded the terms under which it was granted the extensions of its northern boundaries in 1898 and 1912 are less critical issues than the determined effort of Canada and Québec to avoid fulfilling the terms of their lawful obligations. Even an agreement translated into a statute requires the effort and good will of all parties if its terms are to be honored as the basis for a genuine relationship.

In Canada, as in the United States, we like to believe that compliance with the law is the starting point for government policy. The law includes both the plain sense of acts of Parliament as well as decisions of the Supreme Court. Where the plain sense is truly in doubt we rely on the Court's interpretation of the statutes. The belief that governments are no less bound by the law than are ordinary citizens is fundamental to our way of life. When governments act in general disregard of the law then it is really very difficult for the law to command the respect and compliance of ordinary citizens. When a senior official is found to have broken the law, governments tend to react by insisting that the incident is an isolated situation in no way representative of government policy. The *Robinson* case establishes, with the greatest possible certainty, that in this instance the law was not a motive for policy. Indeed, the declared policy was contrary to existing law.

The willful disregard of the law, in this instance, leads us to ask whether this attitude is characteristic of policymaking in Canada's relations with the First Nations. If it is characteristic of First Nations relations, more than of most other areas, then it represents a continuing imposition of a kind of civil disability on Native peoples in Canada. If, however, it is a behaviour that is occasioned by the extremity of the constitutional crisis then we need to recognize that when the going gets tough the government, for the sake of expediency, is free to deprive the First Nations of their most cherished rights. If a crisis between Québec and "the rest of Canada" can be resolved by treating the Crees as the puck in a constitutional hockey match then environmental racism is a process deeply embedded in our constitutional process.

This is not the way in which Canadians, whether Francophone, Anglophone or allophone, would like to view themselves. We would like to think that we are the people who have successfully resolved all the problems which plague the American Constitution. We have a *Charter of Rights and Freedoms* which protects individual rights side-by-side with a recognition of the bilingual and multicultural character of the country. There are prohibitions against all forms of discrimination while still permitting affirmative action for disadvantaged groups. There is great support for recognition and affirmation of Aboriginal people's Aboriginal and treaty rights, together with recognition of a distinct society in Québec.

If, however, governments are allowed to enter into agreements to set aside the laws of the land without most of the people being visibly upset, then all these grand provisions do not prevent the imposition of civil disabilities on any group who are too weak to defend themselves. Even when, as with the Crees in this case, they manage to mount a successful defense we need to ask, at what cost? It would be difficult to estimate the time and effort, let alone the dollars, that were diverted from other programs of the Grand Council of the Crees (of Québec) in order to take cases concurrently through the Québec and Federal Courts and eventually obtain an order directing a federal official to fulfil his legal obligations. That inestimable cost, however, is the amount by which Canada and Québec have deprived every Cree person, man, woman and child, of the supposed benefits of the moneys paid to them under the *James Bay and Northern Québec Agreement.*

At the very least, the *Robinson* decision makes plain why other First Nations are not hurrying to make the *JBNQA* a model for their own development. It also illustrates why the concerns of the Crees and the Inuit need to become the concerns of everyone of good will throughout North America. Canadians, including Québécois, of course, can be said to have a special concern because it is their governments who are acting in the ways described by Judge Rouleau. All Canadians, it will be said, have the opportunity to change these governments through the electoral process.

But federal Canadian governments have been making Indian policy in disregard of general legal principles for a great many years. This has been happening at least since 1927 when it was made a criminal offense to press Indian claims in Canada, or since 1923 when the Six Nations Longhouse chiefs were arrested because they had petitioned the League of Nations to send the case of *Six Nations v. Canada* to the World Court. If we look to broader principles, such as equality before the law, then the disregard goes back much further. The *Indian Act* of 1886 provided that an Indian man lost his rights to reserved land and membership in an Indian community if he became self-supporting.

When that provision was repealed, in 1951, Parliament did not repeal the complementary section which said that an Indian woman lost her Indian rights if she married a man who had lost his. By the time the section discriminating against Indian women was repealed, in 1985, some white, female, liberal parliamentarians were prepared to blame Indian men for the provisions of the *Indian Act*. Few parliamentarians were prepared to demand that the government finally begin to conduct their relations with the First Nations in Canada in a more honorable way. Even fewer were prepared to support the Assembly of First Nations' demand that the reinstatement of Indian women be accompanied by an increased land base. With about the same numbers as the Native American population in the United States, the Aboriginal peoples in Canada have roughly one-twentieth the land base.

The practice described by the Supreme Court of Canada in the *Guerin* case as "equitable fraud" is probably the chief cause of poverty in the First Nations communities, both in Canada and the United States. Selling First Nations lands, on which people have relied for sustenance since time immemorial, at a fraction of their market value, has left one Native community after another without any way to feed, clothe or house themselves. The Court, in *Guerin*, once again described Government behavior in language inspired by the Criminal Code. The press mainly ignored the matter. The public rested secure in the defense of "we didn't know." *Guerin*, like the events at Kanasetake, was about selling Indian lands for a golf course. The difference was that, at Kanasetake, the Warriors' Society decided to prevent the misconduct on which the government had turned its back.

The Need for American Concern

Judge Rouleau's decisions, in the *Cree Regional Authority v. Robinson* case, are important because he sets out the logic by which he comes to characterize Ottawa's and Québec's attitudes toward Aboriginal people. Reading these judgments instills an appreciation of why it was necessary for the Great Whale communities to appeal to American public opinion.

If American utilities were not planning to buy the largest chunks of the power to be produced at Great Whale is there any reason why an Ottawa-Québec conspiracy to disregard a latter-day Indian treaty should interest American citizens? The reasons against such an interest are clearer than those in favor.

There is not, after all, much that either Canada or Québec could possibly teach American authorities about government contempt for the rule of law. There is even less for the United States to learn about how to get around Indian treaties. The *James Bay and Northern Québec Agreement* may be a modern and constitutionally protected treaty. Does this make it very different from the Ft. Laramie Treaty of 1868, which was unilaterally scrapped by the U.S. government when it became desirable to open up the Black Hills of South Dakota for a gold rush? What better model of government contempt for the Supreme Court could be wanted than President Jackson's fabled response when Chief Justice Marshall ruled against the State of Georgia and in favor of the Cherokees in the 1830s? "Mr. Marshall has made the law," Jackson said, "let him enforce it." The president then dispatched the U.S. Army to move the Indians off their land.

This very commonality underlying the superficial differences between Canadian and American political styles, and between Québec and the-rest-of-North-American political styles, may be the first reason why this conspiracy should be of interest to Americans. Other than the distinctive nature of its language and its legal system, Québec may be ethically indistinguishable from any mid-size American state; except that, as a foreign state, it is exempt from most federal U.S. environmental laws. And with enough arm-twisting it is largely also exempt from federal Canadian regulation.

It may also be somewhat helpful for Americans to look closely at this case because it is nominally foreign. The Alice-in-Wonderland nature of the Canadian constitutional crisis may be an ideal looking-glass for Americans to examine what Chief Robbie Dick described as "the bulldozer way of being." Felix Cohen, the leading legal scholar of U.S.-Indian relations in the 1930s and 40s has often been attributed with the statement that "the Indian is the miner's canary." Cohen was suggesting that if the dominant culture of America was not prepared to extend the rule of law to the Indian nations for their own sake, it should do so for the sake of its own members.

Ethical and legal considerations aside, it will be useful for Americans to know something about where their power comes from in order to better decide whether Québec represents a secure source of power. If, as the Crees argued before the United Nations Human Rights Commission in February, 1992, Québec's claim to the Ungava rests on Québec being a province of Canada, an independent Québec may not be a secure source of power for New York, Vermont or the New England Power Pool. A newly independent Québec will, undoubtedly, be more than eager to do business with U.S. state agencies but *the merchandise Hydro-Québec is offering for sale may not be an item owned by Québec* under international law. If Canada is divisible under the principle of the self-determination of peoples, then the question becomes, *is Québec divisible under the same principles?* What if the Crees and Inuit want to secede from Québec?

Québec parliamentarians have reacted with great indignation when this suggestion has been made by international law experts appearing before National Assembly committees. But an independent Québec in search of international respect will not have the advantage of being able to twist arms in Ottawa to get its own way. There could be no better way to jeopardize the prospect of independence than to make promises to the United States about energy when keeping those promises is fundamentally beyond Québec's power.

Hydro Contract Cancelled by New York Governor

On March 28, 1992, Governor Mario Cuomo intervened in the negotiations between the New York Power Authority (NYPA) and Hydro-Québec (Hydro) to cancel a proposed twenty-year contract for power from Great Whale. What was actually cancelled by Governor Cuomo was an agreement which had been made in 1989, which would produce a binding contract if there was no intervention by November of 1992. The agreement was for 1,000 megawatts of firm or assured power to be delivered by Hydro to NYPA. Nothing in the agreement said that it would actually come from Great Whale, but given Hydro's commitment to move existing plants previously used for export purposes to domestic use, there was nowhere else from which the power could come.

The Governor's decision to cancel the NYPA-Hydro contract came at the end of a two-year campaign by the Crees and New York State environmental groups. Whether the Crees can properly be credited for the cancellation is much less clear. The notion that a small group of Indians could exercise enough influence to bring about the cancellation of a contract for New York State's largest power purchase does not jibe with the better known patterns of North American history. At the very least, the idea deserves some examination. Governors have been receiving Indian chiefs for a long time. Not every such visit has stopped a project described by an important neighboring head of government as "the project of the century." Nelson Rockefeller, Mario Cuomo's gubernatorial predecessor, had certainly exhibited almost as much enthusiasm for James Bay One as his good friend Robert Bourassa.

The New York Times, the newspaper which had given the issue the least possible coverage for most of the two-years' debate, noting that the sale to NYPA was critical for financing the project, described the cancellation as a severe set-back for Hydro. Environmentalists and Native leaders reportedly hailed the decision as a major victory.

So far as "victory" means achieving stated goals, nobody could doubt that the cancellation was a major victory. The Grand Chief had met with the Governor the previous fall to present a major brief outlining the human rights issues at stake in the building of the Great Whale project. His brief catalogued the wide range of abuses of the *James Bay and Northern Québec Agreement*. The Grand Chief told the Governor that he had no doubt there were other ways that New York State could meet the needs of its people *without aiding and abetting the devastation of the Cree homeland.*

What the Crees and their southern supporters had succeeded in doing went beyond convincing the Governor that New York's purchase of power from Hydro would make the State complicitous in the consequences both to the Cree people and to the fragile northern environment. The debate, which may have begun at the time of the *Odeyak*, had turned full circle. For months before the Governor's decision the debate had not focused either on the Crees or on the northern environment.

By the time that David Dinkins, the Mayor of New York City, wrote to Governor Cuomo asking him to re-consider the purchase of power from Hydro it was becoming clear that there was a convergence of several different interests. It may well have been that both the Mayor and the Governor would have acted for the environment and for human rights even if it were not financially beneficial for New York State. But there is no doubt that it was the economic arguments which won the day.

Several factors had affected the economic calculations since the initial agreement had been made between NYPA and Hydro three years earlier. The largest factor was a decrease in growth of demand from 1.1% per year to one-sixth of one per cent per year. Some of the decrease was undoubtedly due to the recession. A more long term part of the decrease was the result of dramatic technological changes resulting in much more energy efficient electronics. There was also the matter of alternative energy sources that the Vermont Public Services Board had not been prepared to trust in 1989 but which the New York authorities seemed ready to consider in 1992.

Among the Crees' southern supporters were several major public service unions in New York State whose members would play a leading role in the development of domestic production sites, if the power were not imported from Québec. The unions had come together with less mainstream groups, such as PROTECT, who had been campaigning against electromagnetic effects of the major power lines required to carry power from Québec to New York City since the 1970s.

NYPA and Hydro had been negotiating for new terms for some time when Governor Cuomo ended the discussions by cancelling the contract altogether. The extent to which the energy market had been re-shaped by the combined effects of demand-side management, alternative means of generating electricity and a major surplus of oil and gas following the Persian Gulf conflict is indicated by NYPA's basic negotiating position. The New York state agency was, by the winter of 1991, asking for a one-third reduction of the previously agreed price for Great Whale power.

Whatever else may have motivated Governor Cuomo to cancel the whole matter, it was clear that the negotiators on both sides were beating a dead horse. Even with all the job creation and "northern development," a 33% discount would simply not be credible to the lenders who were expected to finance this twelve billion dollar project. Also, a reduction of that amount would surely have constituted the kind of subsidy prohibited by the U.S.-Canada Free Trade Agreement (FTA) which the Bourassa Government had so strongly supported. U.S. officials were already ruling that the discounted rates at which Hydro was supplying power to smelters was an unfair subsidy under the FTA. Had Hydro been prepared to grant the price reduction NYPA was requesting, the New York domestic suppliers would surely have challenged the deal.

One factor which has been said to have contributed to the timing of Gov. Cuomo's intervention, if not to the cancellation itself, was the death of William B. Hoyt. Bill Hoyt, a 54-year-old Assemblyman from the Buffalo area, had been the leading opponent of the proposed NYPA-Hydro purchase. Hoyt was an enthusiastic white water canoeist and a dedicated conservationist. When Denny Alsop first travelled to Great Whale he had stopped in Albany on his way to Montréal to pick up letters from Bill Hoyt and Maurice Hinchey, another Assemblyman, expressing their support for the *Odeyak* voyage.

As Chairman of the Assembly Energy Committee he had co-sponsored (with Maurice Hinchey, the Chairman of the Conservation Committee) a bill which would have required New York State to have the same kind of environmental impact statement on an out-of-state power source that was already required for in-state sources. Bill Hoyt had been keenly aware that this bill was stepping on sensitive toes. When it had first been introduced he had received a visit from the Consul General of Canada, the head of a trade mission who travelled up from Manhattan to Albany "to reprimand" the Assemblyman "for interfering in Canada's domestic affairs." Hoyt, whose grandfather had taught philosophy at the University of Toronto, and whose district was bounded by the international border, was particularly sensitive to the spurious charges of this merchant-diplomat. His bill did no more than require that his own state not participate in major damage to the environment through its power purchases; or, at least that it be aware of the damage it was causing. It regulated New York's behavior, not Québec's.

Hoyt had co-sponsored hearings in Manhattan and elsewhere on the Great Whale project the previous fall. The forum lent the Crees' campaign enough respectability that *The New York Times* began to take the issue seriously. The appearance at the hearings of Grand Chief Matthew Coon Come provided a story worth covering. The Hoyt-Hinchey Bill had only recently gathered enough momentum to pass the Democrat-controlled Assembly in 1992, when Bill Hoyt collapsed on the Assembly floor on March 25 and was declared dead on arrival at the Albany Medical Center.

Until Bill Hoyt's death, the Hoyt-Hinchey Bill had not attracted the kind of sponsorship it would need to gain approval in the Republican-controlled state Senate. Upon Hoyt's death Republican senators began lining up to sponsor the bill in the state's upper chamber. Governor Cuomo's cancellation of the NYPA-Hydro negotiations took the wind out of the Hoyt-Hinchey Bill's sails just as the proposal was taking off. With no immediate application the bill was suddenly becalmed. Neither those who wanted to honor Bill Hoyt's memory nor those who positively supported his opposition to Great Whale were eager to bind the hands of the state power authorities in some unforeseen future crisis. State officials insisted that the timing of the announcement, two days after Hoyt's death and the day before his funeral, was coincidental. It was a coincidence which left the New York Power Authority and the Governor free to resume negotiations with unregulated neighbors at some future time.

On Becoming Fully Responsible

The Hoyt-Hinchey Bill was almost identical to one introduced in Vermont by state Senator Elizabeth Ready in 1990. More recently a similar bill has been introduced in Massachusetts, the state which would receive the largest block of power from a proposed contract between New England Power Pool and Hydro. The bills, which have come very close to passage in at least three states, have been denounced by several Canadian interests who might not usually be considered natural allies. Both the officially non-partisan federal Department of External Affairs, through Canada's diplomats in New York and Boston, and Québec's official opposition, the Parti Québécois, have denounced these bills as unwarranted interferences into Canada's (or Québec's) domestic affairs.

The Hoyt-Hinchey-type bills are a rejection of reciprocal complicity by American legislators and citizens concerned about the environment. The U.S. *National Energy Policy Act*, a federal law, has long required an environmental assessment of any major power development in the United States. The recognition that the consumer society which finances a project plays an active role in making it happen and is, therefore, co-responsible is a pioneering development in public ethics.

Bernard Landry, the Vice President of the Parti Québécois, insists that an independent Québec would represent a secure source of power for New York and New England. His corresponding objection to interference in Québec's internal affairs by the likes of Bill Hoyt and Maurice Hinchey is, for Mr. Landry, a logical corollary. What he fails to consider is that some people's image of sovereignty requires that they, as individuals or as a collectivity through their legislature, must become fully responsible. It is incoherent to proclaim responsibility for the effect of a project on the environment in one's immediate locale while denying responsibility, but accepting the benefits of, a similar project at a great distance. Neither can the decision to abstain from a project be aptly described as interference in the domestic affairs of another state, any more than turning down a marriage proposal can sensibly be described as interference with the other's autonomy.

The growing attitude of environmental responsibility that threat-ened future Hydro-Québec sales in New England along with the cancella-tion of Hydro's New York contract caused an unfortunate outburst of anti-Cree invective from the government of Québec and its Deputy Premier, Lise Bacon. When the Crees, Greenpeace Québec and several other envi-ronmental groups placed a full-page advertisement in the New York Times outlining their position, she responded by saying, "I blame them for discrediting Québec all over the world. Do you think a Quebecker can accept that? I don't think so."

In this and other statements Mme. Bacon seemed to be saying that only those in Québec who agreed with her government's idea of develop-ment were true citizens of the province. Hydro-Québec responded with its own advertisement with much of the same misleading rhetoric and misinformation as the utility presented in many of its other public rela-tions campaigns. They claimed, for example that "no mercury-related health problems have been recorded as a result of hydro development in Québec." But while no studies had been completed, Hydro-Québec was advising the people not to eat fish from the La Grande River or reservoir, according to a Cree Health Board consultant.

When the New York power deal was cancelled by Governor Cuomo, Lise Bacon told a *Globe and Mail* reporter that the Crees had cost Québec the $17 billion contract. It is likely that statements such as that did a good deal more to bring discredit on Québec than the legitimate and moderate discussion the Crees engaged in over the issue. What is disappointing is that Mme. Bacon's repeated and unparalleled attacks on an identifiable ethnic group went largely unchallenged by either the press or other politi-cal leaders.

Environmental Assessment Starts

Governor Cuomo had intervened on an earlier occasion. On August 29, 1991, he issued a press release announcing that Hydro had agreed with NYPA not to go ahead with plans to build the roads and airports for Great Whale before it had done an entire environmental assessment. Judge Rouleau's decision, which was not handed down until Sept. 11, had been expected the week before. Whether the Governor was beating the judge to the punch or whether Hydro conceded to the Governor, expecting that they were about to lose in the court, is a moot and unanswerable point.

By the time the War of the Ads was taking place in late October, more than a month had passed since the Federal Court had handed down its decision. Had there been a sense of confidence that the governments in Ottawa and Québec were inclined to comply with the court order, in its letter and in its spirit and intent, there would have been no ads.

Not every twist of fate which changes the course of history is for the worse. The environmental assessment which Judge Rouleau had ordered is supposed to take place, according to the provisions of sections 22 of the *James Bay and Northern Québec Agreement*, under the direction of an Evaluating Committee (*Comité d'évaluation* or *COMEV*). The Chairman of *COMEV* rotates annually among the members, i.e., the parties to the *JBNQA*: Canada, Québec, the Grand Council of the Crees and Makivik Corporation. The chairmanship for the year ending March 31, 1992, was Billie Diamond, the first Grand Chief of the Crees (of Québec) and then-president of Air Creebec.

While Ottawa and Québec appealed Judge Rouleau's September decision through the courts, Billie Diamond used the short time available to him to create a Memorandum of Understanding under which work could begin on the environmental assessment which had been ordered. The Memorandum of Understanding provided for the joint assessment which Canada and Québec had been unable to achieve in any legal form in earlier efforts.

The Memorandum incorporated the provisions of a Declaration of Settlement Out of Court between the Whapmagoostui Chief, Robbie Dick, and the Québec Minister of the Environment providing for a single global assessment as far as provincial jurisdiction applied. In other words, Québec would not be allowed to proceed with the split between assessing of infrastructure and assessing of the main project it had earlier announced.

Under the Memorandum, federal and provincial panels would operate independently but could hear evidence jointly. Although the federal Environmental Assessment Review Process (EARP) Guidelines had been repealed during this controversy, in favor of a very watered down statutory formula, they would still apply to the federal review. The terms of the *JBNQA* would also apply. The *James Bay and Northern Québec Agreement* was to remain paramount; neither the EARP Guidelines nor any part of the Memorandum of Understanding were to be interpreted as a modification of the *Agreement*. The Memorandum of Understanding did not set aside any of the seven different cases, including appeals from earlier decisions, still before the courts.

The first task of the various panels under the Memorandum of Understanding was to conduct "scoping hearings" from which Draft Guidelines might be developed. In theory, when the Draft Guidelines are suitably revised they will represent an agreed set of Final Guidelines under which the Great Whale Environmental Impact Study will take place.

The difficulty with the Draft Guidelines is that they were drafted by Hydro-Québec. The proponent of a project typically has the advantage of defining the debate about its project by creating the terms of the proposal. The Draft Guidelines, however, basically represent an exercise in which Hydro adopted all the rhetoric of environmental concern while eviscerating the language of its fundamental meaning. This traditional bureaucratic ploy has a significance beyond the mere borrowing of language. Imitation can, of course, be the sincerest form of flattery. But reconstituting key terms so that they no longer resemble what was previously meant is a way of using language to build communication barriers. *Hydro-Québec set out to build these barriers in both official languages.* The role assumed by government has been to supervise the construction of these communication barriers.

Environmental impact guidelines are a kind of law. Guidelines may be explicit enough to define the standards to which construction will be done or they may be broad enough to set out the criteria by which the need for a project will be demonstrated. Whether broad or narrow, conceptually or behaviorally based guidelines must be clear enough that a panel representing widely divergent views has some chance of agreeing on whether the requirements in the guidelines have been met. Otherwise, there is a danger that the guidelines become meaningless or that compliance is impossible to determine.

When Hydro-Québec proposed that the Great Whale project will be carried out in a sustainable manner according to the criteria established by the U.N.'s Brundtland Commission Report, the proposal was, at very least, assured of attracting attention. But does Hydro really mean "meeting the needs of local communities" and "maintaining or enhancing the Aboriginal peoples' self-reliance," which is what Brundtland means by "sustainable development?" Proponents always need to demonstrate that the projects they are proposing are the least intrusive, least damaging and most efficient alternative. But the Draft Guidelines for the Great Whale assessment require what might be seen as two quite contradictory things. On the one hand they are to ". . . follow the logic inherent in a proposal to develop a project and to insert the project into an existing environment." At the same time they are to ". . . demonstrate the need for the project within the context of sustainable development."

Sustainable development can either become a refrain without currency or it must remain a point of reference about the ecosystem on which a project intrudes. If sustainable development is applied, not to an ecosystem but to a political territory, then it fails to consider not only the natural economy of the Aboriginal people but the effects of a project on the areas beyond the political territory of the sponsor.

Great Whale, and the other James Bay projects, have raised particularly large trans-boundary concerns both in the immediate area and on a continental basis. GB1 (Grande Balaine is French for Great Whale), the most downstream dam site and the first one for proposed development, is only a short distance upstream from Hudson Bay and the Québec boundary. The fate of the many species of marine life, including large mammals in Hudson Bay, may be of no great concern to the Bourassa-Bacon government but they are a critical concern both to the Aboriginal economy and to the future ecological balance of the bioregion. The influx of freshwater is thought to be a decisive determinant in the balance of nutrients shaping the entire food chain. Similarly, the availability of fresh and moving water affects the rate of freezing and thawing and possibly the entire system of currents.

Most important is that no political authority has yet troubled themselves to do sufficient studies even to approximate reliable answers. In an era of global warming the minimal level of responsibility to the entire planet would require that not only Québec but Canada and the United States conduct sufficiently definitive and comprehensive studies prior to any massive northern development.

The United States has both an immediate and a broader interest in ensuring that there is knowledge before development. First, the massive flocks of geese and ducks which summer in the Great Whale area winter in the United States. The Vermont Public Service Board clearly identified migratory birds as an area of direct impact on Vermont. The *Migratory Birds Convention* is a U.S.-Canada treaty which was intended to protect migratory birds and which makes them subject to international regulation. Secondly, any project which potentially reshapes the climate of North America can not help but affect the interests of the United States. Even though local harvesters have observed major changes, governments have not encouraged serious independent studies of climatic change.

The Draft Guidelines, which continue to be a subject of debate, do not address any of these larger questions. The Cree of Whapmagoostui have walked out of negotiations in protest against the lack of any comprehensive approach to the issues which should be properly addressed by an environmental assessment. It is just as well that the Memorandum of Understanding reserves the right to all parties to continue their litigation in court. Mediation is, today, gaining widespread support as an alternative to slugging it out in court. But mediation supposes a degree of seriousness and good will on all sides. That good will has not yet become evident in the battle for the Great Whale River.

Self-Determination

Québec and the Crees both aspire to self-determination, the right of a *people* to control their own destiny, free from alien rule. Self-determination is a concept which has been developed and elaborated since World War I. The Atlantic Charter, of August 14, 1941, sets out certain principles including the idea that signatories to the Charter, "desire to see no territorial changes that do not accord with the freely expressed wishes of the *people* concerned," that "they respect the right of *all peoples* to choose the form of government under which they will live; and they wish to see *sovereign rights and self-government* restored to those who have been forcibly deprived of them."

The 1970 *Declaration Concerning Friendly Relations* calls for states to act internally with the principle of equal rights and self-determination. In other words, large states such as Russia, the United States, Canada or Québec cannot give less respect to these principles within their broad boundaries than small states are obliged to give to their neighbors. Internal self-determination, particularly for indigenous people, has been developed at greater length in the *Covenant on Civil and Political Rights* as well as in the *Charter of the United Nations*.

Indeed, the *Charter* ascribes self-determination not to states but to peoples. It is, perhaps, for this very reason that so much energy in earlier stages of the Québec debate went into asserting that the Québécois are a distinct people. It should not require such a prolonged and emphatic debate to demonstrate that the Crees and the Inuit, two peoples who have lived in the upper and lower portions of the Ungava for thousands of years are also distinct peoples. As Mina Weetaltuk said about the essential message of the *Odeyak*, "It does not take so many words to understand such a thing."

The distinction between "states" and "peoples" is exactly the point which has been repeatedly obscured throughout both the debate on James Bay and the larger debate about the inherent right of self-government of the First Nations in Canada. The same misunderstanding has been carefully cultivated in the debate about the future of the Canadian Confederation. Who benefits from a confusion between the Québec people and the Québec state is easy enough to see. It is the people, and not the territory of Québec, which has a right to self-determination. That right can not be exercised on their behalf. Nor can the exercise of that right be done in a way which deprives another people of that right.

The United Nations has retained a very broad definition of "people" because it recognizes that the term is a troubling and complex one. It also recognizes that if rights such as self-determination were ascribed to anyone else but a people they might soon become a license for the very kind of carnage the U.N. is dedicated to preventing. At the very least, an international concept of peoplehood rests on an inclusive list of factual criteria including: common history, racial or ethnic ties, cultural or linguistic ties, religious or ideological ties, common territory or geographic location or common economic base.

One writer has expressed this by saying that, "Side by side with the objective element, there is also a subjective basis to peoplehood. . . .It is essential to have a present ethos or state of mind. A people is both entitled and required to identify itself as such." The need for a subjective element as the glue to hold together those objective elements applicable to each different peoplehood has led others to observe that "the problems of the Lapps, the Inuit, the Australian Aboriginals, . . . the Québécois, . . . and so forth, are the same in principle but different in practice." This is the very kind of statement that is so threatening, not to the people of Québec, but to those in positions of power and influence. It is, for purposes of their aggrandizement, not enough that the Québec people be recognized as a distinct society. They require that the state within which several other peoples live be considered identical with the Québec people alone.

The Canadian Constitution makes much the same point as international law in provisions as recent as the recognition and affirmation of Aboriginal and treaty rights in section 35 of the *Constitution Act, 1982,* and provisions as old as the *Royal Proclamation of 1763.* Political leaders who find it more convenient to do so treat domestic law with the same regard they show to international conventions.

If it were still necessary to demonstrate the folly of insisting that colonialism can only exist in relation to overseas dependencies the situation of the Crees and Inuit of the Ungava would be the perfect case. Whapmagoostui and Kuujjuaraapik are as far from Québec City as the Atlas Mountains are from Paris. The majority of people in the Ungava, an area equal to all of France, are Aboriginal people. They speak their own indigenous languages as their mother tongues.

A more coherent definition of colonialism is one which is based on the quality of relationship between a local population and a culturally distinct ruling group.

> Internal colonialism results where an ethnic group in control of a government systematically exploits resources of the region occupied by minority ethnic groups "reducing the development of those regions to that of depen-

dencies." . . . Typical results include an inequitable distribution of national wealth and of access to employment and educational opportunities.

The Canadian Human Rights Commission has described the situation of Native communities in Canada as "Our 'Third World'." Based on this observation the Commission made a rare intervention into the constitutional debate by declaring that, "To deny meaningful Native self-government is compatible neither with our domestic nor our international human rights obligations." History, unfortunately, is a better predictor of behaviour than legal obligations.

The Supreme Court of Canada, in the *Sparrow*, case observed that the Musqueam's fishing rights were "in the beginning a regulated, albeit self-regulated right." This recognition of an historical right of self-government by the Supreme Court is one of several strictures limiting the efforts of the federal Canadian and Québec governments to transfer control over the First Nations in Québec and the lands previously guaranteed to them by treaty.

Self-government is significantly different from self-determination. Every people have a right to self-determination. But in recognizing this fundamental human right the international community does not want to foster the endless fragmentation of states. The exercise of self-government, and particularly the extreme act of secession, is justified not simply by a popular will but by the deprivation of human rights under the prior regime. It is this "human rights deprivation test" which is the basis for arguing the need for self-government for the Crees of James Bay and other First Nations in Canada. It is clear that neither Québec nor Canada have respected the rights of the First Nations. Yet it is the recollection of this most basic historical fact which most readily arouses the indignation of Québec ministers and their PQ shadows. The list of witnesses who have advised Québec parliamentary committees of these basic facts has included former Members of the National Assembly, advisors to the federal Prime Minister, and respected Québec experts in international law.

Given the limitations imposed by the *JBNQA* and the *Cree-Naskapi Act* on Inuit municipal councils and Cree band councils nobody could argue that these are self-governing institutions. Several recent statements by the Grand Council of the Crees have emphasized the incomplete extent of their right to self-government under these enactments. These councils are, in the words of Canada's 1867 *Constitution Act*, "municipal institutions." So long as Québec remains within Confederation much of this argument remains academic. The question which is much more vexing, the one which truly arouses the ire of the Québec political elite, is the status of Québec's claim to the Ungava peninsula in the event of secession. Gordon Robertson, formerly Clerk of the Privy Council of Canada (the highest ranking civil servant in the federal government) has speculated on that eventuality.

> If Québec can accede to self-determination, why could the [Aboriginal] peoples not do the same? It has already been proposed before this [Belanger-Capmeau] Commission that the holding of a referendum would permit the Québec people to decide their own future. Similarly, certain Aboriginal groups living in Québec could also demand one or more referendums with a view to determining, as distinct peoples, what will be their future.

Ironically, this is not a move that most Crees are eager to make. Like most First Nations across Canada, the Crees of the Ungava are strongly federalist. Like most First Nations everywhere they have a strong attachment to the land. The "local" nature of provincial authority has tended to make provinces the natural predators of Native peoples. But, in those rare instances where provincial leaders have been willing to build alliances with Aboriginal peoples the shared locale has forged a strong bond between two peoples attached to the same land. But in the general absence of provincial good will the First Nations in Canada have typically argued for continued federal responsibility on the ground that it is the federal government which has the primary trust responsibility to protect their interests against the provinces. But every Indian in Canada knows that the federal government has not always exhibited a commitment to upholding this trust responsibility in the past hundred years.

If the Québec people choose to leave Confederation, it is their self-determination as a people which they will exercise, not the self-determination of the present political territory. Their self-determination may include the land in which the Québec people, however defined, constitute a majority, but the area occupied by the Crees, an area where they are the majority, cannot be deprived of Canadian affiliation without their consent.

The question of who is included as part of the Québec people is a question of great international concern. If it is only the "pure wool Québécois," the people whose ancestors came to Québec about the time the *Mayflower* reached Plymouth Rock, then New England may want to reappraise the kind of people with whom it does business.

If the Québec state is to be the hydro-electric powerhouse of New England, can it tie its economy wholeheartedly to the United States while defining membership in its society by such an anti-American standard? If so, what are the over-riding considerations which allow Lise Bacon's standard of Québec-ness to over-ride free speech, human rights and common decency?

Cree leaders are all too aware of the obvious parallel between the destruction of their food supply, the caribou, fish and fur bearing animals today and the destruction of the buffalo herds by U.S. plainsmen a little more than a hundred years ago. Much more than any claim to self-determination, the northward imperative of Québec today can be better understood by its similarity to the westward imperative of the United States following the American Civil War.

Whether the "Boston States," which did so much to enable previous American expansionist activities, will also want to finance this newest imperial adventure in exchange for twenty years of supposedly cheap power remains to be seen. There is the possibility that New Englanders and New Yorkers will, in the spirit of the *Hoyt Bill* in New York and the *Ready Bill* in Vermont, be prepared to take responsibility for their own impact on the environment, whether within their immediate boundaries or beyond.

We may soon find that such a sense of responsibility is an inextricable part of sovereignty. Self-determination belongs only to peoples and not to states because only a people, and not a state, can grow to become fully responsible.

A Post Script, October, 1993

On Tuesday, August 31, 1993, Hydro-Québec released their long awaited, $400 million feasibility study for the Great Whale project. Reports in the media on the contents of this study were, at best, deceptive. Part of the massive Hydro-Québec offering was a five thousand page document labelled as an "Environmental Impact Statement (EIS)."

This was not a statement from any environmental review panel or any other quasi-judicial body established either by the Canadian or the Québec governments. As a result of the Crees' legal actions, an agreement formally called a Memorandum of Understanding had been signed by Canada, Québec, the Grand Council of the Crees (of Québec), Makivik Corporation representing the Inuit, and Hydro-Québec. The agreement provided for a consolidated environmental review in which evidence would be gathered and testimony heard on behalf of five different panels, representing all the various federal and provincial obligations for various types of environmental assessments. The consolidation offered a more efficient process as well as a more holistic one. It was intended to provide for all parties to the *James Bay and Northern Québec Agreement* to discharge their responsibilities concurrently.

The Environmental Impact Statement released by Hydro-Québec in August, 1993, was nothing more than a consolidation of all of Hydro's studies over the past 15 years. Far from being an environmental assessment, this statement was intended to set out the basis for Hydro's advocacy of the Great Whale hydro-electric project.

During the late winter and early spring of 1992 hearings were held in the northern communities as well as in Montréal. These hearings, however, were restricted to the very limited purpose known as "scoping." They heard only enough evidence to enable the panels to write the guidelines within which the environmental impact statement was to be developed and later hearings of the review panels were to be conducted.

One major requirement of the guidelines was that Hydro-Québec conduct community consultations in the course of developing their environmental impact statement. The review panels expected Hydro to talk directly with the people whose lands are threatened by their proposed project. Rather than fulfilling this obligation, Hydro sent out a questionnaire asking Cree hunters to rank the order in which they value the various kinds of animals which live on their land. "It was like asking me to rate the various parts of my body," Chief Matthew Mukash said.

Although the official Environmental Impact Statement is five thousand pages in length, as yet all that the Crees have received in English is a two hundred page summary. They are presently in the process of translating this into Cree. The EIS will not have officially arrived until Hydro presents a complete English language version to the Crees, the Inuit and other interested English reading citizens and neighbours of Québec.

Meanwhile, opposition to the project continues to grow. Increasing numbers of major American financial institutions are now expressing doubts similar to those which Matthew Mukash was raising during his campaign speeches appealing to town meetings to reject the Hydro-Vermont contract. Robert Blohm wrote a letter in the *Wall Street Journal* of September 28, 1993, entitled "Hydro-Québec Looms as a Possible Whoops." In it he argues that the cautions about the dangers of investing in nuclear power, set out in an article the week before, apply equally to Hydro-Québec. The "five admonitions" arising from the collapse of the "the world's biggest investment in nuclear power" were: "1) avoid political footballs; 2) avoid large projects without established revenue streams; 3) avoid any project requiring a new tax to pay off the debt; 4) don't go by bond ratings alone; and 5) at the first sign of trouble, sell.""

Two days earlier, the *Rutland Herald* carried an article headlined "Hydro-Québec Power Proves Costly to Vermont's Largest Utility." Central Vermont Public Service Corporation's costs and rates were being investigated by the Vermont Public Service Board, the same Board which had enthusiastically allowed CVPS and other members of the Vermont Joint Owners to contract for a massive purchase from Hydro-Québec. The Board was now finding that the purchase by Central Vermont from Hydro was one factor which "will provide significant pressure for a substantial rate increase after 1995." The increasing availability of other smaller, simpler power sources closer to home, combined with decreases in demand from both increasingly efficient electrical appliances and a depressed economy, had left Central Vermont Power holding a large piece of Québec power for which it had no great need, but for which the residents of central Vermont were now to be held liable.

An October, 1993, article in the *Montréal Gazette* documented in substantial detail the extent and nature of Hydro's secret contracts with various aluminum smelters to provide subsidized power at the expense of both the Crees and of the smelters' American competitors. The subsidies violated both the *James Bay and Northern Québec Agreement* because the power is not essentially for domestic use but for export, and the U.S.-Canada Free Trade Agreement. The same article also confirmed the Crees' suspicions that the superficially large sums of money Hydro has been offering for surrender of their claims on the land and the loss of their natural economy represent no more than two per cent of the capital cost of the project. Even so far as the land can be valued, the payments bear no relationship to its value. Hydro has simply applied the same standard they would if they were expropriating a single family dwelling to build a local power station. From Hydro's perspective, it is simply "more of the same."

From the Crees' perspective, it is more of the same policy of denial. Just as the largest financial entity in Québec denied that freshwater seals existed, and that the *James Bay and Northern Québec Agreement* was a binding federal and Québec statute, and Hydro's voice in the Québec Government denied that Crees' were free to discuss politically sensitive issues within walking distance of Wall Street, Hydro now continues to deny that the Crees' interest in the Ungava peninsula extends beyond the narrowest interest of a private property holder.

The failure of Hydro-Québec to attempt to hold community consultations is also "more of the same." The elders who account for the original James Bay trial, *Kanatewat et al* in the 1970s, say that they had to go to court because Hydro would not believe how long their ancestors had lived on the land, or even to come and talk to them. Twenty years later, under a directive from a quasi-judicial environmental review panel, Hydro is still unwilling to sit down and listen to what the elders have been trying to say for such a very long time.

For Matthew Mukash it is "more of the same" in yet another sense. Now that he is Chief of the Cree nation at Whapmagoostui, Matthew continues to travel down south to address one audience after another about the threat facing his community. It is possible that Chief Mukash would travel down south once in awhile because he enjoys travelling. Every local politician in North America appreciates an occasional junket. But not every local leader travels hundreds of miles to appeal to the citizens of other states or provinces to help not to drown his community and destroy an entire way of life.

If it were truly important to the major players in this power game to welcome the Crees and other First Nations as part of the contemporary North American economic culture, they would surely not begin their welcome by drowning the Crees' major resources. If Québec or Canada accepted the principle, voiced by Chief Justice Brian Dickson of the Supreme Court of Canada, that Aboriginal rights must be "unique and contemporary," Hydro-Québec would not be allowed to treat the Crees with an antediluvian contempt that resonates with accounts of the exiling of the Cherokees from southern seaboard states.

Chief Justice Dickson used this phrase to describe Aboriginal rights in a case called *Sparrow*, in which the Court's decision was handed down even as the barricades at Oka were going up. Had the spirit and intention of *Sparrow* been respected by governments in Canada it is unlikely that violence would have ensued at Oka. *Sparrow* was among the recent Supreme Court decisions which Mr. Justice Rouleau reviewed in affirming the rights of the Crees in *Namagoose's* case.

If the recent reports of progress are deceptive it is because so little has changed. Hydro's EIS is all-of-a-piece with their public relations campaigns of a year or two earlier. The Crees continue to cultivate their southern support network despite severe financial constraints.

The caribou continue to be plentiful, and thereby take the pressure off the smaller animals and the fish which are the secondary staples to which the Crees turn when the caribou are scarce. The small, fur-bearing animals are, in the currently low pressure environment, making a comeback. And the people of Chissasibi are not having to eat mercury-contaminated fish. At the same time, the Crees of Whapmagoostui and the Inuit of Kuujjuaraapik continue to face a future in which their river disappears and their fish are no longer fit to eat.

The one major change which has taken place is the growing disbelief among American investors and consumers in the value of a mega-project which will drain money out of U.S. states to buy electrical power from a utility whose credit worthiness is increasingly held in as much doubt on Wall Street as their right to disrupt the flow of the rivers is doubted in the councils of the Crees and Inuit of Ungava.

Bibliography

Books and Journals

MacGregor, Roy, *Chief: The Fearless Vision of Billy Diamond*, Penguin Books, 1990.

Miller, J.R., *Skyscrapers Hid the Heavens: A History of Indian White Relations in Canada*, University of Toronto Press, 1991.

Millman, Lawrence, *Wolverine Creates the World*, Capra Press, 1992.

Richardson, Boyce, *Strangers Devour the Land*, Douglas & McIntyre, Vancouver and Chelsea Green Publishing, Post Mills, Vermont, 1991.

Sam-Cromarty, Margaret, *James Bay Memoirs: A Cree Woman's Ode to Her Homeland*, Waapoone Publishing, Lakefield, Ontario, 1992.

Prodan, Pamela, "The Legal Framework for Hydro-Québec Imports," *The University of Tulsa (Oklahoma) Law Journal*, Vol. 29, No 3, Spring, 1992.

All the Canadian cases discussed in chapters eight and nine can be found in the, *Canadian Native Law Reporter*, University of Saskatchewan, Norman Zlotkin, editor.

Films

Richardson, Boyce, *The Flooding of Job's Garden*, Tamarack Productions, Suite 443, 366 Adelaide St. E., Toronto, Ontario, M5V 1R9.

Power of the North, Wild Heart Productions, 5415 Hutchison St., Montreal, Québec, H2V 4B4.

INDEX